Praise for *Executing Grace*

"This compelling and thoughtful book is a must-read for people of faith who have in many ways been painfully silent about excessive punishment in America. Scripture, history, and conviction make Shane Claiborne's writing essential for anyone serious about grace and mercy."

  —**Bryan Stevenson, author of *Just Mercy***

"Shane is my good friend. I love and respect him deeply, and I am so glad he wrote this book. I wish the whole Church would read it. As Christians, we know we believe in grace, but we must struggle with what that means when it comes to the death penalty, especially when we have a system that is as broken as ours is. So please read *Executing Grace* with an open mind and consider if it might be time for us to live without the death penalty. Might it be time for us to repent and turn from death to life?"

  —**John Perkins, author of *Let Justice Roll Down***

"The best book on the death penalty since *Dead Man Walking*."

  —**John Dear, author of *A Persistent Peace***

"I recommend this clear and passionate book to all who want to follow Jesus, history's most famous victim of state violence."

  —**Jim Wallis, author of *God's Politics***

"Shane Claiborne may well join the ranks of Rachel Carson and John Howard Griffin—storytellers who've pricked the conscience of our nation and nudged us toward a more perfect union."

  —**Jonathan Wilson-Hartgrove, author of *Strangers at My Door***

"Claiborne will not let us off the hook about the radicality of God's grace. Nor will he look away from the social reality of barbarism masquerading as legality. One can only hope this vigorous, inescapable book will make the difference."

  —**Walter Brueggemann, author of *Prophetic Imagination***

"Intelligent, compassionate, and   e most thoughtful moral voices alive to

  —**Brian D. McLaren, author o

D1041130

"*Executing Grace* may be the best book on the death penalty. An indispensable work."

>—David P. Gushee, Distinguished University Professor of Christian Ethics and Director of the Center for Faith and Public Life at Mercer University

"Powerful, urgent, and right. Solidly biblical and full of wrenchingly gripping stories; every Christian should read it."

>—Ronald J. Sider, author of *Rich Christians in an Age of Hunger*

"Timely, relevant, inspiring, and compelling!"

>—Brenda Salter McNeil, author of *Roadmap to Reconciliation*

"Extraordinary. Shane delivers a heavy blow to the death machine. Read it at your own risk: you won't be the same when you're done."

>—Michael T. McRay, author of *Where the River Bends*

"Should be regarded as a warning to those becoming involved in American ceremonial killings. In the middle of the night it's just too late to reach out and blame it on the system."

>—Ron McAndrew, CPM Prison and Jail Consultant

"This book will help lead to the abolition of the death penalty. I ask any Christian who promotes the death penalty to read this book. Best book on the death penalty I have read in the thirty years I have been working to abolish it."

>—Bill Pelke, president of Journey of Hope . . . From Violence to Healing

"With razor-sharp insight, Claiborne rightly divides the Word with the compelling conclusion that our waning American love for executions cannot be attributed to the God of grace and mercy."

>—Dale Recinella, Catholic Correctional Chaplain in Florida's Death Row and Solitary Confinement

"*Executing Grace* is about remembering our humanity in the midst of a culture of death. With no shortcuts or easy answers, Shane has called us to wrestle with capital punishment. An entire generation of evangelicals will find in this work the radical grip of grace."

>—Rev. Dr. Gabriel Salguero, president of the National Latino Evangelical Coalition

Executing Grace

How the Death Penalty Killed
Jesus and Why It's Killing Us

Shane Claiborne

HarperOne
An Imprint of HarperCollinsPublishers

HarperOne

FIRST EDITION

Library of Congress Cataloging-in-Publication Data
Names: Claiborne, Shane, author.
Title: Executing grace : how the death penalty killed Jesus and why it's
    killing us / Shane Claiborne.
Description: San Francisco : HarperOne, 2016.
Identifiers: LCCN 2015042836 (print) | LCCN 2015048394 (ebook) | ISBN
    9780062347374 (paperback) | ISBN 9780062347367 (e-book)
Subjects: LCSH: Capital punishment—Religious aspects—Christianity. |
    Capital punishment—United States. | Executions and executioners—United
    States. | Restorative justice—United States. | Punishment—United States.
    | BISAC: RELIGION / Christian Life / Social Issues. | RELIGION /
    Spirituality. | LAW / Criminal Law / Sentencing.
Classification: LCC HV8694 .C53 2016 (print) | LCC HV8694 (ebook) | DDC
    261.8/33660973—dc23
LC record available at http://lccn.loc.gov/2015042836

16 17 18 19 20   RRD(H)   10 9 8 7 6 5 4 3 2 1

Contents

CHAPTER ONE

Something Just Doesn't Feel Right

At first I thought that I was obsessed with death.
But then I realized that I am obsessed with grace.

There are some fourteen thousand books written on the death penalty, and I didn't want to write another "one of those."

One of my favorite writers once told me, "Don't write unless you cannot *not* write. Make sure it is a fire in your bones, a passion that cannot be contained."

This book chose me.

Growing up, I never questioned the rightness of the death penalty. I was raised in the heart of the Bible Belt, and capital punishment seemed to be pretty clearly ordained by God. I can remember arguing a few liberals into the ground over it. On one occasion, I even argued that homosexuality was a crime punishable by death—and I had verses to back it up.

I'm not proud of that past. But it gives me some compassion for others who still feel the same way I did. Almost every day I get e-mails and letters from folks who have been passionately in favor of the death penalty and are rethinking things. I had one fellow in Texas confess to me, "I want you to know, I'm a redneck. I'm a gun-totin', pickup-drivin', tobacco-chewin', whisky-drinkin' backwoods redneck." Then he went on, "But I've been reading your stuff. And it has messed me up. Pray for me. I'm a recovering redneck now." People change. Convictions change. So I want you to know that I'm not writing this book from a place of self-righteous indignation. I'm not on a soapbox. I'm a bit of a recovering redneck myself. So don't worry about me getting all up in your face.

I once stayed in the home of a pastor who knew I was writing a book about the death penalty, and he was interested in hearing more. Genuinely interested. I told him many of the stories in this book over the weekend, and in just days he told me he had really rethought his position, which had been in favor of capital punishment. He told me he hadn't really thought much about it but had sort of "inherited" his beliefs, and truth be told, he always felt sort of conflicted inside. That pastor is not alone. Since then there have been prosecutors, executioners, judges, and victims who have written me to share that they've become convinced that there are better forms of justice than execution.

I've learned that words really do have power. And so do stories. And so does the Bible. And so do facts. So you'll find all those things on these pages.

I also began to realize that just because we have a strong opinion on something doesn't mean we've thought a lot about it. And it doesn't mean we can't change our mind. I've always been passionate. Even when I've been wrong, I've been passionately wrong.

I know that passionate people change their mind, because I am one of them.

I also know that we can believe something in our head and still have our heart push back against it. This was what happened to me with the death penalty: the stuff I thought to be true in my head didn't jibe with the things I knew to be true in my heart.

My hope is that this book will engage your mind and your heart. And that we can find a way to think about justice, and Jesus, and killing, where our heart and mind are *one*.

So I should just get this out in the open: I have an agenda. It is about grace. I want to build a movement of grace-driven abolitionists—people of faith and conscience who want to put an end to death forever. I want us to make death penalty history.

There, I said it. I believe in grace, and I want you to.

I am not interested in talking about "capital punishment" as much as I am in talking about the ramifications of grace, mercy, forgiveness, and love.

Not only do I believe in grace, but I have seen its transformative power in action.

I want you to read this book—even if you are a skeptic like I used to be—but I want you to read it with an open mind and an open heart. Otherwise, just take it back and get a refund.

The Gut Instinct

If I'm honest, even when I argued for the death penalty, there was something in my gut that just didn't feel right. No one wants to be "for death," but I just didn't know what the alternatives were.

I remember watching a 2011 CNN interview where Piers Morgan talked with Joel Osteen. Joel is the pastor of Lakewood Church, the largest Protestant church in the United States, down in Houston,

John Taylor | James Autry | James Hutchins | Ronald O'Bryan | Arthur Goode | Elmo Sonnier

Texas. (They meet in the former Houston Rockets stadium.) He's a televangelist with over twenty million monthly viewers in one hundred countries, and he's the author of five *New York Times* bestselling books. He's often nicknamed "the smiling preacher" because of how happy he is and how cleverly he avoids speaking of anything negative. It was a great interview—light, winsome, candid. And then . . .

Piers daringly asked Joel about the death penalty. Joel dodged the question with his characteristic sincere smile, saying that issues like the death penalty are way out of his league, and politicians would need to figure that one out. That was unacceptable to Piers; he insisted that since millions of people look to Joel for moral guidance, that answer wasn't good enough, especially from a pastor in Texas, the most deadly state in the country when it comes to executions. Even the governor of Texas has visited Lakewood Church.

So Piers kept pushing. It was clear that Joel wasn't going to be able to avoid the issue. Eventually, he shook his head somberly and said:

> *It's a complicated issue, Piers. I haven't thought a whole lot about it, but of course I'm for second chances and mercy. . . . It's hard for me to say, "Yeah, let's just kill this person because he's so bad."*

Like many of us, Joel hadn't thought a lot about the death penalty and wasn't sure what to say about it. But I could tell, watching the interview, that something in his gut just didn't feel right about killing someone.

There are lots of folks like Joel, who seem to be shaking their heads and saying in their gut, "Something about it just doesn't seem right."

James Adams | Carl Shriner | Ivon Stanley | David Washington | Ernest Dobbert

While opinions are dramatically shifting, and more and more folks are coming out against the death penalty, there are still plenty of people who support it, especially among Christians. But even among these supporters, there seems to be a quiet group of people—perhaps even a quiet majority—for whom something just doesn't seem right. Something in the gut says there must be another way.

Grace and Disgrace

Violence is contagious. Violence begets violence. A rude look is exchanged for a cold shoulder. A middle finger for a honked horn. Hatred begets hatred. Pick up the sword and die by the sword. You kill us and we'll kill you. There is a contagion of violence in the world; it's spreading like a disease.

But grace is also contagious. An act of kindness inspires another act of kindness. A random smile is exchanged for an opened door. Helping someone carry their laundry or groceries makes them nicer. Randomly paying someone's toll in the car behind you invites them to pay it forward. A single act of forgiveness can feel like it heals the world. Grace begets grace. Love rubs off on those who are loved.

But there is a war in the world around us. Both hatred and love seem to be trying to take over our world. The contagion of violence and the contagion of grace are spreading like invasive plants in the garden. The quicker you rip them up, the quicker they spread.

This battle is raging inside every part of our society, and even inside our own souls. We can feel grace and vengeance at work inside us.

There's nowhere you can see the battle of grace and disgrace waged more vehemently than in the criminal justice system. When

Timothy Baldwin | James Henry | Linwood Briley | Ernest Knighton | Thomas Barefoot

Grace is also contagious. An act of kindness inspires another act of kindness.

it comes to words like "justice," people can say the same thing and mean something completely different.

Capital punishment offers us one version of justice. There is a sensibility to it: evil should not go without consequence. And there is a theology behind it: "An eye for an eye . . . a tooth for a tooth."

Yet grace offers us another version of justice. Grace makes room for redemption. Grace offers us a vision for justice that is restorative, and dedicated to healing the wounds of injustice. But the grace thing is hard work. It takes faith—because it dares us to believe that not only can victims be healed, but so can the victimizers. It is not always easy to believe that love is more powerful than hatred, life more powerful than death, and that people can be better than the worst thing they've done.

These two versions of justice compete for our allegiance. One leads to death. The other can lead to life, and to healing and redemption and other beautiful things. For me, the death penalty has come to represent the battle of all battles in the war between good and evil.

It is the eye of the storm, if you will. The death penalty raises all sorts of other questions about race, theology, economics, and inequality. We'll get to those. But at the heart of all of this is a question: When we kill to show that killing is wrong, aren't we reinforcing the very thing we want to rid the world of?

The cure is as bad as the disease.

Death closes the door to any possibility for redemption. Grace opens up that door.

The stories in this book show us humanity at our worst as well as humanity at our best.

Evil is real—and you will hit it head-on in this book. Evil will slap you in the face.

Velma Barfield | Timothy Palmes | Alpha Stephens | Robert Willie | David Martin

But grace and mercy are real, too—not just slippery things, dangling in space like ornaments on a Christmas tree. We will see grace in action, mercy on the move.

It's been said, "Mercy is *not* getting what you *do* deserve, and grace is getting what you *don't* deserve." Both are beautiful, but both can also seem like a betrayal of justice. That's why justice can't just come out of our heads, but it also has to flow from our hearts. Grace and mercy are things, just like forgiveness, that exist in the context of evil—and in contrast to it. When all is well, grace and mercy are hard to notice. But when things are rough, they are hard to ignore. They shine brightly. Just as light shines in darkness, grace is radiant next to evil.

We live in a grace-starved world.

The stories you'll hear are not fairy tales in which there's a villain and a hero; life's way too messy for that. It may very well be that there's a villain and a hero inside *each* of us, and each day we have a choice of who we want to be.

If we look closely, we can see ourselves in the people we read about here: we can see the evil we are capable of, and we can see the good we are made for.

In the end, one of the questions we must answer is this: Is any person beyond redemption?

Could it be that every time a life is taken from us, we lose a piece of God's image in the world?

As you read the stories in the chapters to come, lean in and look for the image of God in every person—victim, murderer, executioner, warden. There is a lot at stake. Life and death, of course, but maybe even more than that.

What may also be at stake is the good news of Jesus. I learned to memorize a scripture passage in Sunday school as a kid in Tennessee that went like this: "For God so loved the world that he gave his one and only Son, that whoever believes in him shall not perish but have eternal life" (John 3:16).

It wasn't until much later that I learned the next verse: "For God did not send his Son into the world to condemn the world, but to save the world."

The wages of sin is death. But the gift of God is life.

Sin and evil are real and terrible things.

But grace gets the last word.

The Faces of Death and Grace

Let me tell you two stories to get us started. First, I want to show you what death looks like.

George Junius Stinney Jr.[1] Have you ever heard that name?

I hadn't heard of him until I started researching for this book. Now I can't forget him, even when I want to. George Junius Stinney Jr. was the youngest person ever executed in the United States; he was fourteen. He walked to his execution by electric chair carrying a large copy of the Bible under his arm.

He was accused of killing two white girls in the Jim Crow South. His trial lasted less than two hours. No witnesses were called, no defense presented. There is no record of a confession or of any physical evidence. And the all-white jury deliberated for a mere ten minutes before sentencing him to death.

In one of the quickest executions in history, George Junius Stinney Jr. was killed eighty-one days after being arrested. One of his last meals was ice cream with the officers who would later kill him. His skinny five-foot-one, ninety-five-pound body was so small that his head didn't reach into the metal helmet of the electric chair, and so he had to sit on the Bible to make it work. *He sat on the Bible.* When the first jolts of electricity hit him, he flinched and the head mask fell off, revealing the terror in his eyes and the tears streaming down his cheeks. Only after several more jolts of electricity did he finally die.

I was so disturbed by George's story, when I first encountered it, that I couldn't stop reading about him. I thought maybe his execution had happened in the 1800s, but it was in 1944. Some of his family is still alive. Part of me wishes his execution had occurred hundreds of years ago so that I could write it off to those less civil days and dismiss it by thinking we've come a long way since then.

But no: it was 1944.

The case of George Junius Stinney Jr. is one of the greatest travesties of justice in American history. But his story raises many important questions. And while it is extreme, it is not exceptional. There are many George Stinneys.

Some things have changed since 1944. But what's also striking, as we will see, is how little has changed since 1944.

Now I want to tell you another story, one that shows you what grace looks like.

It's a story very different from George Junius Stinney's story. His story shows us what it looks like when death wins. This story also starts with horror, but it ends with grace.

In 2006 a troubled gunman named Charles Roberts entered a one-room Amish schoolhouse near Nickel Mines, Pennsylvania. He shot ten girls, ranging from six to thirteen years old, killing five. Then he turned the gun on himself and killed himself.[2]

As always, the shooting massacre immediately became the breaking news story of the day, and of the week to follow. "If it bleeds, it leads," as the old journalism adage goes. So it went.

But what quickly began to steal the headlines was the way the Amish responded. With a distinctive commitment to nonviolence, the Amish families put their faith into action as they built a bridge to the shooter's family and went to visit them— Charlie's widow, children, and parents. They were neighbors. In fact, Charlie was a milk truck driver who delivered to the Amish farms, and he had three children of his own. One of the Amish men massaged the shoulders of Charlie's sobbing father for an hour as he wept.

The response stunned the world.

People from around the globe, moved by compassion, began to send the Amish gifts and money . . . and the Amish used that money to create a fund for the family of the shooter. As the funerals rolled around, the Amish attended service after service of their own children who had died . . . but then they went to the funeral of Charlie Roberts, the man who had killed their kids, so they could grieve with his family and hold hands with them as they found a way forward together.

Marie Roberts, Charlie's widow, wrote an open letter to the Amish community, thanking them for their forgiveness, grace, and mercy. "Your love for our family has helped to provide the healing we so desperately need," she wrote. "Gifts you've given have touched our hearts in a way no words can describe. Your compassion has reached beyond our family, beyond our community, and is changing our world, and for this we sincerely thank you."[3]

James Roach | Charles Bass | Arthur Jones | Daniel Thomas | Jeffrey Barney | David Funchess

I was in Australia speaking when the shooting happened, and I will never forget one of the front-page headlines in the Australian newspaper. It read: "Amazing Grace: Why Would the Amish Do What They Did?" Though this was not a capital case since the killer committed suicide, you can imagine how things might have unfolded had the man lived. Undoubtedly, the Amish would have refused to create another set of victims by seeking the death of Charlie Roberts.

The incident morphed from a horror story to a grace story, inspiring books such as *Amish Grace.* I got a chance to talk with one of the authors of *Amish Grace* as I researched this book.[4] He explained to me that the willingness to forgo vengeance is a core value of Amish culture. This grace does not undo a tragedy or pardon a wrong, but it becomes the first step toward a more hopeful future.[5]

The grace and love extended by the Amish to the Roberts family not only touched people around the world. It moved the Roberts family themselves to action. Check this out.

Charlie's mother, Terri Roberts, began to visit with one of the Amish girls that her son had shot and almost killed.[6] The girl, Rosanna, was six at the time of the incident. She survived the shooting but is not able to enjoy life as it was meant to be lived. She's in a wheelchair, eats with a feeding tube, and is unable to talk. But she is not unable to love and be loved. Terri visits Rosanna regularly; she helps bathe Rosanna, and reads to her, and sings to her. Spending time together helps to heal the wounds of this tragedy. Every time Terri visits with Rosanna, she is forced to confront the damage her son caused. But she is also reminded that violence does not have to get the last word. We don't have to be held hostage by the worst moments in our lives. Healing is possible even when the wounds are deep.

Grace gets the last word.

Stories like this have the power to change the way we think and the way we act. I'm convinced that one of the things we suffer from when it comes to the death penalty is imagination. And the Amish captured our imagination for a moment.[7]

It's hard to miss, even from the two stories above, that there is a dark, evil finality when it comes to death and killing, and there is something spectacular about the possibilities opened up by grace.

Bad News and Then Good News

Before we dive into the darkness, one bit of explanation. I remember hearing the evangelist E. V. Hill speak before he died. We were at a conference together, and I'll never forget his words. He spoke about how we all love the good news but sometimes need to hear the bad news first. He told a story about a charismatic woman in his church who always sat in the front row. Her nickname was Eighteen Hundred, because she was so elderly that everyone said she must have been born in the 1800s. Seen as the matriarch of the congregation, she was beloved.

But the problem was, she wanted to hear only "the good news"— perhaps because she had lived through so much bad news. She wanted to hear about Jesus, resurrection, life. At first glance, this might not seem like a problem, but here's what happened. Every Sunday old Eighteen Hundred would sit in her usual spot in the front row. As Pastor Hill started preaching, she'd begin muttering, "Get to the good news, Pastor; get to the good news." And her commentary would get louder and louder as the sermon progressed. The longer he talked, the louder she got. He'd be talking about how Jesus died on Friday, and she'd yell back, "Don't leave him there. Get to the empty tomb on Sunday!" He'd be talking about how hatred, sin, and racism are still alive today, and she'd shout back, "Move on, Pastor. Get to the good news!" Eventually he *would* get to the good news, and she would shout "Amen!" at the top of her lungs.

It's one of those "preacher stories" that, if it isn't true, should be.

Old Eighteen Hundred reminds us of something important. In the end, the gospel, the story of Jesus, is good news. It's not okay news, not bad news . . . it's *good* news. But E. V. Hill was right. We must take a plunge into the darkness before we can fully appreciate the light.

The good news is also the story of a God who hears the suffering of people, who enters into that suffering, who experiences the pain and suffering of our world.

In Jesus, we have a God who dies. Enduring the most famous execution in history, he turned one of the worst symbols of violence, the cross, into one of the greatest symbols of hope.

And he died with love on his lips, forgiving the people who were torturing and killing him. Every week, every day, every moment, we who follow Jesus identify with a grace-filled, forgiving victim of violence. That alone should change everything for us, reorient us, cause us to pause and reconsider how we think about death—that is, in light of God's grace.

In writing this book, I initially started out with a lot of really heavy, dismal bad news and was saving the good news until the end. But I kept getting stuck. It felt so dark that I wasn't sure anyone would be able to read this book all the way through and make it to the good news. In fact, *I* couldn't make it through my own book without tears streaming down my face as I reread it.

As I often do when I get stuck, I went for a run—miles and miles, like Forrest Gump. As I ran I prayed, and I had one of those all-too-rare experiences (for me anyway) in which I felt a clear whisper from heaven say, in effect, "Jesus deserves more than a chapter. Jesus is the thread of hope that connects it all. Don't leave Jesus until the end."

So you will see that I have woven Jesus throughout. Jesus is present in the lynchings. Jesus is present in the section on innocence. Jesus is there when we talk about those who have been executed. Jesus is there when we think about the victims of violence. This is the good news—not just that Jesus rose from the dead, but that Jesus is with us, in death and in the triumph of grace. So for anyone reading this book who, like old Eighteen Hundred, can't wait to get to the good news . . . you won't have to wait long.

CHAPTER TWO

Let's Begin with the Victims

The death penalty has failed victims' family members in virtually every way, and many of us— including many who support the death penalty in principle—have come to support its end.

—Vicki Schieber, whose daughter Shannon was murdered in Philadelphia[1]

Nearly every time I write or speak about the death penalty, one of the first questions to surface is: "What about the victims?" Thank God it is. I believe in a God who cares deeply about the victims of violence and injustice. Whether we care about victims of violent crime should never be in question. The real issue is *how* we care, and what we can do to best care for the victims of violent crime. The victims are front and center, as they should be. That's why we are going to start this book with them.

Jimmy Glass | Jimmy Wingo | Elliot Johnson | Richard Whitley | Connie Evans | John Thompson

"What about the victims?" is not just a fair question; it is an essential question.[2]

As we will soon see, most people (including representatives of our courts) make the assumption that those who are the victims of violent crime support the death penalty. While that is indeed sometimes the case, victims and their families often provide some of the most compelling arguments for abolishing the death penalty.

Here are some voices of victims and their families that we often do not hear:

> *When my brother was murdered I thought I was supposed to support the death penalty.... Little did me and my family know then that when Michael Ryan was sentenced to death, we were sentenced too. Our sentence has been going on for 20 years and there has been no execution. For 20 years it has been all about Michael Ryan. He is all my family and I ever hear about. Jim is never mentioned.... Having seen what the death penalty has done to my family, I have since changed my mind and now think it should be abolished.*
>
> —Miriam Thimm Kelle, whose brother, Jim, was tortured to death

> *So, if it's not a deterrent, if it's not cost effective, if it begets more violence, if it releases a murderer from his earthly punishment, if it puts the victim's family through years and years of reliving the event, if it does not change our life without our loved one, and if it makes us no better than the murderer, what possible reasons could you have, could we have to have a death penalty?*
>
> —Bruce Grieshaber, who led the fight to restrict parole for violent felons in New York after his daughter, Jenna, was murdered

Willie Celestine | Willie Watson | John Brogdon | Sterling Rault | Wayne Ritter | Beauford White

You may know that my father was gunned down by an assassin's bullet in 1968. My grandmother was gunned down in 1974 by another person. Certainly, I should be one to support the death penalty, but our family has always been against the death penalty.

—**Martin Luther King III, son of Martin Luther King Jr.**

We are family members and loved ones of murder victims. We desperately miss the parents, children, siblings, and spouses we have lost. We live with the pain and heartbreak of their absence every day and would do anything to have them back. We have been touched by the criminal justice system in ways we never imagined and would never wish on anyone. Our experience compels us to speak out for change. Though we share different perspectives on the death penalty, every one of us agrees that . . . our state is better off without it.

—**Letter to the New Jersey State Legislature (May 10, 2006) signed by sixty-three New Jerseyans who lost loved ones to murder**

As I said, one of the most unchecked assumptions in our society is that the victims of murder are all in favor of the death penalty. To advocate for victims, from this assumed perspective, necessarily means one version of justice, closure, and finality: execution.

This assumption has caused many murder victims' family members who are less inclined to pursue execution to ask, "Ain't I a victim?" just as Sojourner Truth famously asked, "Ain't I a woman?"[3]

Sadly, in many cases the state's answer to this question has been no. In fact, the state often assumes that it is inconceivable to be a victim of horrific violence and not want to see the killer killed. Victim advocacy offices run by prosecutors operate under this assumption.

Dale Selby | Billy Mitchell | Joseph Starvaggi | Timothy McCorquodale | Robert Streetman

Prosecutorial offices operate under this assumption. Media folks often look for the voices and stories that support this version of "justice."

It is an assumption so pervasive and so repressive that many murder victims' family members have formed groups to unify their voices against the death penalty.[4] Three of the most prominent groups are Journey of Hope . . . from Violence to Healing, Murder Victims' Families for Reconciliation (MVFR), and Murder Victims' Families for Human Rights (MVFHR).

But the more victims I have gotten to know and love, the more I have realized that there is not just one way to heal from trauma.

When it comes to the family members of the murdered, some of the most amazing stories of healing and closure I have heard or read are from families who found alternatives to execution for the offender. (Many of those stories you will see scattered throughout this book, primarily in the "grace stories" at the end of each chapter.) In contrast, some of the folks who still seem overcome with pain and anger and resentment were able to witness the execution of the offender. In other words, the idea that an execution will bring closure or final justice is a mirage. For many families, execution has simply meant reliving the horrific event year after year, decade after decade, through the slow process of carrying out a death sentence.

Without a doubt, some of the strongest voices against the death penalty, and some of the most credible voices, are the victims of violent crimes who know that there are better forms of justice than execution.

But there is a reason we don't hear as many victims speak out *against* execution on the news and in the headlines as we do victims who support it. And it's not because execution-opposing victims aren't out there. Rather, it's because those victims are actively discouraged from expressing their views.

One of the most disturbing things I discovered in writing this book is that victims of crime who, for whatever reason, are not in favor of the death penalty are routinely marginalized, silenced, and even threatened. When victims are *for* execution, they are given a media platform, massive assistance from the government and from victim assistance programs, and even compensation for participating in public events in support of capital punishment.[5] However, when victims are *against* execution, they are sometimes ordered not to talk publicly (via a so-called gag order), are excluded from public hearings and victim assistance conferences, and are sometimes threatened with obstruction of justice by people for whom the only version of imaginable justice is to take "a life for a life."

There's the fascinating case of Bob Autobee, whose son was a prison guard killed by one of the men in the prison. Initially, Bob was in favor of the death penalty for his son's killer and was a key witness in the case. But eleven years later, there was a retrial, and Bob had changed his mind about the death penalty. As he considered what his son would want, along with his own faith convictions, he no longer wanted execution—and in fact, he met with his son's killer, Edward Montour, and publicly forgave him. Bob's witness against the death penalty became so compelling that the state tried to keep him silent—and since he was no longer in favor of the state's version of justice, he was of no use to them in court as a witness.[6]

Something is wrong with a system that rewards victims when they are *for* execution but punishes them when they are *against* it. As you survey the various responses of victims outlined in this book, you will discover that many of those who have healed best have not

James Messer | Donald Franklin | Jeffrey Daugherty | Raymond Landry | George Mercer sought the death penalty but have instead found closure in forgiveness and restorative justice, or even in life in prison for the killer. You'll meet some of these victims soon.

Silencing the Victims

Even those in favor of capital punishment can agree, I hope, that silencing a victim of violence because we disagree with him or her is not right. Victimization is about powerlessness, and justice is about amplifying the voices of those who have been silenced. Healing requires being able to process, to grieve, to make choices freely, and to feel acknowledged in that journey. There are many families who feel that execution adds to their pain and does not help with healing or closure; others do not want to spend the next ten years of their life in trials (the average time it takes for an execution to happen), forcibly reliving the horror of the incident while hoping for an execution that may never come; while still others are opposed in principle to any taking of a life. Whatever their individual reasons, these victims simply want society to recognize that opposition to the death penalty is a valid response to the trauma of murder, that not all victims' families want the death penalty. Certainly *every* victim should have a voice and a choice and not be silenced. Sadly, this is not the case today.

It is this bias that has caused many victims' family members to relegate themselves to the status of "second-class victims." Indeed, the Lamm family learned that because they opposed the death penalty, they weren't victims at all!

In 1980, Victoria Lamm and Janet Mesner were murdered in a Quaker meetinghouse in Lincoln, Nebraska. They were killed by a man named Randy Reeves, who was the adoptive cousin of Janet Mesner.[7] Perhaps because of their faith (Quakers are known for their respect for life), members of both families were opposed to execution. In 1999 the Nebraska Board of Pardons met as they considered the death sentence for Randy Reeves, handed down in 1981 and finally about to be carried out. Three family members asked to present testimony, but only one was permitted. Victoria's sister, who supported the death penalty, shared and went on record. Both Gus, the husband of the murdered, and Audrey, the daughter of the murdered, were denied the right to speak.

However, Nebraska is one of thirty-two states[8] that have amended their constitution to give special rights to victims, so the Lamms filed a suit to fight for their right to have a voice in sentencing. A district court ruled against the Lamms, the judge saying, "The Lamms are not victims, as that term is commonly understood." *They lost their wife and mother but were not victims because they were against execution.* The Board of Pardons never got to hear the words of Audrey (who was only twenty-one at the time). "It pains me to think that in some indirect way, my mother's death could cause another person to lose his life," she said. "Killing another person doesn't do any honor to her memory."

To oppose the death penalty, in this case and many others, was seen as opposing the state, and thus as being more closely associated with the defense than with the prosecution. In the Lamms' case, opposing the death penalty meant that they were not even recognized as victims of violence. In fact, the judge went on to characterize the Lamms as "agents of Randy Reeves"! The court failed to recognize that a victim's family, even a faith-filled family with no political agenda, could be against execution. Gus Lamm had this to say: "What began with an event that marginalized my life to a certain extent—the murder of my wife—was now turning into a situation where I was marginalized even further by the state of Nebraska." The state of Nebraska considered Gus and his daughter personae non gratae. The state would only help victims when those victims were willing to help the state seek the death penalty.[9]

Clearly, then, the fact that a victim is able to imagine a form of justice outside the punitive system we have now does not guarantee that the judge involved will have that same moral imagination. In this case, having an anti–death penalty family member of a murder victim was simply incomprehensible to the court.

Sadly, the Lamm case is not an isolated incident. There are countless cases of the silencing and repression of murder victims' families who are against execution. Some of the most disturbing cases are family members who are threatened with contempt of court if they do not seek execution.

Consider the troubling case of SueZann Bosler.[10] A deranged man broke into her father's home and violently attacked both her and her father. Her father died, but SueZann, who was stabbed repeatedly in the head, miraculously survived by playing dead and holding her breath until the attacker left. The man was eventually caught and brought to trial. During the proceedings, SueZann wanted to honor her father's opposition to the death penalty. When she was called to the stand as a witness during the sentencing phase, she talked about her father, his faith, and his opposition to the death penalty.

The judge interrupted her, saying, "There will be no discussion about the death penalty, period, and I'm advising you right now that if you violate my order, you will be in direct criminal contempt, and you face six months in county jail and a $500 fine."

I wish I could say that this was an isolated case of a bad judge, but it's not. Thankfully, this one was caught on tape. A video recording of the scene in the courtroom shows SueZann on the stand, weeping as she says, "I don't know what to say. I feel like if I say one word I'm going to go to jail. I don't want to go to jail." Years later she reflected back on this moment and said, "I was wondering who was a criminal in that courtroom. They were treating me like I was the bad one."

Mind-boggling, isn't it? A young woman barely survives a violent attack and watches the brutal murder of her father. Not only is she not seen as a legitimate victim, but she moves from victim to defendant because her version of justice, or perhaps even her deceased father's version of justice, is different from that of the state of Florida. To say that anti–death penalty victims do not exist, or that they are not "real" victims, or that they are in danger of contempt of court or obstruction of justice creates further victimization and powerlessness and adds salt to the massive wounds these people have already endured.

The silencing of anti–death penalty victims also robs us of the perspectives, information, and evidence that these victims possess. Survivors' opposition to the death penalty can mean that they are denied the right to legal proceedings, or that they are not given information about proceedings related to their case. In one Texas case, when Jeanette Popp began to publicly oppose the death penalty, she stopped receiving information about court hearings related to her daughter's murder.[11] Two men were convicted of the rape and murder of her daughter, only to be found innocent and released twelve years later. It's entirely possible that Jeanette's testimony could have saved these men twelve years of their lives and the grave injustice that occurred had the prosecution not excluded her from these legal proceedings.

These victims' voices are invaluable. They must be heard and amplified, which is why you will encounter them scattered throughout

Countries with the
Most Executions:

#1 China

#2 Iran

#3 Saudi Arabia

#4 Iraq

#5 United States
of America

the book. But that doesn't mean we should silence the *other* victims, those who are in favor of execution. Their grief and trauma likewise give them credibility to speak out of their pain.

Ironically, the pain experienced by a family traumatized by violent crime is not that different from that of a family traumatized as their loved one is taken away for execution. And in some cases both things happen to the same family. The children of Kelly Gissendaner, in Georgia, lost their father to murder; eighteen years later, in 2015, they lost their mother to execution.[12]

The murder victims have families and the execution victims have families. Some of the groups I'm working with for this book (and donating proceeds to) have brought together the loved ones of the murdered and of the executed to join forces in calling for an end to all killing—both legal and illegal. They are all heroes of mine.[13]

We need to listen to people's pain.

Passionate death penalty abolitionists are faced with the temptation to avoid or ignore the victims and thereby to turn a blind eye toward evil. Some activists can come across as unreasonable, giving the impression that real evil does not exist or that every person on death row is innocent. We always have to be careful that in exposing one truth we don't cover up another. Or that in amplifying one person's voice we do not silence another.

Sister Helen Prejean, the Roman Catholic nun whose death row ministry was depicted in the book and film *Dead Man Walking* (and arguably one of the biggest champions for life on the planet), has said that one of her early mistakes was advocating for those on death row without being equally committed to the victims of crime. She has since promised to come alongside both victims of crime and those facing the death penalty.[14] There is something powerful about

Dalton Prejean | Thomas Baal | John Swindler | Ronald Simmons | James Smith the consistency of being against *all* killing, both legal and illegal, since *any* time a life is taken, that event creates new victims and new trauma.

So caring for the families of the victims of violent crime and caring for the surviving family members of the executed must go together. And as expensive as it is, execution may actually be "cheap" justice because it doesn't require that the offender take responsibility in repairing the harm done. Many crime victims feel that execution circumvents true justice. These survivors would rather see the offender take responsibility for what they caused rather than just terminating their lives. Arguably, facing the reality of what you have done to someone and taking responsibility for the pain you have caused may be harder than facing the electric chair. Caring about justice means considering *both* the victims and the offenders; and as we'll soon see, sometimes their healing can be inextricably connected.

In recent tragedies, including the Boston Marathon bombing, the Sandy Hook school shooting, and the Charleston church massacre, if you listen closely you will hear whispers of grace. After each of these tragedies, there were families who'd lost someone they loved saying that justice should not mean death for the one who had caused their pain; that death is the problem, not the solution.

So let us open up our moral imagination and not box in victims as exclusively pro-death. There are hundreds of victims of violence who refuse to respond to their loss with a pursuit of execution. They insist that their loved ones deserve a more honorable memorial and that executions do not help *anyone* heal.

Victims Against the Death Penalty

Here is a sampling of the voices we often are not allowed to hear:

Anthony Aversano.[15] Anthony's father was killed in the September 1, 2001, attack on the World Trade Center. In memory of his father, Anthony spoke out against the death penalty for Zacarias Moussaoui, the one person tried in connection with the attack, and Anthony now works with New Yorkers Against the Death Penalty.

Jo Berry.[16] Jo's father, a member of the British Parliament, was killed by an IRA bomb in 1984. The person who set the bomb was arrested but later released as part of the ongoing work to resolve the conflict in Ireland, which became known as the Good Friday peace process. Jo has not only met with the man but also works with him to promote peace and understanding.[17] A few years ago, I was speaking in Belfast, and the two of them were speaking together. (I thought of telling everybody at my event, "Let's go listen to them!")

Jennifer Bishop Jenkins and Jeanne Bishop.[18] Jennifer and Jeanne's three-months-pregnant sister and her husband were murdered in their home by a high-schooler. To honor what their sister would have wanted, they opposed the death penalty, and the high-schooler received life without parole.

Ron Callen.[19] Ron's eighty-six-year-old mother was murdered by a robber who had been surprised by her presence. Ron and his family did not support the death penalty for the man, even though the courts pushed for it.

Charles Coleman | Charles Walker | James Hamblen | Wilbert Evans | Raymond Clark

Clementina M. Chéry.[20] Clementina's fifteen-year-old son was killed in the crossfire of a gang fight while he was on his way to a meeting for teenagers against gang violence. Clementina does not support the death penalty because her son did not support it; in fact, she founded a peace institute in her son's name, the Louis D. Brown Peace Institute.

Robert Curley.[21] Robert's ten-year-old son was killed after two men tricked the youngster into getting into a car with them. Initially Robert was for the death penalty and worked to bring it back to his home state, Massachusetts, but he has since heard stories of other murder victims' families and changed to an anti–death penalty position.

Loretta Filipov.[22] Loretta's husband, Alexander, was aboard one of the hijacked flights that flew into the World Trade Center on September 11, 2001. Alexander and Loretta had been against the death penalty, and Loretta worked for life sentences for the one person charged in the attacks. She is part of September 11th Families for Peaceful Tomorrows.

Aba Gayle.[23] Aba's nineteen-year-old daughter was murdered in 1980, and her killer has been on death row since he was convicted. Aba originally supported his sentence but eventually changed her mind and connected with her daughter's killer. She met the man after many years of grief as a step toward healing.

Susan Hirsch.[24] In the 1998 bombing of the U.S. embassies in Tanzania and Kenya, over 200 people were killed. Susan was injured and her husband was killed. It changed the course of Susan's life. She opposes the death penalty and does incredible work as a legal anthropologist and professor of conflict resolution. Among her books is the remarkable title, *In the Moment of Greatest Calamity,* which speaks of her grief and her heart for better forms of justice than execution.

Bill Jenkins.[25] Bill's sixteen-year-old son was killed during a robbery, and as the state pursued the death penalty, Bill and his wife requested they take the death penalty off the table. Bill now writes and teaches about juvenile crime and traumatic loss. He has published a book to help other victims of traumatic loss, entitled *Street Talk.*

Bess Klassen-Landis.[26] Bess's mother, Helen Klassen, was beaten, stripped, raped, strangled, and shot multiple times in Indiana. By publicly telling her story, Bess was able to expose and release pain and trauma inside of her. She believes that we are all instruments in healing the hatred in this world and that we will never do it with violence. As many political figures say the death penalty is for the worst of the worst, Bess realizes that in reality it is for the "poorest of the poor." She has put out a CD of original music called *Beauty So Close,* a collection of songs of hope.

Art Laffin.[27] Art is a revolutionary for grace. He's a dear friend, sort of a "brother-from-another-mother." He has been a longtime leader in the Catholic Worker Movement, a passionate advocate for peace and nonviolence for decades. But in 1999, there was a tragic incident that tested his ideals. Art's brother Paul, who worked in a homeless shelter in Connecticut, was killed by a mentally ill man. In the eulogy for his brother, Art asked everyone to pray for Dennis, the man who killed Paul.

Andrew Jones | Albert Clozza | Derick Peterson | Maurice Byrd | Donald Gaskins | James Russell

Some weeks after the funeral, Art attended Mass at the church where some of Dennis's family were parishioners. He held hands with Dennis's sister-in-law and her husband, Dennis's brother, as they prayed the Lord's Prayer together. Art says this event "took him to a different place" than he had ever been before. And it fueled his conviction that we cannot fight violence with violent justice. Dennis was deemed mentally incompetent to stand trial and is now serving a sixty-year sentence in a Connecticut prison hospital where he is receiving treatment for his mental illness. Art was able to send Dennis a message that he is praying for him, that he may experience God's forgiving love. Art has been jailed for his courageous witness for nonviolence, most notably when he and seventeen others were arrested for holding a banner on the steps of the U.S. Supreme Court that said, "Stop Executions." Since his brother's death, Art's conviction to challenge the culture of death and fear has only grown stronger.

Yolanda Littlejohn.[28]   Yolanda's sister Jacquetta Thomas was beaten to death and her body left in the streets in Raleigh, North Carolina. Yolanda became convinced that the man convicted of her sister's brutal murder was not guilty. She visited this convicted man in prison, spent time with him, wept with him, and became deeply troubled that he was not guilty of the murder . . . and that he could be executed for a crime he didn't commit. Year after year police assured her he was the killer, and that man, Greg Taylor, waited for seventeen years before he was exonerated in 2010. Yolanda and Greg now unite their voices against the death penalty. Yolanda has now been waiting for over two decades for the real murderer to be found. She longs for an end to the broken death penalty system and for better forms of restorative justice.

Marietta Jaeger Lane.[29] Marietta was camping with her family in Montana when her seven-year-old daughter, Susie, was kidnapped from their tent during the night. For a year, the family knew nothing of Susie's whereabouts. On the first anniversary of Susie's disappearance, the kidnapper telephoned Marietta and inadvertently revealed sufficient information to enable the FBI to identify and arrest him.

Marietta asked that the mentally ill man be given the alternative allowed in capital cases: a mandatory life sentence instead of the death penalty. Only then was the kidnapper willing to confess to Susie's murder and to the deaths of three other young people in the same county. He committed suicide just hours later.

Marietta insists that the claim that the execution of an offender is "just retribution" is an insult to the immeasurable and irreplaceable worth of the victim. For her, to kill in retaliation is to violate and profane the goodness, sweetness, and beauty of Susie's life.

Robin Theurkauf.[30] Robin's husband was killed in the September 11, 2001, attack on the World Trade Center. She testified against the death penalty at Zacarias Moussaoui's trial and remained outspoken against the death penalty until she died of cancer in 2009. Before she died, she wrote this: "Each of us is always a child of God. In our brokenness, we are called to forgive so that we may be forgiven. The act of forgiving, of giving up the demand for vengeance, is an act of transcendence. To let go of the anger is to let go of some of the pain."

Ricky Rector | Johnny Garrett | David Clark | Edward Ellis | Robyn Parks | Olan Robison

Jonnie Warner.   Jonnie's brother Dennis was killed in 1980. Months later, the accused killer was murdered after being released from prison for lack of evidence; Jonnie's other brother, Larry, was charged in the second killing.[31] Convicted, Larry was executed in 1995, but in 2005 an investigation concluded that Larry was most likely not the person who committed the crime. Jonnie now speaks across Missouri about the effects of the death penalty on victims' families.[32]

SueZann Bosler.[33]   As noted earlier, in 1986 SueZann and her father were attacked. Her father, a pastor, had told her before his murder that he was against the death penalty, and so SueZann worked for ten years to lift the death sentence from their attacker. She eventually succeeded. As she offered forgiveness to the attacker, SueZann says, "a weight lifted from my shoulders."

Maria Hines.[34]   Maria's brother, a state trooper, was killed while on duty in Virginia. After seeing the movie *Dead Man Walking,* Maria resolved to fight against the death penalty for her brother's killer. Though she was not successful, she befriended the killer and held a prayer vigil during his execution.

Cathy Harrington.[35]   Cathy's twenty-six-year-old daughter was murdered at the hands of her housemate's friend. At first, Cathy agreed that his punishment should be the death penalty, but by the time of the sentencing three years later, she and her sons had changed their views. After the trial Cathy met the killer's mother and found relief and forgiveness in that encounter.

Judith Toy.[36]   Judith's sister-in-law and two nephews were killed by a teenage neighbor. Judith struggled for years with hatred, until she began practicing Buddhism. With meditation she was able to understand the young killer's story, and she forgave him.

Terry Caffey.[37]   Terry's wife and two young sons were brutally killed by his teenage daughter's boyfriend and another accomplice, in a crime that she was convicted of helping to plan. Terry was also wounded but managed to escape to his neighbor's house to call the police. Terry had a profound experience with God that convinced him forgiveness was possible, and that the death penalty was not the way forward. Terry prayed each day that he would be able to forgive his daughter and the men responsible, a stunning story of courage. He has written a book entitled *Terror by Night*.

Rebecca DeMauro.[38]   Rebecca's twelve-year-old daughter was kidnapped, raped, and strangled by a relative who confessed to the crime after a statewide search for the girl. Rebecca supported the death penalty at his sentencing. Her mind was later changed, however, as she watched a news program on the case of another murderer. In a scene included in the program, the father of one of that man's victims told the killer that he forgave him, and Rebecca decided to forgive her daughter's killer so that she, too, could have peace.

After almost every tragic event—like the massacre inside Emanuel AME Church in Charleston, South Carolina, where nine people were killed during worship—the victims speak about grace and public forgiveness. Over and over you hear the whisper of mercy that slows the rush of revenge.

Remember the Boston bombing in 2013? Over 250 people were

injured, sixteen people lost their limbs, and three people died, one of them eight years old. But what was truly remarkable was the response of many of the victims, who were the first to say they did not want the death penalty for Dzhokhar Tsarnaev.[39] The families of the Boston bombing victims shared their opposition to the death sentence, providing evidence of the hundreds of murder victims' family members who believe that there are better forms of justice than execution but who rarely make headlines.

The family of eight-year-old Martin Richards released a five-hundred-word statement detailing their opposition.

And these are the words of Jennifer Lemmerman, the sister of the slain MIT police officer: "Whenever someone speaks out against the death penalty, they are challenged to imagine how they would feel if someone they love were killed. I've been given that horrible perspective and I can say that my position has only strengthened." She went on to say, "I also can't imagine that killing in response to killing would ever bring me peace or justice. I choose to remember Sean for the light that he brought. No more darkness."

Jessica Knesky and Patrick Downes, a newlywed couple who each lost limbs in the attack, also asked prosecutors to take the death penalty off the table: "In our darkest moments and deepest sadness, we think of inflicting the same types of harm on him," they confessed. But then they went on, "However, we must overcome the impulse for vengeance."

Amidst the horror, the voices of grace sang a different song.

Edward Fitzgerald | William Andrews | Curtis Johnson | Willie Jones | James Demouchette

FACES OF GRACE

A Journey of Hope

In 1985, Bill Pelke's grandmother Ruth, a beloved Sunday school teacher everyone called Nana, was brutally killed, stabbed thirty-three times in an unthinkable act of violence. More troubling still, it was four of the teenage girls from the local high school who killed the elderly Bible school teacher. One of them was Paula Cooper, then fifteen years old.

I first heard about Bill when CNN reported that he was one of the first people to celebrate Paula's release from prison, after twenty-eight years behind bars. It was such a wild story I had to rewind it a few times and make sure I'd heard it right.

Few stories exemplify grace and redemption like this one. And there aren't many people I've met who embody compassion like Bill Pelke.[40]

But this story is no fairy tale. Ruth's murder was real—and horrific. Naturally, Bill's instinct was to seek the death penalty. He was a believer in capital punishment for the worst of the worst, and this seemed about as bad as it could get.

Then he began to think about his grandmother, and he replayed in his mind the Bible stories Nana had told. At the very heart of her message were forgiveness and grace.

These were things that seemed pretty far off for him right after the incident; they existed in a dream world a long way from the real world of thirty-three stab wounds. But he wanted compassion

Ricky Lee Grubbs | John Gardner | Jeffrey Griffin | Cornelius Singleton | Kavin Lincecum and love to have the last word, and he knew that's what his grandmother would want. So, with little else to lean on, Bill began to pray.

In response to his prayers, he says, he recalled Jesus telling us that forgiveness was the only way forward. Bill didn't know where to start, so he asked Jesus to help. After all, Jesus seemed to be pretty good at forgiveness. Praying for forgiveness and compassion, Bill turned the matter over to Jesus.

Then reality hit. The death penalty, once a theoretical matter, became real: Paula Cooper, the teenage ringleader of the crime, was given the death penalty. On July 11, 1986, Bill sat in the courtroom as the judge sentenced her to die in the electric chair.

At that moment it seemed as if justice had been served, even to Bill. His grandmother's life had had value, and now her death would not go unpunished. It didn't matter to him at the time that Paula was only fifteen years old. If she was old enough to kill someone, she was old enough to face the consequences.

And yet it wasn't long before his life began to change in a most unusual way. To be exact, it was November 2, 1986. He was a crane operator at the Bethlehem Steel Mill, and it was a slow night at work. As his mind wandered, he thought of Nana.

He remembered her Sunday school lessons about Jesus, about how we will be forgiven as much as we forgive. If we do not show mercy to others, Nana had taught, then we shouldn't expect God to show mercy to us. But what did it all mean for him? How much should he forgive Paula?

He remembered the apostle Peter asking Jesus how much we should forgive someone: seven times? And Jesus responded by saying seventy times seven. Bill says he realized at that moment that the point was not that we should forgive 490 times and stop, but that forgiveness must become habitual; it must become a way of life—part of who we are and how we live, woven into the very fabric of our being. And only God could accomplish that.

As I interviewed Bill he told me that he recalled Jesus's own execution and how Jesus had found the strength to forgive his murderers. Now Bill wondered: Could it be that Jesus might help him find the strength to forgive Paula Cooper? He knew very well he couldn't do it without some help from above.

Bill recalled the courtroom scene from four months earlier, when Paula had been sentenced to die, and wondered what Nana would have done. When the sentence was announced, Paula's grandfather had had to be removed from the courtroom—his wailing was so loud. Bill thought of Paula being strapped into the electric chair, and what her grandfather would feel as he watched the voltage hit her. Bill was convinced that Nana and Jesus would have chosen a different path.

These are his words as he remembers that quiet November night in the steel mill:

> My grandmother would have been appalled that this girl, Paula, was on death row. I was convinced that my grandmother would have had love and compassion for her and her family, and I was convinced beyond a shadow of a doubt that my grandmother wanted me to have that same love and compassion. I did not have any. But I was so convinced that's what she would have wanted that I begged God in a short prayer to please, please—please—give me love and compassion for Paula Cooper and her family.[41]

God answered that prayer beyond anyone's wildest dreams (including Bill's). Bill was convinced that Nana would want love, not execution, to have the last word, and that responsibility fell on his

James Red Dog | Robert Sawyer | Syvasky Poyner | Carlos Santana | Ramon Montoya shoulders now. He decided to write Paula and tell her about Nana and about Jesus. He wanted her to know the faith that had driven his grandmother to welcome her and the other girls into her home for Bible study.

Not only did he write a letter, he wrote lots of letters back and forth with Paula, one every week or so. And he began to visit her in prison. Not only did Paula get to hear about Nana, and about Jesus, but Bill learned about Paula. He got to know her—not Paula the murderer, but Paula the little girl who had been abused, beaten with electric cords, locked in a car to die. At fifteen *that* Paula Cooper was convinced she was unlovable.

Bill visited her in prison over and over through the years. They became family. What began as compassion led to forgiveness. And forgiveness led to healing.

But it wasn't just about Paula. Bill felt his own heart healing too. In the early months after the murder, when he thought about Nana his mind immediately went to the crime scene. Sometimes it felt like her murder had overpowered the other memories of her. But now he began to remember *her* and to share about her life, not her death. More than how she died, he remembered how she'd lived, what she'd believed, and who she'd been.

Bill is the first to say that forgiveness did not mean forgetfulness. He never forgot what happened to Nana, and he never will. Nor did forgiving mean condoning; it certainly didn't mean there should be no consequences for the murder.

Paula spent many years in prison, at one time the youngest woman on death row. But her life was ultimately spared—just a few years after her initial conviction, her sentence was commuted to a set term of imprisonment—in part because of the friendship and

James Clark | Robert Henderson | Darryl Stewart | Larry Johnson | Leonel Herrera dedicated advocacy of Bill Pelke (a little help from the pope didn't hurt).[42]

To Bill, Paula was no longer the woman who had killed his grandmother. She was his sister. Bill watched as she got first her GED and then a college degree, and—still in prison—they shared dreams through letters and visits.

Paula spent thirty years in prison before her release in 2013. It's hard to imagine what it must have been like to reenter society after spending her adult life in prison, including several years in solitary confinement—total isolation twenty-three hours a day in a space the size of a bathroom.[43] When she was finally released, after being in jail since she was fifteen, Paula did her best, and she had a lot of great friends and support. She got a job at Five Guys, from a manager who made a point of hiring folks coming out of prison in need of work. It wasn't long before Paula herself became a manager. She got the chance to give back to the lawyer who had helped her since she was a teenager, working alongside her at the legal clinic as an assistant.

Bill Pelke watched from a distance, perhaps a distance farther than he might have wished. The system doesn't always have room for things like reconciliation and grace and forgiveness. But Bill kept an eye on Paula from afar, praying for her continually.

All who knew Paula described her contagious joy, her strong spirit, her passion for life. But on Memorial Day in 2015, less than two years after her release, Paula Cooper was found dead. Her death was ruled a suicide.

Sadly, Bill Pelke never got to see Paula on the outside.

As I said, this is no fairy tale; none of these stories are. They don't have Hollywood endings.

John Sawyers | Andrew Chabrol | Thomas Stevens | Markham Duff-Smith | Curtis Harris

As for Bill, he's one of the grandfathers and key leaders of the death penalty abolition movement now.[44] He is unstoppable—more passion and energy and love in one body than you can imagine. Bill made two promises to God in the steel mill that November night. One was to always point to God as he speaks about forgiveness. The other was to walk through any door that opens up an opportunity to teach others about grace, love, compassion, and Jesus. He's kept both promises for the past thirty years.

And Bill is not alone. There is an all-star team, a whole host of characters on the side of grace. He brings together family members of the murdered and family members of the executed to stand together against death in all its ugly forms—both legal and illegal. These folks are sort of like the superheroes of love. But the weird thing is, they're people just like us—normal people who experienced something terrible but decided to answer it with grace.

CHAPTER THREE

Death and Grace in the Bible

The Bible Belt has become the Death Belt.

—Dale Recinella, chaplain for Florida's death row[1]

H ere is a troubling question: As a nation, how have we justified things like lynching, the death penalty, and the wicked glorification of death?

And the answer is: the Bible.

To be more accurate, the answer is the Bible, the Koran, the Torah, the U.S. Constitution, and all sorts of other holy and unholy stuff. When it comes to execution, few cultures do it more passionately than those compelled by their understanding of their religion. That's true both of Christians and of Muslims.

But for our purposes in the United States, executions are happening almost exclusively in deeply Christian territory.

Here is a stunning fact: Over 85 percent of state executions in the last thirty-eight years occurred in the so-called Bible Belt.[2] As Brother

David Mason | Ruben Cantu | Michael Durocher | Richard Wilkerson | Kenneth DeShields

Over 85 percent
of state
executions in
the last
38 years have
occurred in the
"Bible Belt."

Dale Recinella, a chaplain on Florida's death row, puts it: "The Bible Belt has become the Death Belt."[3]

After much reflection on the causes and consequences of capital punishment, my friend Bryan Stevenson, devout Christian, all-star death penalty lawyer, and bestselling author—"America's young Mandela," according to Desmond Tutu—implicates Christians. With the cartoon character Pogo, he says, "We have met the enemy, and it is us."[4]

The death penalty did not flourish in America in *spite* of Christians but *because* of us. So it is pertinent to ask: Does the Bible really support the death penalty? And even more precisely, does the Bible support the contemporary practice of execution *as it exists today?*

In the Beginning

One of the first stories in the Bible is about a murder: Cain kills his brother Abel (Gen. 4:1–16).

Remember, death itself was a consequence of the "original sin" in the Garden of Eden, when Adam and Eve ate the forbidden fruit. Death was not a part of the original plan. Sometimes, in our obsession with original sin, we forget *original innocence*. Before there was sin and death, there was life. God is the author of life, the one who created life by breathing into dirt. And, as my friend Paul Young puts it, "God goes to great lengths to protect our ability to say no—without that freedom, love cannot exist."[5] We humans said no to love, perfection, life. We chose death. And we continue to choose death over life.

Let's take a closer look at that first biblical story of death. After

Adam and Eve's initial rejection of life, things start to unravel. Relationships fall apart.

Some years after the Garden of Eden, Cain kills his brother Abel. Murder is thus the inaugural act of human beings outside the garden. Cain commits the first homicide in human history. But what is just as important is how God deals with Cain.[6]

The background is clear. God made life. Sin entered the world. Death is the fruit of sin. God has a different dream and a different plan. God is and always has been on the side of life.

So God does not execute Cain. In fact, after condemning the murder, God protects Cain from avengers. God even goes so far as to promise sevenfold vengeance on anyone who might kill Cain (Gen. 4:13–15).

God deals with Cain by banishing him from the community that he has betrayed (Gen. 4:10–12). God's justice is exile rather than vengeance. One could argue that that punishment is similar to life in prison. Exile is sort of a reverse imprisonment, after all; but rather than being locked up, Cain is locked out, banished to the wilderness.

Only in Cain's case, he is allowed to marry, have children, and raise a family; he even builds a city (Gen. 4:17).

One of the beautiful things that begins to surface in the Hebrew scriptures is the subversion of violence. There are killings aplenty, to be sure, but there are also stories that demonstrate something other than retaliation, which scholars point out is very rare in the ancient world. Stories like that of Joseph (Gen. 37). A totally innocent victim of violence, Joseph is nearly killed by his own brothers. His response: forgiveness. Another story concerns David and Saul (1 Sam. 24). Saul and his three thousand soldiers are pursuing David to kill him. When Saul enters the cave David is hiding in, David has the chance to kill

Saul, but instead David snips off the corner of Saul's robe—just a subtle little way of saying, "I could've . . . and didn't."

Throughout the Bible there is a movement away from violence, toward "beating swords into plows" (Isa. 2:4), transforming the instruments of death into tools that can cultivate life. The climax of this is the cross. But let's not get ahead of ourselves.

A Shorter Bible Without Grace

Defenders of the death penalty often point to the Old Testament law given to Moses, with its explicit instructions about which crimes deserve the death penalty (more on this later), as the best expression of God's will on the matter. But we might not want to go down this road too quickly.

The Bible is full of messed-up people. And that seems to be one of the points. The whole story is not about how good we are, but how good God is, even when we're not.

Think about it. If held to the letter of the law, one of the first people to face the death penalty would have been none other than Moses himself, one of the first prominent murderers in the Bible. He commits premeditated, first-degree murder (Exod. 2:11–12). He has at least four "aggravators" (circumstances that elevate a crime to a capital offense), and only one would be needed to land him on death row in America today.

God does not kill Moses, though God does rebuke and punish him. Moses, like Cain, is sent into exile. If God's most perfect will were for everyone who kills to be killed, God would have killed Moses. But God did not.

Johnny Watkins | William Hance | Freddie Webb | Richard Beavers | Roy Allen Stewart

Then there is David, one of the most prominent heroes of the Bible and author of many of the Psalms. In Sunday school, growing up, I remember hearing all sorts of stories about David, "a man after God's own heart" (Acts 13:22). But if you read the Bible carefully, you discover that in two chapters (2 Sam. 11–12) he breaks pretty much every one of the Ten Commandments: he lies, covets, lusts, commits adultery, and even commits murder. He takes another man's wife, Bathsheba. Has sex with her. Then has her husband, Uriah, killed. David, like Moses, was a murderer! Let me just point out as well that David, at the time, already had six wives and a dozen concubines. The man had a problem. He was a womanizer and a murderer. *And a child of God.*

What does God do in response? God rebukes David through a prophet named Nathan and forgives David. It's clear: God's grace is bigger than David's mistakes.[7] *Bigger than our mistakes.* That starts to sound like good news, doesn't it?

Then of course there's Saul of Tarsus, who wrote more books of the Bible than any other person and is arguably the most influential person in Christian history other than Christ himself. Saul of Tarsus was also a murderer. By every definition he was a religious extremist. Before his conversion, he terrorized the early Christians, going house to house trying to "destroy the church," imprisoning and persecuting those who followed Jesus (Acts 8:3). One of those followers was a young man named Stephen, who is known to be the first Christian martyr. It's easy to forget that Saul oversaw his execution. As Stephen was being killed by a mob, Scripture says Saul was there "giving approval of his death" (Acts 22:20).

As they were stoning Stephen, the young man cried out for mercy—not for himself, but for those killing him: "Lord, do not hold this against them" (Acts 7:60). Sound familiar? He had heard those words before—as Christ pleaded for forgiveness for those nailing him to the cross. It was the cry of grace, of agonizing, scandalous love. Those same words would be heard over and over from the mouths of martyrs and Christians throughout history. They form a prayer that brings redemption. A prayer that *converts* those doing evil rather than killing them.

I don't think it's a coincidence that when you flip over a page or two from the story of Stephen's death, what happens next is that Saul has a radical conversion (Acts 9). He gets knocked off his horse and blinded, and he hears Jesus say, "Why are you persecuting me?"

Saul has such a radical conversion that even his name changes—to Paul. He goes on to write half the books in the New Testament. One of the things he will write is this: "Christ Jesus came into the world to save sinners—of whom I am the worst" (1 Tim. 1:15). When making such an audacious claim—"the worst" of sinners—he wasn't exaggerating. Most of his life, he looked more like ISIS than a saint. But God's love is unstoppable. Paul goes on to describe the depths of God's love, saying "neither height nor depth" nor anything in the world can separate us from the love of God—not even death itself (Rom. 8:38–39). God's love is bigger than our sins—and perhaps even bigger than our imaginations.

The Bible is a love story—it's about a God who so loved the world that Jesus was sent to save it—not to condemn it to hell.

God's love is good news to those who suffer. It's good news to the victims of violence. But God's love is good news also to those who have killed someone. Mercy triumphs over judgment (James 2:13). That's the promise of grace.

If we believe that murderers are beyond redemption, we can go ahead and rip out half the Bible. Get rid of the whole book of Psalms.

Edward Pickens | John Thanos | Charles Campbell | Stephen Nethery | Denton Crank

Tear out the first few books of the Old Testament. Ditch Paul's fourteen books in the New Testament. We wouldn't have much left.

Much of the Bible was written by murderers who were given a second chance. Moses. David. Paul.

The Bible would be much shorter without grace.

And our churches would be empty if we killed everyone who deserved to die according to Old Testament law. Let's take a closer look at the Bible, which has far too often been used as a weapon.

God Said It; That Settles It

There are some major problems with the simple view that "the Bible has the death penalty in it, and so it's okay." Think about it for a minute. The Bible also has passages that support polygamy, animal sacrifice, and many other things from which we have moved on. (I say that as a committed Christian with a very deep love for scripture.) So how do we decide what in the Bible was meant for the ancient Hebrew people and what is still God's intention for us today?

There are only a handful of verses that are used to legitimate execution, but these few verses have gotten used and abused throughout the church's history. It is not unusual for prosecutors to quote these scriptures, even during trial and sentencing, to clear the conscience of any conflicted jurors by affirming that God is on the side of execution.[8]

The Bible—or, more accurately, a certain interpretation of the Bible—has laid the foundation of the death penalty in America and the moral justification for it. If you look at the list of death-worthy crimes in America's history, you'll discover that many of them have their origin in texts in the Old Testament—as we see in the infamous

Salem witch trials. In 1665 New York, striking one's parents was a capital crime, and in 1647 Massachusetts, witchcraft, adultery, cursing your parents, and being a rebellious son were all death-worthy (and you can see the clear biblical parallels). There is even a case (Thomas Granger) where a teenager allegedly caught in an act of bestiality was executed, along with the sheep (as mandated in Lev. 20).[9]

There are over thirty death-worthy crimes in scripture. The crimes punishable by death according to the Bible include not just murder but also rape, incest, adultery, bestiality, sorcery, idolatry, blasphemy, witchcraft, kidnapping, striking a parent, insubordination to a priest or judge, working on the Sabbath, and cursing your parents.

Don't take my word for it. Here's a list of capital crimes along with the verses where you'll find them:

- Murder (Exod. 21:12)

- Adultery (Deut. 22:22–24)—they shall both die

- Rape (Deut. 22:25)

- Kidnapping (Exod. 21:16)—incidentally, this would include the trafficking of women and children

- Fornication (Deut. 22:13–21)

- Cursing one's parents (Exod. 21:17)

- Incest (Lev. 20:11–12)—sleeping with one's father's wife or one's daughter-in-law; they shall both die

- Bestiality (Lev. 20:15–16)—with both man and beast being executed

- Sorcery (Lev. 20:27)

- Idolatry (Deut. 17:2–5)

- False witness in a capital case (Deut. 19:18–21)

- False prophecy (Deut. 18:20)—the televangelists predicting the end of the world would have seen their own end of the world

- Rebellion in a son (Deut. 21:18–21)—we'd have smaller youth groups

- Working on the Sabbath (Exod. 31:15)

What would happen if we really tried to import all the Mosaic law's death penalties into our times? We'd have a much smaller population, to begin with. Pretty much everyone on *Jerry Springer* would have to go. Almost every business in America, except Chick-fil-A, dishonors the Sabbath; those workers would be goners. And sadly, the cursing one's parents bit would take out most of our young 'uns. If Jesus is right that looking at a woman lustfully is a form of adultery (Matt. 5:28), then most men are in trouble, since statistics consistently show a majority of males look at porn (and a good chunk of others probably lie about not looking at porn), so men would be pretty sparse on earth. Let's not let the ladies off the hook, though. Studies have shown that two-thirds of young women have had premarital sex,[10] a crime biblically punishable by death. Heck, people would get nixed for consulting a psychic or reading their astrological forecast or playing with a Ouija board.

It is especially noteworthy that bearing false witness is cited as being punishable by death. Hundreds of prosecutors, witnesses, police officers, and forensics examiners guilty of lying in court would not only do time, but be killed.

My point is that we have never followed what the Bible teaches as literally as the church thinks it has. That does not mean we have to throw out the Bible. I am still a deeply committed Christian who believes that scripture is God's Word to us.

Many Christian leaders and teachers, throughout the church's history, have pointed us to a better way of understanding how best to use scripture as a guide for discerning how to govern. Many point out that the ancient Hebrew laws reveal the moral fabric of these ancient communities—showing us what they valued and what they deemed toxic. These laws help us see how severe the people understood certain violations to be, seeing them as poisonous to the common good of all. And, of course, since God is helping form and shape these communities as God's own people, they show us the things God cares about.

Every society establishes its values and laws and identifies those actions that are offenses, along with appropriate punishments. What we can learn from the Bible is that the Hebrew people and their God identified the above-listed offenses as so destructive to the life of the community that they were deserving of death. They were the worst crimes against God and community.

If we look closely, we can see that these criminal acts fundamentally betrayed love for God and love for neighbor, and thus the offenses began to rot away the core identity of the Hebrew people.

The Surprising History of Jewish Law

There's one more thing worth noting in regard to the Old Testament as a whole. And this is monumental.

In practice, the Jews abolished the biblical death penalty ages ago, even though Christians continue to use Old Testament texts to justify it.

Historically, the Jews have never been comfortable with the death penalty. The rabbis did not like the killing of people. They made it all but impossible to jump through all the strict legal requirements needed to warrant an execution. The Talmud, which collects rabbinic wisdom and guidance about the scripture, says of the process required for execution, "They rendered the execution of a death sentence all but impossible."[11] The Mishnah, another source of rabbinic reflection, considers a court that passed the death penalty even once in seven years to be overly zealous.[12] Other rabbis said one execution in seventy years is too many.[13]

Don't miss that. The Jews themselves said one execution in seventy years is too many!

It is of huge significance that even though there are dozens of death-worthy crimes in the Hebrew scriptures, there were not many executions over the centuries.

The death penalty was not practiced widely; indeed, it was so limited as to be almost impossible to enact. Surely that's because, as we just saw, if every person who was worthy of death were killed, who would be left? This point, emphasized by Jesus in a passage that we will turn to later, was understood by the Jews.

Here is the sad irony. The Christian community has used the Hebrew scriptures to execute people with more passion and conviction than the Jews themselves ever did. And as we will see, to this day Jews are not big fans of execution. It's Christians who use the Old Testament to justify the contemporary practice of the death penalty. The rabbis of old must be turning in their graves.

Dale Recinella has written a stellar book on this. He has pored over the thousands of pages of Jewish teaching on the death penalty—

from the biblical text itself, to the Talmud and the Mishnah.[14] As he juxtaposes the biblical death penalty with how it works in America, Recinella asks questions such as, What were the criteria for executions? What was the process for execution? What he discovers is stunning.

One of Recinella's central findings is that the rabbis' top priority was to make sure they never condemned or executed an innocent person: they had an explicit bias toward the defendant. Among the ancient Jewish community, the court for capital cases (known as the "Small Sanhedrin") was composed of twenty-three judges. One of the criteria for serving on the court was a general reluctance to sentence people to death. Anyone who seemed too inclined toward death was removed from the court. (Imagine if the same were true of our juries!) In addition, for someone to be put to death, many conditions had to be met.

Christians need to exercise the same care with the biblical death penalty that the Hebrews always have. As a person who has a very high view of scripture, I think we must take the argument that "the Bible has the death penalty in it" seriously. Brother Dale does exactly that, and he does it meticulously.[15]

His conclusion is that if the ancient Hebrews looked at the contemporary practice of the death penalty in America, they would be absolutely shocked, appalled, and offended.

One of the most fascinating observations Dale Recinella makes is this: the old-school biblical practice of the death penalty ended around the time of Jesus: "What we are realizing is that biblically based capital punishment ceased to function at the same time that Jesus Christ died on the cross on Calvary."[16]

Jesus died around 30 AD. The second temple was destroyed in 70 AD. Check this out: "Forty years prior to the destruction of the

Second Temple, the right of Israel to try capital cases ceased, for though the sanctuary still existed, the Sanhedrin was exiled and no longer held sessions in the place assigned to it in the sanctuary."[17] It ended, and never again resumed, at least not in the same way capital punishment was originally laid out in scripture.

There's something really cool about it. The ancient Jews stopped practicing the death penalty around the time of Jesus. Just as scripture says the veil of the temple split open when Jesus died, could it also be that the whole punitive system took a death blow? What if the entire system of ancient Jewish capital punishment ceased as the sacrifice of Jesus was given for all. Wow. Now if we can just get the Christians on board. More on that later.

All this is to say, when you take the biblical practice of the death penalty and try to compare it to the contemporary practice of the death penalty in the United States, there are some insurmountable problems. This takes the argument that "the Bible has the death penalty in it" seriously—so seriously, in fact, that we see how impossible it would be to implement the *biblical* death penalty today.

Sin, Evil, and Other Ugly Things

Let's talk about evil. Sometimes folks accuse people who want to abolish the death penalty of being unrealistic, utopian, or oblivious to the fact that evil is real. What do we do with someone who is a threat to society? How do we deal with pathological killers, terrorists, and vicious murderers? These are good questions.

This is also one of the reasons the victims of violence against execution inspire me so much. They have looked evil in the face, experienced it firsthand—and have found better ways forward than execution. And it is why Jesus inspires me: he was very familiar with the evil humans are capable of, and yet he was undeterred in his love for us.

The Bible has a lot to say about evil. That's because evil is real. Sin, too, is real. All we have to do is look at the news or, if our vision is good enough, look in the mirror.

As I read, interviewed, and researched for this book, I heard some of the most horrific stories I've ever come across.

Upon hearing a story about four men raping an eleven-year-old and killing her by stuffing her panties down her throat, any reasonable person is prone to think lethal injection seems like a pretty tame punishment in comparison to the crime. As U.S. Supreme Court Justice Antonin Scalia said regarding that case, "How enviable a quiet death by lethal injection [is] compared to that."[18] Sadly and ironically, the man convicted of the horrific rape and murder of this eleven-year-old girl, Henry McCollum, was later proved innocent by DNA evidence and released, after thirty years in prison.[19]

Yes, people are capable of unfathomable evil. To ignore evil is to become an accomplice to it. So the question is not, *Do* we respond to evil? but *How* do we respond to evil?

My concern is, How do we deal with evil without becoming it? If we aren't careful, our "justice" can be as bad as the crime itself. Yet, as noted earlier, we don't want the cure to be as bad as the disease.

I want to go out on a limb and make a bold assertion: God loves people and does not want people to die. That is not a universally accepted assertion. As you hear some Christians talk about sin and God's wrath, you get the impression that God hates people.

Here's what it boils down to. God hates sin, because God loves people and sin destroys us. So divorce is bad because it breaks people's hearts and rips families apart—not just because we broke a law. God hurts when we hurt. God cannot stand to watch us hurt ourselves and others. Sin leads to death—it eats away our bodies and our souls like a cancer.

"For the wages of sin is death," says Romans 6:23—but don't stop there. It goes on, "but the gift of God is eternal life in Christ Jesus our Lord."

Every day we are given the choice between life and death.

Sin is not just things we do; it is a condition we live with, an illness of our soul. When it comes to the law, it is not that we were made for the law, but that the law was made for us—which is what Jesus taught. The law was created to protect us—from ourselves. God wants to set us free.

So when it comes to this thing we call sin, it is not about breaking obscure laws that God put in place, like booby traps, to test our obedience. Instead, just like household rules established by a good parent, God's laws are put in place to protect the "children" from harm. God loves us infinitely more than even the best mom or dad, which is hard for me to imagine (having the greatest mom in the world). Missouri pastor Brian Zahnd tweeted it well: "We are punished more *by* our sins than *for* our sins." That's why parents—and God—set rules: they don't want to watch those they love get hurt.

The starting point, then, must be this: God loves people. And God wants us to love as richly and fully as God does. That's another reason God hates sin: it is a failure to love as God intended us to. It is a falling short of what love requires of us. This is why the Bible says, over and over, some variation on "All the law is summed up in this: love God and love others."[20] As we read the biblical story, it seems pretty clear that God's justice is not just concerned with "getting what we deserve"; it is also about stopping the cycle of destruction. I want to be clear that I am not putting compassion and justice at odds with each other. Both of them are part of God's character. But God's justice may look different from ours—in part because God is more compassionate than we are.

As the author of life, God is concerned with preserving life, not ending it. Think of stories like the one about plagues. They depict, in effect, God slapping our hand to save us from losing our arm. Even the story of Noah and the flood, in which humanity is decimated, shows a God who is committed to keeping the human experiment going, even though humans were (and still are) doing a good job of sabotaging things. And so painful was that experience to God that God "repented"—rethought things—after the flood, promising not to do that again and giving us a rainbow as the symbol of that covenant to preserve life.

One thing is for certain: the author of life is on the side of *life*.

FACES OF GRACE

An Execution Interrupted in Iran

A grace story from Iran recently went viral and made news around the world.[21] Iran puts more people to death than any country except China. In fact, Iran and Iraq constitute two-thirds of the total recorded executions around the world. And the executions are still held in public. But in April 2014 something stunning happened: an execution in Iran was interrupted—by the victim's mother.

A man named Balal was facing execution. Seven years earlier, Balal had stabbed another young man, Abdollah Hosseinzadeh, in a street fight. His crime was a capital one, and the time for death had

Sylvester Adams | Barry Fairchild | Jimmie Jeffers | Carl Johnson | Charles Albanese come. In Iran, the victim's family traditionally helps carry out the execution; it is customary practice in the Sharia law of retribution for the victim's family to push away the chair on which the condemned stands, leading to his death. But this time something went wonderfully haywire.

Balal was ushered through a crowd to the gallows where he would die. A noose was placed around his neck, up he went onto a chair, and the crowd awaited his death. As the victim's mother and father approached Balal, people watched with anticipation.

To everyone's surprise, the mother slapped Balal in his face—and then forgave him! The victim's father removed the noose from his neck, and his life was spared.

Balal's mother hugged the grieving mother of Abdollah, the young man her son had killed. They sobbed in each other's arms. One victim was enough. They wept together over their sons.

CHAPTER FOUR

The Limits of an Eye for an Eye

If it's not right to torture someone for torture, abuse someone for abuse, rape someone for rape, then how can we think we can kill someone for killing?

—Bryan Stevenson[1]

We have established that God is biased toward life, not death. Still, there remain two biblical principles that stand at the center of those who want to argue that the Bible supports the death penalty. The first is a cornerstone of the Western idea of justice, the idea from Moses that justice is achieved through "an eye for an eye and a tooth for a tooth."

The second is the idea, often attributed to the apostle Paul, that all governments are established by God and given the sword in order to restrain evil and exact justice. Christians are enjoined, then, to obey these authorities.

Let's take those principles one by one.

Robert Sidebottom | George del Vecchio | Anthony LaRette | Jerry White | Phillip Atkins

What About "An Eye for an Eye"?

The injunction to take "an eye for an eye" is one of the best known and most misunderstood scriptures in the Bible.

I'll admit, in my younger days I tended to just ignore passages that I didn't like. I figured that's why God invented highlighters.

But tunnel vision is dangerous. As we'll see, highlighting a few verses at the expense of others is actually what led to our country's current death dilemma. We can end up constructing a version of God that lines up with our worldview rather than reorienting our worldview so that it lines up with the character of God. As I've heard it said, "God made us in his image, and we decided to return the favor."

Let's resist that temptation.

As we look at scripture, our guiding principle should be this: the law was made for people, not people for the law. In other words, God created things like the Ten Commandments to protect life, to shelter us from harm. Jesus consistently challenges religious folks when they use the law to *oppress* people rather than to set people free. This is where we get the old distinction between the "spirit of the law" and the "letter of the law."

God is reconciling all things—setting them right again. God is restoring healthy relationships—between people and God, people and people, people and creation.

With that reconciliation in mind, let's dive right into "an eye for an eye." I'll warn you: we are going to find what restorative justice guru Howard Zehr found: "There's more to an eye for an eye than meets the eye."[2]

How "An Eye for an Eye" Came to Be

The idea of "an eye for an eye, a tooth for a tooth" that appears in the Pentateuch (the first five books of the Bible and the foundation of ancient Israel's laws) is nearly as old as humanity.[3] Often referred to as "parallel retaliatory justice" or "lex talionis" ("law of retaliation"), it is the origin of our concept of retaliation. The idea behind this ancient concept was that a person who had been harmed could retaliate and return the same harm done to the person responsible for the crime—like for like. Lex talionis appeared in primitive cultures thousands of years before the compilation of the Bible. As a guide to justice, it was used virtually universally in that era.

The Code of Hammurabi, a Mesopotamian law code even older than the Old Testament, included a similar philosophy of justice, but with an important exception: if the offending person was of higher social status, you did not have the right to retaliate. Too bad. This particular justice was only for social equals. And obviously if those of lower status, such as slaves, did harm to the social elites, the "eye for an eye" thing went out the window. The offenders were mercilessly killed, or worse.

So the Old Testament/Hebrew remix "eye for an eye" was an improvement on the primitive idea; it was more fair. Unlike the Mesopotamian code before it, with its explicit bias toward those of higher social status, the biblical law applied equally to everyone, a radically new idea. *All* people, no matter their ethnicity, social status, rank, or class, were to be treated fairly and equally—"eye for eye," tit for tat. ("Equal justice under the law" was God's idea long before it was America's.)

The Hebrew version of lex talionis also limited the scope of retaliation to people, not property or possessions. Finally, the biblical law restricted retaliation to the offender alone; neither vicarious nor collective punishment was allowed.

It's worth noting that retaliation was seen as very different from revenge. It was simply about balancing the scales, finding a way to reconcile harm done. While the Hebrew law left room for retaliation, it did not endorse revenge—though there's undoubtedly a fine line between "making things right" (retaliation) and "getting even" (revenge). The Hebrew law (like the New Testament) explicitly *forbids* revenge (Lev. 19:18, Deut. 32:35, Prov. 20:22, Prov. 24:29).

For our purposes, it is important to see that the "eye for an eye" standard presented in the Hebrew scriptures was a radically fresh revision of a really old idea. While "an eye for an eye" has become a cliché to contemporary ears, it was a powerful concept for the ancient Hebrew people.

It served two purposes. First, it limited destructive cycles of violence (such as feuds and escalating conflicts between clans or families). Second, it provided a way to make restitution or reparation for harm done.

Here's the key: the "eye for an eye" law was intended to be a *limit* to retaliation—not a *license* for it. The goal was to stop the cycle of violence rather than validate or escalate it.

Prior to the Old Testament laws and the guidance of God, there was unregulated violence. Clan conflicts and tribal wars had no boundaries. Vengeance was limited only by the human spirit, which can be brutally vindictive.

Escalating violence is not just a thing of the past, of course. I see it nearly every day in our North Philadelphia neighborhood. What starts as words (or a Facebook post) turns into yelling. Yelling leads to fighting in the streets. Fists turn into knives and two-by-fours. Knives turn into guns. Lesser weapons turn into bigger weapons. A gunshot turns into three return shots. Other neighbors and family members get involved, and before long we have a full-on riot in the streets, with lots of collateral damage. (Let me be clear, I love my neighborhood; this is just one of the demons we battle.)

Escalating violence is not just a demon of the ghetto, but also of our government. All we need to do is look at what has happened since September 11, 2001, to see the wisdom of the Old Testament "eye for an eye": it would have limited our retaliation to 2,977 (the number killed on U.S. soil) rather than the estimated tens of thousands who have died in the Iraq and Afghanistan wars.

As we think of the "eye for an eye" principle, it is helpful to remember yet again that God is on the side of life, not death. God is about interrupting death, not promoting it. God is the author of life, and Satan the father of death. Consistent with the idea that God made people and pronounced them good, God doesn't like it when blood is shed and life is destroyed. Limiting violence is a good place to start. God limits our urge to escalate violence by saying to us, "You can go this far, but no farther." If someone breaks your arm, you can't go break both his arms. If someone knocks your tooth out, you can't go knock all his teeth out. An eye for an eye and a tooth for a tooth, *no more.*

Legal scholars make an important distinction that can help us here. There are laws of mandate and laws of limitation. Mandate means *you must;* limitation means *you can.* So, for example, one law of mandate says that if you want to drive a car, you must get a license. One law of limitation says that you can drive up to fifty-five miles per hour on a particular stretch of highway, but that doesn't mean you have to. Likewise, just because the law allows you to drink alcohol up to a certain blood alcohol content doesn't mean doing so is the best idea. Just because there's a minimum driving age but no maximum doesn't mean folks should still be driving at ninety-five years old. You get the idea.

This gives us a helpful angle when thinking about the death penalty. The laws of Moses were intended not to endorse violence but to harness it, to keep it from spiraling into more violence and revenge. Not *more* than an eye for an eye, not *more* than a fracture for a fracture, not *more* than a tooth for a tooth, not *more* than a life for a life. The punishment should never exceed the crime.

When we understand that the "eye for an eye" concept was a law of limitation, not a law of mandate, it makes complete sense that Jesus would tell us to take the next step and apply an even more rigorous limitation: not even to return the harm done to us, but to forgive. He makes that connection explicit, saying, "You have heard that it was said, 'Eye for eye, and tooth for tooth.' But I tell you, do not resist an evil person. . . . Love your enemies and pray for those who persecute you" (Matt. 5:38–39, 44). Don't poke anyone's eye out. The fact that it's *legal* doesn't mean it's *right*.

When it comes to transplanting the "eye for an eye" concept to contemporary society, there are a number of problems, as you can probably anticipate (one being Jesus, whom we will get to soon).

For starters, the retaliation of an eye for an eye, a tooth for a tooth, a life for a life did not apply just to capital crimes, as many people today want to apply it. Lex talionis meant that the injury suffered by the victim, whatever that injury was, could be inflicted identically upon the perpetrator. It was permissible to punish in proportion to the harm done in all sorts of crimes. So why would we today use this biblical mandate to apply only to the most egregious cases of

murder, but not to other cases, lesser crimes? Why do we allow reciprocal murder but not, say, reciprocal maiming?

Perhaps because we think it is cruel to rape someone who raped?
Or barbaric to gouge out the eye of someone who took the eye of
another? Perhaps it seems unthinkable to saw off the arm of someone who cost another person their arm? Perhaps we think there
must be another, better way to punish someone than by reciprocat-
ing the offense?

Death penalty lawyer Bryan Stevenson had this to say on the
subject:

> *The only reason we don't rape people who rape or torture people
> who torture, allegedly, is because we can't imagine requiring a
> healthy person to do that. What healthy person could we pay to
> go rape somebody as punishment for rape? It's just too distorted.
> And yet we think it's very easy to hire healthy people to kill people.
> Somehow killing doesn't implicate the same kind of immorality or
> decadence or lack of character that engaging in an act of torture
> does. The truth of it is: you can't safely, comfortably, conveniently
> kill a human being without it having an impact on you. And that
> same principle that affects how we think when we think about
> hiring people for rape ought to apply to killing people.*[4]

If we believe that people—*all* people—are not beyond redemption, it does not seem right to torture and traumatize them, even
though they may have done that very thing to someone else. Perhaps they need help, we think, rather than hurt.

While "eye for an eye" justice is still practiced in parts of the world,
I don't think many of us would argue that it's a move in the right
direction. The above-mentioned reluctance to harm others holds us

back. And certainly, given the teachings of the New Testament, it would be inconceivable to suggest that it's the direction Jesus wants to take us next.

There's much more that could be said about the Old Testament and its many examples of grace, mercy, forgiveness, and nonretaliation, but let's turn to Jesus now. I'm convinced that he did not come to negate the law, but to fulfill it. He shows us the most excellent way—perfect justice, perfect judgment, perfect love.

And Then Comes Jesus

No matter how much we study the Bible, folks come to different conclusions about the death penalty, just as we did with slavery, war, sexuality—well, most everything. That's why for Christians the most important revelation of God is Jesus. His life and words interpret scripture for us.

I love the Bible, and if I were stranded on a remote island for the rest of my life, a copy of the Bible would top the list of things I'd want with me. And yet I'm so very thankful that God did not send us just words on paper, but the Word made flesh, with skin on. Jesus is the full revelation of God. I like how my pal Bruxy Cavey puts it in a tweet: "We believe in the authoritative, inerrant, infallible Word of God. His name is Jesus."

Jesus is the lens through which we understand the Bible—and the world around us. If we want to know what God is like, we look at Jesus. If we want to know what love looks like when it stares evil in the face, we look at Jesus on the cross. As we look at Jesus, it becomes harder and harder to justify retaliation, revenge, even the sort of punishment that passes as "justice" in the world we live in. And it takes some theological gymnastics to reconcile the death penalty with the One who said, "Blessed are the merciful for they will be shown mercy" (Matt. 5:7) and "Forgive, and you will be forgiven" (Luke 6:37).

It's easy to understand why some early Christians had a hard time reconciling Jesus with the things they saw in the Old Testament—episodes of anger and violence. As we will see when we look at those Christians in chapter 6, one of the earliest Christian heresies was Marcionism, which contended that Jesus was God, but not the same God we see in the Old Testament. He was *better*.

Even today, some people suggest that between Malachi (the last book in the Old Testament) and Matthew (the first book of the New Testament), God got born again, or at least went through some anger management classes. But I don't buy that.

I want to suggest that something much deeper and more wonderful is going on. God is being more fully revealed to us—in Jesus.

Jesus is the climax of the Bible's story of grace and of justice. The character of God is fully fleshed out in Jesus. Jesus is the incarnation of God's love. He is grace with skin on. Everything reaches a pinnacle of perfection in Jesus.

Moses's law limited violence. Jesus wanted to heal us from violence altogether. Moses's law said that many deserve to die for the evil they've done. Jesus went even further, teaching that while all *deserve* to die—for even if you call someone a fool you have committed murder in your own heart (Matt. 5:22)—we all receive from God the gift of *life*.

The law of Moses was a good start, an improvement on earlier law. But that Mosaic law is fulfilled in Jesus. No law can heal the human heart. No law can reconcile enemies or break the chains of hatred.

Jesus came to do what the law cannot do: he finally saves us from sin, reconciles us to one another, heals the wounds of hatred and evil, and rescues us from the contagion of violence. When it comes to justice and the law, Jesus is not a contradiction to the law, but the consummation of it.

Consider these words from the apostle Paul: "Therefore there is now no condemnation for those who are in Christ Jesus, because through Christ Jesus the law of the Spirit who gives life has set you free from the law of sin and of death. For what the law was powerless to do because it was weakened by the flesh, God did by sending his own Son" (Rom. 8:1–3).

So what does Jesus, who sets us free from the law of sin and death, do to our understanding of "an eye for an eye"? He upends it. Let's take a closer look.

As we saw in the previous chapter, the law of Moses lists over thirty crimes punishable by death, including adultery, disrespecting one's parents, and working on the Sabbath. Interestingly, though, there are very few stories in the Old Testament in which people are actually executed according to these laws. But then, as was noted earlier, if these laws were *fully* enforced, few of us would be left.

This is precisely the point Jesus makes. Not one of us is above reproach. Conversely, no one is beyond redemption. We were all dead according to the law, but the gift of God is eternal life through Christ. It's not that the law has no meaning; it's just that grace has the last word.

Jesus takes us back to God's ideal. Moses moved us toward that ideal, toward the original dream, by limiting violence and divorce and other ugly things. But Jesus takes us even farther. Return evil with good. Do not fight fire with fire. Jesus admonishes us not to engage in retaliatory violence *at all*—not to take an eye or a tooth or a limb, ever. In essence, Jesus brings us a new law . . . and he does it without negating the old law, but by moving beyond it.

In replacing "an eye for an eye" with "love your enemies," Jesus teaches us to wear evil down with love. He teaches us that no one is beyond redemption; all of us are better than the worst mistake we've made. That new law of love is absolutely critical to understanding what Jesus meant when he said, "Do not think that I have come to abolish the law or the prophets; I have not come to abolish them but to fulfill them" (Matt. 5:17). The law condemns us to death. God's grace in Jesus means life. The wages of sin is death, but the gift of God is eternal life. Hallelujah!

Limiting violence was a good place to start. Abolishing it is a good place to end.

"Let Any One of You Without Sin Pull the Lever"

In 2014, Southern Baptist leader Albert Mohler wrote a piece defending the death penalty. In his twelve hundred–word argument for why Christians should support the death penalty, I saw a major problem: he did not mention Jesus a single time. In this official pro–death penalty statement of the Southern Baptists, there was not a single reference to Jesus or the gospels.[5]

I wrote a response entitled: "If It Weren't for Jesus, I Might Be Pro-Death Too."[6] Any Christian inclined to favor execution has what Brother Dale Recinella calls "the nagging problem of Jesus" to deal with.

There are plenty of other problems with the scriptural maneuvering used by some Christians to justify the contemporary practice of

Kirt Wainwright | Billy Waldrop | Randy Greenawalt | Eric Schneider | Michael George the death penalty. The use of a few verses from the Bible, in isolation, is as problematic in justifying the death penalty as it was in justifying slavery and lynching. But for now I want to stick with the nagging problem of Jesus, the greatest obstacle for pro–death penalty Christians.

Consistently, Jesus emphasizes redemption, saying things such as, "It is not the healthy who need a doctor, but the sick. I have not come to call the righteous, but sinners" (Mark 2:17, Matt. 9:12, Luke 5:31); "Blessed are the merciful, for they will be shown mercy" (Matt. 5:7); "Forgive, and you will be forgiven" (Luke 6:37); "Do not judge, or you too will be judged" (Matt. 7:1); "You've heard it said 'an eye for an eye' but I tell you . . ." (Matt. 5:38–39).

There is one place in particular where Jesus really brings it home. It's an incident in the gospels where Jesus is asked about the death penalty. Here's the scene: a woman has been humiliated and dragged before the town, ready to be killed. Her execution would be legal; her crime, adultery, was a capital one. It was a death-worthy crime. But as we've seen before, just because it's legal doesn't make it right.

Jesus interrupts the scene—with grace. He tells the men who are ready to kill the woman, "Let any one of you who is without sin be the first to throw a stone at her" (John 8:7).

A friend of mine has said of this incident: "Jesus turned water into wine, but his greater miracle was turning that mob into people."

You can practically hear the stones drop as the men walk away.

The only one who is left with any right to throw a stone is Jesus, and he has absolutely no inclination to do so. In Jesus we see that the closer we are to God, the less we want to throw stones at other people.

We cannot ignore Jesus when it comes to the death penalty. As was the case with slavery, many Christians ignored Jesus, misused scripture, and ended up on the wrong side of history. Let's not do it again and have to apologize one hundred years from now. Let's stand on the side of grace. And redemption. And *life*.

Obedience and the Governing Authorities

Some defenders of the death penalty point to another biblical passage for support, saying, "But what about Romans 13?"

I'm glad you asked.

One of the New Testament's MVPs (most valuable passages) when it comes to legitimating execution is Romans 13:1–5, written by the apostle Paul. Here it is:

> *Let everyone be subject to the governing authorities, for there is no authority except that which God has established. The authorities that exist have been established by God. Consequently, whoever rebels against the authority is rebelling against what God has instituted, and those who do so will bring judgment on themselves. For rulers hold no terror for those who do right, but for those who do wrong. Do you want to be free from fear of the one in authority? Then do what is right and you will be commended. For the one in authority is God's servant for your good. But if you do wrong, be afraid, for rulers do not bear the sword for no reason. They are God's servants, agents of wrath to bring punishment on the wrongdoer. Therefore, it is necessary to submit to the authorities, not only because of possible punishment but also as a matter of conscience.*

Paul's argument, in summary, goes something like this. All governmental authority is established by God. Governments are God's instruments for restraining evil, and rulers have been given the sword to bring punishment on those who do evil.

Let's begin with what should be obvious to anyone who has ever watched a news show highlighting governmental antics. Just because God establishes authority doesn't mean God approves of every official, every law, every policy; likewise, just because God can use government for good doesn't mean *every* government is good. Even the best human government isn't perfect. Without getting knee deep in theology, it's important to distinguish between what God *permits* and what God *most perfectly wills*—or, as theologians like to say, between God's permissive will and God's perfect will. This distinction is similar to that between the law of mandate and the law of limitation, which we looked at earlier.

God permits polygamy, but that doesn't mean it's part of God's most perfect plan. And God permits all sorts of evil in monarchies, dictatorships, and even democratic governments in order to ensure our human freedom to make choices—even bad choices. I'd go so far as to say that God advocates vehemently for our freedom to make bad decisions, such as giving our governments too much power—power that should belong to God.

Look at the Old Testament. When it comes to kingship among the Israelites, God makes it really clear that they don't need a king (1 Sam. 8). God warns them of all the terrible things a king will do to them—enslave them, force them to fight wars. But the people demand a king. So God establishes the kingship. I get the sense that God is continually working with a self-imposed handicap in order to allow humans to have free choice.

And sometimes we make bad decisions.

Lots of times we make bad decisions.

There aren't many folks who are going to argue that God put Hitler in power, or Saddam Hussein, or Putin, or Stalin, or Castro, or that God handpicked both George W. Bush and Barack Obama. Not many of us are going to say that the leaders in Uganda who recently wanted to make homosexuality a capital crime were established by God, even though they may have claimed to be.

That's true even for Paul. We often miss the irony that the same Paul who writes "submit to the authorities" goes to jail and is condemned for subverting the authorities! He ends up writing the book of Ephesians, where he says, "Our struggle is not against flesh and blood, but against . . . the authorities . . . of this dark world" (Eph. 6:12)—and he uses the same word ("authorities") here that he used in the pivotal Romans passage. We are both to submit and to transcend—what theologian John Howard Yoder calls "revolutionary subordination."[7] In the end, there is a more Supreme Court than the U.S. Supreme Court, and a King that all human kings and presidents and governors will be accountable to.

It's important to see that *submit* does not necessarily mean *obey*. In fact, Paul himself openly disobeys any authorities who are disobeying God. Many Christians, including Augustine (who affirmed that "an unjust law is no law at all"), insist that it is a Christian duty to obey good laws and disobey bad ones.

There are two ways to submit to authority, then. One is by obeying the good laws; the other is by openly suffering the consequences of disobeying the bad laws—that is, by revolutionary subordination. We see it in Paul and many of the great saints throughout history.

So it's clear that Paul did not mean for us to simply follow whatever the government says. This Romans 13 passage has been used and abused through the ages. It was used in Germany to stifle opposition to the Nazis and was quoted in South Africa to defend the racism of apartheid.[8] It was used to legitimize slavery, and I hear it regularly used to justify the death penalty. So let's dig deeper.

There's the issue of the "sword" here in Romans, which has often been assumed to mean the executioner's sword. We may think of beheadings or of the guillotine, both of which involve swords or blades, but this is imposing our world onto scripture. In ancient Rome, there were many ways of executing—crucifixion, stoning, and being fed to beasts—and execution by sword was one method they used. The problem is the word "sword."

There were different Greek words for what we would translate unilaterally as "sword" in English. But they had different kinds of swords, just as we have different kinds of guns today—and these "swords" conveyed dynamically different uses. A machaira was a short sword worn on the belt, a dagger. It was not the instrument of decapitation in capital crimes. That was the other sword—the rhomphaia. It was a long sword, a saber. Just as we don't use an AK-47 to hunt deer or a pistol for a firing squad, the Romans did not use a machaira, the word Paul uses in Romans 13, for execution.[9] And just to go one step farther, the word sometimes translated "execute" in verse 4 merely means to "bring about." So if we were to translate it, "execute" would only imply execute in the sense of "executing" a football play or "executing good judgment." It was not the word for state murder.

Just as it is unthinkable to execute with a cross today, it is unthinkable to suggest that Paul, in Romans 13:1–5, was sanctifying state execution—especially given that his fellow Christians were among those who would have faced execution.

Leaving Jesus Behind

Not long after the sword passage in Romans, Paul says, "For the wages of sin is death, but the gift of God is eternal life through Christ Jesus our Lord" (Rom. 6:23). In these words Paul affirms both life and Jesus—further evidence that his sword passage was never intended to endorse state-sponsored execution.

If the Bible turns out not to support the death penalty as so many Christians think, how do we explain how so many of us got this so wrong?

Here's how.

When it comes to the death penalty, we've put Jesus on the back burner, buried him in the closet, mistaking the things he said for good advice relevant to certain individuals but not applicable to the real world of politics. We've somehow separated his execution by the state from our contemporary context of executions. We've divorced heaven from earth, something that Jesus consistently challenged his own disciples on. *That's* how we ended up with the current crisis.

Here's when I realized that the death penalty was a spiritual issue, not just a political one. I was visiting a man on death row, and he told me his story. He confessed to having done something terrible, which he will regret for the rest of his life. But then, when he told me about his trial, it got even more interesting. During the course of his sentencing, the victim's family had argued that his life should be spared, that he should not be sentenced to death.

"They were Christians, so they talked a lot about mercy," he told me matter-of-factly, as if every Christian were against the death penalty. He went on, "They believed that Jesus came not for the healthy but for the sick. And they argued that God might not be done with me yet. So I was spared the death penalty because of the victim's family."

He added, "I wasn't a Christian then. But you better believe that I am one now."

Over the years, I've heard many other marvelous stories just like that one.

FACES OF GRACE

The Legend of Ahmed Shah

There is a story told of Ahmed Shah, a legendary tale based on real-life events that happened hundreds of years ago in the troubled land of Afghanistan. I first encountered it through my friend Michael Frost.[10]

Ahmed Shah was a ruler in Afghanistan, known for bringing peace in that country traumatized by endless wars and tribal conflicts. The story has a Moses-like feel to it: Ahmed is remembered for leading his people to a promised land, out of the war-torn region and into a secret valley bordered on all sides by cliffs. The valley was accessible only by a secret, hidden passageway that was never to be revealed. The people's very existence depended on its remaining a secret.

Sadly, one day a lieutenant discovered that the location of the hidden passageway had been revealed. What's more, the person responsible—the traitor—was Ahmed Shah's own mother! Guards took the woman into custody. The lieutenant informed Ahmed, nervously, about what had happened—that his mother was in custody and that everyone was waiting on him to decide what to do next.

One option, of course, was to kill all the witnesses and guards and cover up the whole matter. But it would have been next to impossible to keep that action hushed up in such a small community. Besides, Ahmed was known for his fairness and integrity. He decided he would think the matter over during the night and make an announcement the next morning.

As the next day arrived, word had already begun to spread, and folks had gathered in the town square. Ahmed came out to make the announcement of penalty: his mother must receive one hundred lashes, which would almost certainly mean her death. The woman was led into the square and bound; then soldiers began the lashing. After two lashes, her body was already bloodied and bludgeoned, buckled over in pain.

Ahmed could not bear it any longer: he halted the proceedings, untied his mother, and carried her inside to dress her wounds and restore her back to consciousness. A few minutes later he emerged from the hut, faced the crowd, and made another pronouncement: "The penalty for my mother's crime was one hundred lashes. She has paid two of them. I will receive the other ninety-eight."

And he did. By the end of the ninety-eighth lash, Ahmed was near death, bloodied, bruised, barely breathing. It was unclear if he would survive. Eventually, though, he recovered, and his act of courage and grace was never forgotten.

CHAPTER FIVE

The Most Famous Execution in History

*Have the same mindset as Christ Jesus: Who, being
in very nature God, did not consider equality with
God something to be used to his own advantage; rather,
he made himself nothing by taking the very nature of
a servant, being made in human likeness. And being
found in appearance as a man, he humbled himself by
becoming obedient to death—even death on a cross!*

—Phil. 2:5–8

I n 2014, Tennessee brought back the electric chair as a legal means of execution—and they did it during the week of Easter. To be more precise, Tennessee reinstated the electric chair on what Christians call Maundy Thursday, the day before we remember the brutal crucifixion of Jesus (on Good Friday). In the heart of the Bible Belt, during the most holy of Christian holidays, when we remember Jesus's agonizing execution, passion, and love for all, Tennessee

Mario Murphy | Jessel Turner | Samuel McDonald | Benjamin Stone | Johnny Cockrum brought back the electric chair as a means to execute criminals. The only thing more ironic would have been deciding to bring back *crucifixion* as a legal form of punishment during Holy Week.

Just as we needed to take a fresh look at scripture, we also need to take a fresh look at the crucifixion of Jesus—the most famous execution in history. How we understand what happened two thousand years ago on the cross may very well have deep implications for how we understand capital punishment in our own time.

At the heart of Christianity is an executed Savior. He was a convicted felon, tried and found guilty, jailed, shamed, and sentenced to die at the hands of the state. That alone should stop us in our tracks. Before we get to the theological implications of Christ's death and resurrection, we first have to recognize this: Jesus was given the death penalty and executed.

Yes, his trial reeked of injustice. One of his own disciples sold him out for a few pieces of silver, betrayed him with a kiss, and then hung himself out of remorse.

As Jesus was arrested, one of his closest friends, disregarding all Jesus's teachings on love, pulled out a knife and cut an ear off one of the arresting officers. (Jesus called his friend out and healed the other guy.)

Once arrested, Jesus was passed back and forth between politicians and bureaucrats. He appeared before Caiaphas the high priest, the Sanhedrin (a council of Jewish elders), Pontius Pilate, the crowd. Everyone seemed to want him dead, but no one wanted blood on their hands. Even Pilate washed his hands clean.

Jesus's various opponents had all kinds of accusations: insurrection, inciting a riot, conspiracy, terrorism (plotting to destroy the temple), tax evasion, treason, claiming to be king, blasphemy.

Despite the absence of substantial evidence, witnesses, or signs of any crime committed, Jesus was eventually pronounced guilty and sentenced to die.

As he awaited his fate, he was bullied, interrogated, harassed, tortured, beaten. The authorities humiliated him and stripped him naked. They mocked the claims of his divinity, ramming a crown of thorns onto his head and wrapping him in a royal purple robe as they laughed.

And so it went. This man, who many believed was the holy one that the prophets had spoken of—the long-awaited messiah, God incarnate, love with skin on—was executed, brutally. He died with his body convulsing as his lungs collapsed. Vultures were undoubtedly swarming overhead, hoping to clean up after the execution.

Most of his friends had deserted him, leaving him to fend for himself. Some of them were so scared that they denied even knowing him. Only the women stayed. The long, painful loneliness up on that cross was so agonizing, so gut-wrenching, that Jesus felt like God had bailed on him. Among his last words were these: "My God, my God, why have you forsaken me?" (Matt. 27:46, Mark 15:34).

But here's the good news: death did not get the last word.

A convicted felon, executed by the state, hanging dead on the cross, was not the end of the story. On the cross Jesus made a spectacle of evil. He exposed the hatred we all are capable of. And he triumphed over that hatred with love. He died with forgiveness on his lips. And then he rose from the dead.

The whole Jesus event that has shaped human history, even how we date history itself, is about a God who suffers with us, bleeds with us, cries with us, hopes with us. And dies with us. *That* is the most famous execution in history.

Aaron Fuller | Earl Matthews | Dawud Majid Mu'Min | Durlyn Eddmonds | Walter Stewart

An Executed Savior

Yes, Jesus was sentenced to death, and he died a real death on a real imperial cross.

There is a danger in forgetting the terrible, bloody, torturous, gory, sickening part of Jesus's death and thinking of it only in an abstract, transcendent, spiritual way. One concrete way to remember the grit and horror of it all is to speak of Jesus's death as an *execution*. It might help if instead of saying that Jesus was crucified two thousand years ago, we said that Jesus was hanged.

Up until Jesus, no one had anything good to say about a crucifixion. It's been said that the cross could become a religious symbol only a generation after anyone had seen a real one in use. For sure, the earliest Christians saw the cross as a powerful symbol of God's love—but this was a scandalous notion. Prior to Jesus and in the generation after him, the cross of old was something to be looked on not with admiration but with disgust. It was not to be adored but feared. It was a symbol not of hope but of defeat.

Two thousand years ago people did not go to a religious store to buy a cross; the Roman Empire gave them away for free.

The cross was an agonizing instrument of death. It was a brutal form (and symbol) of execution. Biblical scholars disagree on a lot of things, but on this they agree: crucifixion was a very common, and very brutal, way to die in the first-century Roman Empire. Countless historians tell of how commonplace it was to see a public execution by crucifixion. Crosses sometimes filled the horizon, the hillside so cluttered with them that it was hard to enjoy a decent sunset.[1]

Alexander the Great is reputed to have crucified two thousand people at once, and the Roman general Marcus Crassus crucified six thousand people at one time. The Jewish king Alexander Jannaeus crucified eight hundred people in the middle of Jerusalem. Even as Jesus died, we see that there were others being crucified "on his right and on his left."

It was a terrible way to die. Wild dogs and birds crowded around the crosses to feed off the carnage of the naked, exposed, bloodied bodies.

This is the way Jesus died: a brutal "legal homicide," a torturous, state-sanctioned execution reserved for the "worst of the worst," which in first-century Rome meant traitors, rebels, and insurrectionists—agitators, prophets, failed messiahs, and folks who disturbed the status quo. This is the company Jesus joined on the hillside at Calgary.

It's easy to lose sight of the original, "old rugged" cross of Jesus when we see harmless crosses of gold (sometimes sprinkled with diamonds) around people's necks, tattooed on people's bodies, and adorning the altars of fancy churches. The truth is, wearing a cross two thousand years ago would be like wearing an electric chair around your neck today.

Let's get even more graphic about crucifixion, a slow, painful form of execution in which the person was tied or nailed to two perpendicular wooden beams. This form of execution, common from the sixth century BC until AD 337, was such a brutal way of killing someone that it gave birth to the word "excruciating."

As if plain old crucifixion weren't bad enough, the ancient historian Josephus writes that executioners would often amuse themselves by crucifying people in different positions.[2] It was an utterly cruel and humiliating punishment, but sadly not unusual.

It was not uncommon that the condemned would be forced to carry their own instrument of death, as was the case for Jesus. The cross often weighed over three hundred pounds, so in many cases the condemned carried only the horizontal beam.

The length of time it took to die ranged, but the process could last for days, and the cause of death varied from heart failure to dehydration, asphyxia, shock, or blood loss. In many cases animal predators contributed to the death as they came to feed off the dying body. Family members were known to set up camp beside the cross of their loved one, holding vigil day and night, primarily to try to keep predators from picking at the dying body or outright devouring it.

When we see a cross, we think of Jesus—and rightfully so. But perhaps we should also think of the thousands of other victims of execution who died by means of crucifixion. Some of those deaths were legal, others were illegal, but *all* were brutal.

Crucifixion has been the means of execution for many Christians throughout history, including Andrew (Peter's brother) and Peter, who was crucified upside down. In more recent years, crucifixion was reintroduced in Japan in the sixteenth century as a legal means of execution after 350 years without capital punishment. In 1597, twenty-six Christians were crucified in Nagasaki, marking a long history of persecution. Archbishop Joachim of Nizhny Novgorod was reportedly crucified upside down in Sevastopol, Russia, in 1920. Crucifixion is still a legal means of execution in some parts of the world today such as Iran and Saudi Arabia, though it is rarely used.[3]

Interestingly enough, it was the first Christian Roman emperor, Constantine, who abolished crucifixion throughout the Roman Empire. He's not a man known for his mercy; he killed his own son, among many others. But he came to see that crucifixion was an offense against Christ, and so he got rid of it.

Jesus died the same way lots of people have died throughout

history, some innocent, some not—by execution. So, as suggested earlier, I invite you (whether you consider yourself a Christian or not) to think and speak of Christ as one who was "executed." That language connects the most famous execution in history to the world we live in today.

That change doesn't detract from the sacredness, the mystery, the transcendent power of what Jesus did on the cross. Just the opposite: you may find, as I have, that speaking of Jesus as among those who have been executed adds depth to what happened on the cross, allowing you to see a dimension of God's grace that is even more glorious, more beautiful, and more scandalous than you ever imagined.

The Great Paradox:
Dying to Save Us from Death

What happened on the cross is one of the greatest mysteries in the world. One of the most offensive events in history—the crucifixion of Jesus—became the conduit of God's grace and salvation. One of the most horrific instruments of death was transformed into an icon of hope. How bizarre indeed for us to sing songs about Golgotha, a word that means "place of the skull," as the spot from which our hope comes.

Jesus died to save us from death.

At the heart of Christianity is that great paradox: a crucified Savior. God got lynched. Christ was executed. As we've seen, that was much harder to miss in the first century, when crucifixion was the customary means of execution. It was today's electric chair, gallows, lynching tree. When we lose sight of that, we lose sight of one of the most important truths of the Christian faith: Jesus was fully human, just as he was fully God, and on the cross Jesus died a real death, suffered a real execution.

You'd think that having an executed Savior who died forgiving his killers would mean that Christians identify with the victims of violence and have a special propensity toward mercy. Sometimes that's been the case. But there are other times—as with the death penalty—that we Christians have been the champions of death rather than its challengers.

Just as the cross has inspired millions of Christians to stand up for life, and to come alongside victims of violence, there have also been times when the cross has been twisted.

Deadly Theology

Bad theology gets people killed.

I once heard Catholic peace activist and priest Father Daniel Berrigan put it bluntly: "When you twist the cross, you get a swastika."[4] And yet many of us twist the cross, in subtle ways, to suit our purposes or ideologies.

I remember a friend who joked about his occasional cravings for revenge: "I know the Bible says, 'Vengeance is mine, saith the Lord,' but sometimes I just want to be about the Lord's business!" That was the late singer-songwriter Rich Mullins. He was kidding; he was actually one of the most grace-full people I've ever met. Unfortunately, some other folks aren't joking when they say things like that.

One politician who is a professing Christian was asked how he could support the death penalty when Jesus tells us that we should not judge, lest we be judged. The politician's response: "It is God's job to judge but our job to arrange the meeting."

When we miss the central message of God's love and the cross gets twisted, it can be used as a weapon. Some of the most horrifying things in history have happened at the hands of Christians with poisonous theology, divorced from grace. It's what happened with Hitler and the Holocaust. It was the case with slavery and the lynching of black folks in the United States. It's the story of the Ku Klux Klan (KKK). It's behind the abortion bombers, and the Inquisition, and the Crusades. And I think it's bad theology that we're using to justify execution today.

Bad theology is dangerous.

As a Christian who worships the loving, forgiving Savior on a cross, I find it particularly troubling when the cross is used as a weapon to justify violence, bloodshed, and vengeance—the very stuff I'm convinced Jesus came to heal the world of.

After the KKK threatened violence to protesters in Ferguson, Missouri, last year, I went on their website. While in Ferguson after the racial strife that broke out there, I was disturbed by what I heard from the KKK—they were invoking Christ in their threats—and so I did a little snooping. Not only did their threats in Ferguson invoke God's blessing, but their entire website was sprinkled with how Jesus and God blessed their activities. One part in particular caught my attention: under the heading "Tradition," I found one of the most disturbing things I've ever seen—a theological explanation of why KKK members set the cross on fire in those iconic images of lynchings and hate-filled mobs.

Glennon Sweet | Joseph Cannon | Jose Villafuerte | Lesley Gosch | Frank McFarland

This is the statement from the KKK website:

> *The lighted cross of The Knights is no different than the average church that has a lighted cross either on top or in front of their church building. The light of the cross symbolizes the Light of Christ dispelling darkness and ignorance. It is the fire of the cross that reminds us of the cleansing "fire" of Christ that cleanses evil from our land. The fiery cross is a symbol that has long been popular with the Christian faith. . . . We don't burn the cross, we Light the cross. We recognize that Christ is the light of the world. The lighted cross is a symbol of freedom—freedom from sin—freedom from tyranny. When a Klansman or Klanswoman participates in a cross lighting ceremony they are making a public declaration to Jesus Christ of their continued commitment to the Christian faith.[5]*

It's easy to write off the KKK as a bunch of fanatics. But most bad theology is more subtle than that of the KKK or the folks who hold signs that say, "God Hates Fags." Most bad theology sounds good in the head but doesn't feel quite right in the heart.

This is why my pal Tony Jones says our theology needs to pass "the smell test." Does it smell like love? Does it smell like Jesus?[6]

Consider this. After the terrible botched execution of Allen Lee Davis in 1999, graphic pictures began to circulate showing Davis after his death in the electric chair. The surge of current had been so powerful that blood had poured from his mouth onto the collar of his shirt, then spilled down his chest, leaving a large stain. Florida Supreme Court Justice Leander Shaw called it a picture of a man who, "for all appearances, was brutally tortured to death by the citizens of Florida."[7] But then Florida State Senator Ginny Brown-Waite, a professing Christian, saw the photo. While at first she was shocked by the blood, she says she then realized it formed the shape of a cross and that it was a message from God saying God supported the execution.[8]

The way we interpret the execution of Jesus can affect the way
• we think of execution today. Makes me wonder how Senator Ginny Brown-Waite interprets Christ's death.

What does it mean, what *should* it mean, that this man Jesus died to save us from death? Let's spend a little time on this question.

Recently, I got a note from a young woman who was confused about how God could be against the death penalty since Jesus had been executed. After all, hadn't God sentenced God's own son to be killed? Hadn't God condemned Jesus to death?

For her, as for many others, the theology in her head was in collision with the God in her heart: she was tempted to give up on God because she couldn't reconcile her doctrine with her deity. She didn't understand how a loving God could kill God's own son—and how an omnipotent God could not manage to work out a better solution to sin.

She's not the only one wrestling with why Jesus died on the cross, or confused by the questions raised by the great paradox at the heart of the Christian faith. Over the centuries, Christians have worked hard to wrap their heads around the execution of Jesus.[9] They've used language like "penal substitution" and "ransom" and "sacrifice" and "atonement."

Some have suggested that God's wrath had to be appeased, blood needed to be shed; so Jesus shed his blood in order that we don't have to shed ours. It can be confusing. As I once heard a seven-year-old kid trying to make sense of Jesus's death say, "I wish God didn't have to kill himself for me. I wouldn't have asked him to do that." In other words, some would say God was pointing a gun at humanity but decided to swing it away from us and take aim at Jesus.

Others have said that sin created a debt owed to God (like money owed to the bank), but Jesus paid the bill. Still others have said that Jesus was the "victor" on the cross—that he plunged himself on it as a condemned man might throw water on an electric chair to short-circuit the whole system. Others have said that on the cross Jesus became a "mirror" to the world, showing us the evil that humans are capable of and the grace that God bestows on us in the face of such evil.

Each of these explanations is a human attempt to "see in a mirror dimly,"[10] trying our best to understand one of the greatest mysteries of all time.

Alas, our feeble attempts to put language to what happened on the cross will always fall short and feel inadequate. This is probably a good thing, since we finite beings are trying to wrap our heads around an epic act of an infinite God.

Nevertheless, let me suggest a few things that happened during that execution two millennia ago that may very well shape the way we think about execution today:

- Jesus made a spectacle of death.

- Jesus joined the ranks of the despised.

- Jesus reconciled all things.

- Jesus was the sacrifice to end all sacrifice.

The solution to bad theology isn't *no* theology. The answer to bad theology is *good* theology. So let's dig a little deeper.

Making a Spectacle of Death

Scripture says this about Jesus at his execution: "And having disarmed the powers and authorities, he made a public spectacle of them, triumphing over them by the cross" (Col. 2:15). Another way to put this is to say that Jesus, on the cross, became a victim of violence to expose the systems of violence. He revealed the evil we are capable of. He did this—and this is clutch—not to glorify death but to overcome it. Love stole the show. Jesus became the water that short-circuited the electric chair.

One of the things the death penalty does, both two thousand years ago and today, is put death on display. It is eerie how the condemned becomes iconic and the event becomes an eerie ritual. It happened with Jesus, and it happens every time there is an execution.

The prisoner is moved to the death chamber. Changes into an execution outfit. Is shaved one last time. Then the last meal. Final words. And . . . death. The whole process is meant to have a theatrical effect, to register terror and awe on all who watch. That's as true now as it was with the public executions and lynchings of yesterday.

It is what professor and theologian Mark Lewis Taylor calls the "political theatrics of terror."

But in that execution two millennia ago, something goes haywire. As Taylor says, "Jesus steals the show."[11] In the very familiar theatrics of death, there is a surprise ending.

Genaro Ruiz Camacho | Johnile DuBois | Delbert Teague | Kenneth Stewart | David Castillo

We can see in the broken legal system the need for a Savior. And Jesus comes through, delivering us from the sin within us and the sin around us.

The cross has the power to invert the systems of domination and power with the upside-down news that the last are first and the first are last, that the mighty are cast from their thrones and the lowly are lifted up. Theologian James Cone said it like this: "The cross was God's critique of power . . . snatching victory out of defeat."[12] Hallelujah! Tweet that, baby.

In Jesus, the whole system is exposed for what it is—sickening. His was *not* just another crucifixion. Jesus exposes the powers and principalities. But then he makes a spectacle of them. He robs them of their power. He short-circuits the electric chair.

Jesus counters the theatrics of death with the theatrics of grace. What is made holy is not death but the ability to face death without fear—with love and grace and life enduring.

Jesus leaves the empire stripped naked as he himself hangs naked on that tree. He unveils the broken systems of power, empire, and domination. He shows us the dead-end road of sin, hatred, and our systems of "justice"—as he dies forgiving his killers.

In the face of unimaginable evil, Jesus dies with grace on his lips.

The sun stands still, the sky splits open, the veil in the temple is ripped in half—the world is torn apart.

And then grace wins.

The resurrection can be understood only in light of the cross.

The cross is not just an obstacle on the way to resurrection. It is ground zero for grace. The worst thing imaginable—an execution on a cross—has become the conduit of God's love for the world.

Joining the Ranks of the Despised

The prophets foretold of one who would come to save the world by suffering:

> *He was despised and rejected by mankind,*
> *a man of suffering, and familiar with pain.*
> *Like one from whom people hide their faces*
> *he was despised, and we held him in low esteem.*

—Isa. 53:3

At his execution, Jesus joined countless victims of violence and torture who, over the centuries, have experienced agonizing pain and wondered where God was in the face of such evil. Jesus joined all who suffer in any way as he died on the cross.

The cross offers us a cure from the pieties and theologies that would keep God at a distance, in heaven, above the suffering people on earth. Jesus brings God "down to earth" and shows us a God who is present in the world's pain and injustice. Jesus experiences an agonizing loneliness so deep that he cries out, with victims all over the world, "My God, my God, why have you forsaken me?" (Matt. 27:46).

Jesus feels the absence of God. And God feels the agony of losing a child. Try and wrap your mind around that: in one moment, God feels the pain of the victims of unspeakable violence, and God feels the agonizing pain of seeing a beloved child executed at the hands of the state.

When we think of lynchings, and the electric chair, and the myriad sadistic ways people have taken the lives of others, it's hard to keep from shouting with Jesus, "Why have you forsaken me?" It is the cry

Dwayne Wright | Ronald Fitzgerald | Tyrone Gilliam | Kenneth McDuff | Kenneth Wilson of the blues. It is the cry of oppressed people around the world. It is the cry of all victims of murder. It is the cry of folks on death row. On the cross Jesus joined and united the agonizing pain of victims of violence everywhere: My God, my God, why have you forsaken me?

Now we see how radical it was for the first followers of Christ to admire, let alone worship, a crucified Savior. That stance aligned the early Christians with the most despicable people on earth—the worst of the worst: monsters and villains. It was an act of political incorrectness, even resistance—a fist in the air to the deity of Rome. No wonder the early Christians were called "enemies of the state." The followers of Jesus were now aligned with the shamed and condemned as they made the contentious proclamation that the crucified One had risen from the dead. For that they too would be killed, numbered among the vulgar, ignoble, bottom rungs of society.

Here's how Paul puts the status of the early Christians:

> *It seems to me that God has put us apostles on display at the end of the procession, like those condemned to die in the arena. We have been made a spectacle to the whole universe, to angels as well as to human beings. We are fools for Christ, but you are so wise in Christ! We are weak, but you are strong! You are honored, we are dishonored! To this very hour we go hungry and thirsty, we are in rags, we are brutally treated, we are homeless. We work hard with our own hands. When we are cursed, we bless; when we are persecuted, we endure it; when we are slandered, we answer kindly. We have become the scum of the earth, the garbage of the world—right up to this moment.*

> *—1 Cor. 5:9–13*

John Noland | Kevin Cardwell | J. D. Gleaton | Larry Gilbert | Daniel Corwin | Jeff Emery

This is what it means to follow a crucified Savior.

And this is why suffering people around the world have found a home in the cross and a friend in the crucified One.

Oppressed people all over the world identify with the cross and with the suffering of Jesus. Salvadoran theologian and martyr Ignacio Ellacuria spoke of "the crucified peoples" of the world who resonate with the message of liberation at the heart of the Christian faith, a message that cost him his life.[13] I'll never forget one of the murals I saw when I visited El Salvador, outside the home of Oscar Romero, an outspoken Catholic archbishop who was killed (and later beatified). It is a painting of a crowd of people, young and old, men and women. Looking closely, you can see that they all have the stigmata—the scars of Jesus on their hands.

Now we can understand why black folks, the lynched and the long enslaved, have found a home in the cross. They have looked into the naked, bloodied face of Christ and found a friend. James Cone, himself black, has done magnificent work in his book *The Cross and the Lynching Tree,* showing the eerie connection between those two means of execution. Both the crucifixion and lynchings were public spectacles accompanied by torture and agonizing pain, and both were carefully designed to humiliate and shame. They were also both used as "public service announcements"—to say, "Do what these folks did, and you too will hang from a tree."

Cone begins *The Cross and the Lynching Tree* with these words:

> *The cross and the lynching tree are separated by nearly 2000 years. One is the universal symbol of Christian faith; the other is the quintessential symbol of black oppression in America. Though both are symbols of death, one represents a message of hope and*

salvation, while the other signifies the negation of that message. . . .
Both the cross and the lynching tree were symbols of terror,
instruments of torture and execution, reserved primarily for slaves,
criminals, and insurrectionists—the lowest of the low in society.[14]

During the era of lynchings, black Americans identified deeply with Jesus and his suffering. It is stunning to see the depth of this connection for black folks in their struggle for freedom—and equally stunning to see how white folks missed this connection.

For black folks during the era of lynching, looking at the cross was like looking in the mirror: in Jesus they saw their own struggle and hope. You can hear it in hymn lyrics like "Were you there when they nailed him to the tree? . . . Sometimes it causes me to tremble, tremble, tremble," and "Nobody knows the trouble I see; nobody knows but Jesus. Nobody knows the trouble I see, glory hallelujah." You can hear it in jazz and see it in black art.

Cone says this: "The cross has helped me deal with the brutal legacy of the lynching tree, and the lynching tree helped me to understand the tragic meaning of the cross."[15]

One of the greatest evidences of the Holy Spirit is that the faith of black folks survived despite all the horrible things white Christians were doing to them. This, despite the fact that white Christians justified the unspeakable evil being done to black people with the same Bible being read by black brothers and sisters!

In Galatians 3:13 Paul writes: "Christ redeemed us from the curse of the law by becoming a curse for us, for it is written: 'Cursed is everyone who is hung on a [tree].'"

The cross, and the lynching tree, show us the worst that human beings are capable of, and simultaneously they also refuse to let that evil have the last word.

James Cone points out that Jesus was the first "lynchee."[16] As we read in Acts: "They put him to death by hanging him on a tree" (Acts 10:39, paraphrase). There, on the cross, Jesus joined the ranks of the most despised people on earth, and he died with an equally despicable person hanging on each side of him. He hung—tortured, bloodied, mocked, humiliated—with all the victims of violence, and he survived to tell the story.

My friend Tony Jones, who is also inspired by James Cone's work in understanding Jesus as the first lynchee, says this: "If we can heed Cone's words and see a noose every time we see a cross, we have the potential to avert future atrocities. But it seems that first we must face the horror of our own past."[17] Perhaps we might even say Jesus was not the first nor the last lynchee—but on the tree he joins a long list of victims of horrific violence.

If we can see a noose every time we see a cross, we can prevent the kind of atrocities that have left bloodstains on this land.

And the blood cries out to God.

Clarence Jordan, a pecan farmer and revolutionary theologian from Georgia, is a really helpful teacher when it comes to a proper appreciation of the cross. Clarence was one of the founders of Koinonia Farm, where black folks and white folks committed to defy racism by living together as brothers and sisters in the thick of the Jim Crow segregated South. It's been said that Koinonia Farm may have inspired these words of Martin Luther King Jr. in his "I Have a Dream" speech: "I have a dream that one day on the red hills of Georgia, the sons of former slaves and the sons of former slave owners will be able to sit down together at the table of brotherhood."[18]

Clarence's most famous work is *Cotton Patch Gospel,* in which he retells the story of the gospels but situates them in the deep South in the early 1900s.[19] Jesus is born in Selma. The climax of Clarence's

Mark Sheppard | Joseph Atkins | Martin Vega | Darrick Gerlaugh | Sean Sellers | Tony Fry retelling is when Jesus is executed. Jesus once again hangs on a tree—only this time, he is lynched.

Reconciling All Things

So how is it that lynching, that execution, was transformed into a message of hope? Consider these words of Paul:

> *All this is from God, who reconciled us to himself through*
> *Christ and gave us the ministry of reconciliation: that God was*
> *reconciling the world to himself in Christ, not counting people's*
> *sins against them. And he has committed to us the message of*
> *reconciliation. We are therefore Christ's ambassadors, as though*
> *God were making his appeal through us.*

—2 Cor. 5:18–20

Let's look at what that means.

Through his long-ago execution, Jesus not only exposed evil. He also healed the world. He showed us a way to overcome death and hatred. He showed us a way to heal the world of it. Still today, he shows us a way to stop the pattern of violence and hatred and death. That has all sorts of implications for how we think about healing the harm done by violent offenders today. We're going to look at "restorative justice" later, but before we look forward, let's look back.

If we all fell with Adam, now we all rise with Jesus. What was lost in the Garden of Eden is restored on the cross.

"Atonement" is one of the most basic ideas in Christian thought and theology. It's about how God is reconciling all things, as Paul noted above. And it has everything to do with the death penalty, as we try to find better forms of justice than execution. The Greek word *katallage,* which Paul used in his quote, is often translated "atonement," but "reconciliation" captures its essence even better.

Atonement sounds like a fancy theological word, but its meaning is pretty basic: *at-one-ment.* What Jesus did on the cross is reconcile all things and make them "at one" again. What Jesus did on the cross is nothing short of put the world back together again.

The early Christians understood several dimensions of this, symbolized in the cross: the vertical dimension—reconciling people to God, making them one again, healing the separation caused by sin and fallen humanity; the horizontal dimension—reconciling people to each other, tearing down the walls of division and isolation, making them "at one" with each other; and a third dimension, symbolized by the cross being anchored in the earth—reconciling people with creation again, healing a suffering earth.

A closely related idea is the Hebrew notion of *shalom.* It is the core belief that laid the very framework for justice in the ancient world. The common translation is "peace," but "all-rightness" might be a little better—a state in which all is well. Shalom is God's dream for the world, God's most perfect intention: that things exist in harmony and are one. From this foundation flow the other ideas of salvation, atonement, forgiveness, and justice. And so when things go haywire, the goal of justice is shalom. It encompasses our relationships with each other, our relationship with God, and our relationship with creation. Scholars point to deeper resonances of shalom that include honesty, truthfulness, transparency.

So in the earliest days of Christianity, believers understood the cross to be the ultimate act of atonement, the restoration of shalom. That understanding is a fundamental building block for Christians

James Rodden | Norman Green | Karl LaGrand | Walter LaGrand | George Quesinberry

today who want to find ways of doing justice that go beyond punishing wrongdoing to truly heal the wounds of sin and evil.

If one act in the Garden of Eden caused it all to go haywire, then
one act on the cross put it all back together again—achieving at-
one-ment, reconciling everything. If the fruit of the sin in the garden
was the original murder of Cain killing Abel, then the resurrection
was the final victory over death. Christ has triumphed over death.
Death is dead.

Serving as an End to the Sacrificial System

Just as we have a system for justice, so did the ancients—and it was
a system based on sacrifice. Death was part of that justice system.

In the ancient Hebrew world, sacrifice played a role in restoring
shalom, setting things right again. It's worth digging a little deeper
into that idea of sacrifice, because understanding Jesus's death as a
voluntary, loving sacrifice may help us have new language for what
he did as he died.

As long as there have been humans, there have been sacrificial
offerings to God. To the ancients, the gods were bloodthirsty, and
sacrificing humans (generally virgins, children) was how you got
them to chill. Even in scripture we see an early story where God asks
Abraham to sacrifice his son Isaac; fortunately, God stops things
short and provides a ram instead.

Human sacrifice then led to animal sacrifice, well represented in
scripture (for example, Lev. 3, Lev. 17, Lev. 22, Ezek. 43). One of the
central Jewish holy days is Passover, when the Hebrew people wiped
blood on the outside of the houses so their lives would be spared—
literally, "saved by the blood of the lamb."

There are clear parallels to Jesus, the "lamb of God" who takes away the sins of the world. The image of the Christian lamb is a sacrificial image. Jesus is often seen as the fulfillment of the ancient prophecy of a coming messiah, who is "led like a lamb to the slaughter, and as a sheep before its shearers is silent" (Isa. 53:7).

Jesus's execution, then, is a turning point in history. After Jesus, everything changes. There is no need for more blood.

One of my friends grew up in Africa in a tribe where he made sacrifices to appease God and the ancestors. When missionaries came and explained that "there is no need for more blood," he had a powerful conversion. He was drawn to Jesus because it meant an end to the bloodshed. Interestingly enough, it also led him to a theology of absolute nonviolence, since there truly is no need for more blood.

Hosea 6:6 puts it succinctly: "I desire mercy, not sacrifice."

As we've seen, the contemporary practice of the death penalty glorifies death and disgraces the work Jesus did on the cross. Over and over, we've seen spectacles made of executions—the hanging of Saddam Hussein, the seeking of the death penalty for the Boston bomber.

Yet any time we rejoice in death, we disgrace the cross.

Contemporary thinker René Girard writes in depth about the "scapegoat mechanism," sort of a release valve for our violence and hostility.[20] It creates the illusion of finality and closure and offers us an outlet for our rage, pain, and fear—even under the guise of "justice." To hang the head of a dead king on a stake at the city gate. To throw the body of Osama bin Laden into the sea. To lynch a person from a tree.

Girard argues that without some release valve we become unrestrainedly violent people, as sin and hatred and jealousy reach a

Any time
we rejoice
in death,
we disgrace
the cross.

boiling point. On the brink of mob violence, a victim is sacrificed and the desire for violence dissipates, at least temporarily. Without that release valve, without a way to let off steam, the pent-up violence becomes combustible.

That's why people feel "at one," or reconciled, when they have "paid the price" with someone's blood. That was true of tribal conflicts of old that ended in death. Likewise, contemporary "honor killings," common in certain parts of the world, are efforts to resolve issues of "crime" or "wrongdoing." (I put those latter words in quotes because often the sacrificial victim hasn't committed an actual crime, but may simply be, for example, a woman not wanting to be forced to marry a man she doesn't love.) There were "avengers of blood" even in scripture—stories like the slaughter of Jephthah's daughter (Judg. 11)—that were all about making things "at one" again, with blood as the magic formula.

In Girard's view, then, blood becomes like a medicine, curing the disease of sin and violence. Perhaps it's a sort of vaccine—a little bit of blood prevents the spread of the contagion of bloodshed; a small amount of the virus in a controlled environment prevents great harm.

You see where we're headed with this? The death penalty has served a very similar purpose for us.

But eventually the sacrificial system came to an end. Sacrifice, as the ancients used it in their justice system, failed. The shedding of blood did not prevent further bloodshed. Even as we see today in the United States and across the globe, regions where executions happen do not become less violent (often exactly the opposite). The vaccine didn't last; people were inoculated against violence for a short time only. As with heroin, our addiction to violence needed a "hit," and then another and another. The trade-off of violence against one victim to satiate a bloodthirsty mob had proven to be a dead end. So God weaned people off that sacrificial system, off the need for blood. From human, to animal—to Jesus.

And Jesus dazzled. In one public spectacle, the entire system was exposed as a farce. With the spiral of violence continuing like a skipping CD, Jesus came to break the cycle of violence. He came to cure the contagion of sin and bloodshed—once and for all.

It was not that Jesus was *obligated* to die as much as he was *willing* to die. Perhaps that's why Jesus pleaded with God for another way. But in the end, love was *willing* to die. And in that willingness, Jesus toppled the entire sacrificial system. The sacrificial system could not stand up to God.

Jesus was the "sacrifice to end all sacrifices." He was the whistleblower who called out the lie of the entire system—and brought it to an abrupt end, forever. He was the ultimate subversion, the divine monkey wrench—the water that short-circuited the electric chair. He ripped away the curtain completely and showed the myth behind the entire enterprise of sacrifice. It was bankrupt. It was a lie. And it was over.

Jesus's sacrifice was the ultimate sacrifice, or the counter-sacrifice—the end of the sacrificial system. He did what all the laws in the world could not do. Laws can only show us where we fall short and try to regulate our sin and violence. Jesus came to save us from evil altogether.

Hebrews 10:1–18 unveils the tedious monotony of the sacrificial system "repeated endlessly year after year," with no end . . . until now. The sacrifices were a reminder of our evil and our need for a Savior; but no matter how much blood was spilled, the curse of sin still reigned . . . until now. Hebrews says, "Sacrifice and offering you did not desire," but now Christ has reconciled all things "once for all." Now, says God in Hebrews, "Their sins and lawless acts I will remember no more." And where there is grace, there is no longer any blood needed.

"The wages of sin is death," says Paul (Rom. 6:23). In the end, sin leads to bloodshed; it kills us, it kills others. But the gift of God is life. Jesus is "the way and the truth and the life" (John 14:6), freeing us from death.

Now we have a truly innocent victim who shed his blood. But he did it with love on his lips, forgiving the people torturing him, forgiving *us*. It is the triumph of grace.

When we see the crucifixion as a legal transaction in which Jesus "paid the bill," we run the risk of cheapening the work of restoration at the heart of the cross. After all, God is healing the wounds of sin, not just paying off the mortgage. And by making it a simple legal transaction, a "ransom" of sorts, we run the risk of circumventing our response to Christ, which *should* be a life transformed by the grace we have received.

If we fail to see the depth of pain and love behind Jesus's death on the cross, we can end up feeling a little like we're paying a "sin tax" to God—as if we had an occasional parking ticket that we owed God, now made right. Jesus wasn't reinforcing this kind of exchange. His life and death and resurrection were much more meaningful, more potent, than paying taxes.

It's a fine line. One of the dangers Christians face is that we can give punishment too much power. Punishment alone doesn't heal and restore. Thus the cross is not just about punishment.

Conversely, we can give sin too little weight. More than just a debt we owe to God, sin is a disease; it is a pathology. Jesus recognizes

Michael Poland | Bruce Kilgore | Stanley Faulder | Brian Baldwin | Robert Walls | Charles Tuttle this, which is why he pleads from the cross on behalf of those hurting him, "for they know not what they do" (Luke 23:34, KJV).

Healing from sin is a process we get to participate in. God doesn't just do it for us. Certainly Jesus died to save us from death (one of the core themes of this book); but when we receive the gift of grace, it should transform us into grace-filled people who want to see other people given a chance, and other people loved back to life again. If you're really sorry for breaking someone's window, you don't just pay for a new one; you help that person get it installed . . . and you might even mow their yard a few times. God's love and justice are much more dynamic than many of our theologies allow for.

It might be helpful to step back and see that Christ suffers not as a third-party substitute victim, but *in solidarity with us;* Christ feels the weight and loneliness of the human condition. The one who had no sin became sin (2 Cor. 5:21). The crucifixion is the ultimate act of divine solidarity. And of divine love.

Scholar N. T. Wright puts it this way: "God's justice is his love in action to right the wrongs of his suffering world by taking their weight upon himself. God's love is the driving force of his justice, so that it can never become a blind or arbitrary thing, a cold system which somehow God operates, or which operates God."[21]

God's love is bigger than a system—and it is dynamic, alive, vital.

It's helpful to see sin with that same dynamism. It's not just about immoral incidents that need to be accounted for (as if we'd piled up debt on a moral credit card). Sin is a disease that has infected us and all of creation. *That* is what Christ came to heal.

Christopher Marshall says it well: "Sin is an alien power that distorts personality, corrupts relationships, and enslaves human will."[22]

On the cross, we see a remedy to sin and to violence. We see what love looks like as it stares evil in the face. And we see a God whose mercy triumphs. Jesus shows us how evil people and systems can be, and how good God is in spite of it all.

God is justified in forgiving us, not on the basis that God has received enough blood compensation to make up for our sins—but because God's mercy triumphs over judgment. God can forgive us because God's love is bigger than any system—be it the sacrificial system of antiquity or the punitive justice system of today. I want to invite you to consider this: God did not need blood. God *chose* to bleed with us and show us a way to stop our patterns of bloodshed.

The crucifixion was an act of divine solidarity and costly forgiveness. As God continues to remain loyal to a disloyal people, we now are invited to extend that same grace to others. We are to be like God and forgive. We are to see people who do evil with the possibility that *they* can be healed. And we are to extend to them the same grace God extends to us. We are all victims of the crushing power of sin, and all in need of liberation.

Sorry, didn't mean to preach. But I hope you enjoyed it.

Identifying with the Executed Jesus

Christians around the world regularly identify with a Savior who was a victim of violence. Shouldn't that make us more sensitive to the violence around us? Shouldn't it make us skeptical of state-sanctioned violence, which simply creates another set of victims?

The Latin word for the wafer of the Eucharist (often referred to as "the host") is *hostia,* which literally means "the victim." All the sin and violence in the world crashes into Jesus, "the victim," on the cross. We can see what we have done—the angry mob, Pilate, Judas, the Sanhedrin, Herod, you and me. We killed God. We executed love.

Ricky Blackmon | Charles Boyd | Victor Kennedy | Kenneth Dunn | James Earhart

When we take Communion we remember the blood; we remember Jesus's broken body. We sing songs like "Nothing but the Blood." But we still tend to think of the crucifixion as a mystical event rather than a real execution. Not only can the crucifixion be both real and transcendent, it must be both—just as Jesus was both God and man. Just as we appreciate the mystery of what happened, we must also remember that it was a real execution. The blood he shed on the cross was not metaphorical blood but real blood. His tears were real tears. His agonizing loneliness was as real as our own long loneliness. That perspective should radically reorient us and cause us to identify with *all* victims of violence—whether the victim is a little girl raped and murdered, or a mentally ill man facing execution; whether it be an unarmed black man in Ferguson, or two police officers in New York City. We weep with those who weep.[23] We bleed with those who bleed.

What's more, on the cross Jesus died not only for the victims, but also for the victimizers, for whom he interceded with God. Again those words from the cross: "Forgive them; for they know not what they do" (Luke 23:34, KJV).

The scandalous part of grace is that it is big enough to include both the oppressed and the oppressors. God is setting both groups free. That is good news indeed. That is the gospel.

What's more, death is not the end of the story. In the end, the tomb is empty. Death has lost its sting.

So what does all this mean for the death penalty?

I'd like to suggest that it means . . .

The End.

The life-giving power of grace is a call for us to advocate for victims, to empathize with those who suffer, to seek forgiveness from people we have wronged, and to forgive as we want to be forgiven. It is a call to end the bloodshed of execution and lynchings and torture and hatred and all the things that destroy life. It is a call to dismantle the apparatus of death. We are called to love people back to life. We are called to love the world back to life. We are invited to join the holy work of making all things "at one" again—reconciled through the executed and risen Savior of the world. How about that?

If we take the Bible seriously, we must admit that "all have sinned and fall short of the glory of God, and all are justified freely by his grace" (Rom. 3:23–24). Or, stated in reverse, "There is no one righteous, not even one" (Rom. 3:10).

Even the most grueling understandings of God's wrath and punishment will agree on certain things. We humans are all guilty. We are all deserving of death. And we were spared the death penalty by the supreme sacrifice of Jesus's death.

God, the Judge above all judges, has decided: mercy triumphs over judgment. And God carries out the judgment in love: "God demonstrates his own love for us in this: While we were still sinners, Christ died for us" (Rom. 5:8).

Jesus came to show us what perfect love looks like. And he exposed the most vicious evil that humans are capable of. Love was nailed to a cross. Grace died for a moment. And the world went dark. And then . . .

There was resurrection. Jesus rose from the dead. He triumphed over all the hate-filled, violent, ugly things we do. By his wounds we are freed from wounding others, even our enemies. Death is now dead. Execution has been abolished. Life has triumphed. Love has won.

Willis Barnes | William Davis | Everett Mueller | Richard Smith | Willie Sullivan | Harvey Green

How can we who follow this love-bestowing Jesus be so quick to call for the death of another human being?

Following the Executed Jesus

To identify with the executed Jesus is one thing. To *follow* him is another. But that is exactly what we are invited to do: "To this you were called, because Christ suffered for you, leaving you an example, that you should follow in his steps" (1 Pet. 2:21). And of course, Jesus even gets specific with the invitation to come and suffer: "Whoever wants to be my disciple must deny themselves and take up their cross and follow me" (Matt. 16:24).

All this theology talk isn't just about ideas "out there." One of the most powerful things Jesus did was give us an example—one that we are to imitate and follow. We are to love and forgive as Christ did.

The way we think about God affects the way we live. If our understanding of the cross is based on the punitive justice of God, then we will be inclined toward punitive models of justice, like the death penalty. But if on the cross we find grace and forgiveness, then as we follow Christ we become more gracious and more forgiving.

Whatever our faulty, limited human understanding of the cross, the elephant in the room is this: If we really believe that we are all worthy of death and Christ died to spare us from the ultimate death penalty, who are we to argue for someone else to be killed? To be like Jesus is to spare sinners death and to offer them forgiveness and grace—even unrepentant sinners like the ones Jesus forgave as they nailed him to the cross.

If we think that Jesus was punished in our place, this means, in effect, that Jesus spared us the death penalty and suggests that we too should stand on the side of life. I am greatly encouraged to see a whole bunch of folks from all traditions—Calvinists and Lutherans too!—seeing that their own theology and their own relationship with God need not be an obstacle to grace, but can motivate us to become some of the most passionate advocates for grace. We see Christians everywhere turning up the volume for grace. "Where sin increased, grace increased all the more" (Rom. 5:20). Amen!

Christians throughout history have pondered why Jesus had to die, and we've understood the crucifixion in a lot of different ways. That's not to say these different ways are equally valid or totally incompatible, or that the various interpretations necessarily disagree; it just means that there is something mystical, mysterious, sacred, and magical about the whole event. We should see it as a treasure to be explored rather than a puzzle to be solved. But some ways of interpreting the death of Jesus are toxic, because they end up perpetuating the very patterns of violence that Jesus came to expose and free us from.

What's just as important as what we do with the crucifixion of Jesus is what it does to us. Regularly identifying with a grace-filled, loving, forgiving victim of violence and execution should so transform us that we stand with all victims of violence. It should make us into people who stand on the side of life and grace. And who with the Christian poet John Donne declare—in the name of the executed and risen Jesus—"Death, thou shalt die."

Forgiving Alessandro

In the years since Jesus's death, the Christian church has been no stranger to gruesome death. There are countless Christians who have died from tragic murders, brutal assassinations, and legal executions at the hands of the state. In two famous examples, Oscar Romero, an archbishop in El Salvador, was killed in 1980 while serving Communion. Dietrich Bonhoeffer was hanged by the Nazis in 1945.

But when it comes to the mystical power of grace in the face of evil, few saints stand out like Maria Goretti. I hadn't heard of her until I was telling my neighbor, a devout young Catholic, about my book on the death penalty. After she mentioned Maria Goretti as an icon of forgiveness, I realized that one of my close friends, a nun who goes by Sister Goretti, is named after her. I got curious and started reading about the young saint.[24]

Maria Goretti died at eleven years old in 1902 after a violent, sexually charged attack. She grew up in a poor family in Italy. Her father had died when she was younger, and her mother, Assunta, was now a widow with six young children. It was a hard life of poverty and manual labor. Forced off their own farm when they couldn't make ends meet, they became sharecroppers, joining another family on a larger plantation. The kids weren't even able to attend school; they were needed in the fields.

In their new living situation, things got even more difficult. Assunta, little Maria, and her siblings all lived in one room, in a house they shared with two men: Giovanni Serenelli and Alessandro, his son. A second son had ended up in a mental hospital, as had the boys' mother; she had died there. Alessandro was a lonely, moody teenager, and he and his father were obsessed with violence and sex. Posted all over the walls on their side of the house were photos and magazine articles about sexually charged crimes.

Assunta knew better than anyone that her neighbors, Giovanni and Alessandro, were less than ideal. They were lazy and belligerent and inappropriate, to be sure—but she didn't imagine that they were dangerous. She had talked to them about taking down the sexual images from their walls, and they had refused, but for the most part they kept their distance. Besides, she didn't have much choice. She would have loved to take her kids back to their old farm, but there was no way that they could survive there financially. If they weren't willing to hunker down and make ends meet, they would be out on the streets.

Maria, at only ten years old, took over the running of the house while her mom was in the fields. When Assunta headed off to work, Maria would look after the children, tend to the farm animals, cook, clean, do laundry, go shopping.

She seemed to be a special kid—not just because she worked hard, but because she had a deep hunger for God. Every morning she'd wake up in the early hours, often before her mom, to pray. And she insisted on evening prayers every day, putting the little ones to bed by saying prayers with them.

Because of that hunger for God, she begged to take Communion, but she was told that First Communion was not offered until kids were twelve. Besides, they had no money for a special dress, no free time for confirmation classes. And there was another obstacle: she couldn't read. She had never been to school.

But Maria was persistent; she insisted. She got a friend to come read to her and help her learn the catechism. She borrowed a dress, shoes, veil, and even a candle, and she managed to bypass the age requirement. At ten years old she began participating in the Eucharist, already a woman of faith, deeply in touch with God.

Things got more difficult with the men next door, especially Alessandro. He began encroaching on the Gorettis' side of the house. Sometimes it seemed innocent enough; he'd join them for prayers, genuinely longing for a family he'd never had. He began to pester Maria, and kid with her, but there was a darker side to him.

One afternoon, while Assunta was in the fields, Alessandro, twenty years old by that point, visited Maria and asked her to have sex with him. She refused awkwardly; after all, she was only eleven. He threatened to kill her if she told anyone, so she hid. From then on she locked the doors when her mother was away, and she prayed for Alessandro. Night after night she prayed for him, and for her safety.

But it was nearly impossible to hide all the time, since they shared a house and a kitchen. About a month after his first attempt, Alessandro came home from the fields early and trapped her in a room. As he tried to rape her, little Maria simply said, "God does not want this. You are in danger of hell." Her response infuriated him. In a frenzied assault, he grabbed a needle-like tool used for making brooms and viciously stabbed Maria over and over. She was taken to the hospital in a horse-drawn ambulance, a trip that took nearly four hours. During this time she was bleeding internally; many of her internal organs had suffered severe damage.

Meanwhile, back home, an angry mob had gathered and surrounded the house where the Giovannis and Gorettis lived. Having learned of the attack, people began hurling stones and calling for the death of Alessandro. Eventually they burst into the house, bashing in the door. Moments later, armed officials arrived and took Alessandro into custody.

Maria had received fourteen major stab wounds that had done irreparable damage to her internal organs, including her heart. There was little the doctors could do. As she lay in her bed, she began to see visions. Over and over she prayed aloud—for Alessandro. She spoke of how he was in danger of hell. A parish priest arrived to offer her Communion. They talked about Jesus. He reminded her of Christ's love, and the cross, and his forgiveness for even those who murdered him. How great is the love of God! And little Maria, eleven years old, told the priest that she forgave Alessandro and did not want him to go to hell. While she surely hated what he had done to her, she said that she would like to see him in heaven and did not want him put to death. He needed help. He needed Jesus.

Maria received Communion on her deathbed. It was only her fifth Eucharist. As she ate the Body of Christ, she fell asleep, still muttering about forgiveness for her killer in a scene that looked very similar to Christ on the cross. The situation seems scandalous, almost offensive to us now—this innocent girl trying to save her killer. Our inclination is to demand, "But what about justice?"

That was not Maria's concern, however. Not long after taking Communion, she died with love on her lips, died in the arms of Jesus. Her death was so moving that one of the priests asked if he could keep one of the towels used to care for her, as a relic of her life—Catholics are into things like that—because he was convinced she was a saint.

Indeed there *was* something special about Maria Goretti, but also about how her life and her death bore witness to Christ's love and forgiveness.

The papers told the story of her vicious murder with headlines like this: "Human Beast: Ferocious Murder at Nettuno." It was indeed a ferocious murder. The outrage against Alessandro was so great that many folks believed he would be killed in prison.

Making things worse, Alessandro showed no remorse. He was outraged that he was in prison and insisted that he was innocent. He had the audacity to claim that he was a victim of injustice, wearing an offensive air of arrogance throughout the trial. Overwhelmed by the evidence, Alessandro eventually admitted his guilt but dodged all blame, pleading insanity and citing his mother and brother as examples of mental illness in his family.

He was sentenced to thirty years in prison. At first he mocked his punishment, singing a song he had written for the occasion: "Only twenty-nine more years, and I'll be welcomed home with cheers." He even shouted at a priest that this was all the cleric's fault.

But then something stunning happened. After many years in jail, Alessandro had a vision that changed everything. In the dream he was in a garden, and he saw Maria. She was wearing a white dress and picking flowers. When she had collected a beautiful bouquet, she approached Alessandro and offered it to him. He took the flowers gladly, but as he took hold they caught on fire, burning in his hands.

This vision changed Alessandro's life. He finally owned the evil in his heart. He accepted the gift of forgiveness from Maria—and from Jesus—and allowed that grace to transform him. He wrote a letter on November 10, 1910, that read: "I am deeply sorry for what I have done. I have taken the life of an innocent girl. . . . I publicly renounce the evil I have done and beg the pardon of God and of her injured family. Only one hope encourages me—that I may one day obtain God's pardon as so many others have."[25]

As for Assunta, she publicly spoke of her forgiveness of Alessandro.

He spent nearly two more decades in jail, living an exemplary life behind bars. He was released four years early on good behavior, in part because Assunta advocated for this.

Sometimes folks would ask him about his past, and he would simply say that he had committed a terrible crime in his youth and was spending the rest of his life trying to atone for and heal from it.

Oh, and he saved up his money to make one trip. He went to visit Maria's tomb. And then, on that same trip, he went to visit Assunta—this was around Christmas in 1937—to personally ask for her forgiveness. She assured him that he *was* forgiven—by her, and by Maria, and by Jesus. She then asked him to stay at the presbytery where she was the housekeeper so that they could share the Eucharist. So he did: at the midnight Christmas mass, Assunta led Alessandro to the altar and they took Communion together.

Alessandro spent the latter part of his life as a gardener in an isolated monastery, where he died in 1969 at the age of eighty-two. His last words were, "I am going to be with Maria."

Maria Goretti was officially recognized as a saint (with a capital S) on June 24, 1950. Half a million people attended the ceremony, which had to be held in the open air to accommodate the huge crowd. The president and prime minister of Italy were there. But so was Alessandro. He was there with Assunta and the rest of Maria's

Anthony Bryan | Betty Beets | Odell Barnes | Freddie Wright | Ponchai Wilkerson | Darrell Rich family, a mind-boggling demonstration of the power of grace and forgiveness.

The depth of such forgiveness makes no sense outside of Christ— and even still, it is hard to believe. Love *is* stronger than death. It was the first time in history that a mother was present for the canonization of her child. And I'm pretty sure it was the first time a murderer was present for the canonization of the person he killed.

CHAPTER SIX

The Early Christians and Execution

Though it took many centuries for the Christian church to come around on slavery, the patristic writers were already pointing a new direction on the death penalty. It is time for us to take another look at what Jesus and those earliest Christian writers had to say about the value of human life, no matter how sinful that life may have been.

—David Neff, former editor-in-chief of *Christianity Today*

As I mentioned in the previous chapter, there's a saying that suggests that the cross could become a religious symbol only a generation after anyone had seen a real crucifixion. The cross was not just an icon of hope, it was also a terrifying reminder of Roman imperial power.

That's got to be the starting point as we consider how the early Christians thought about capital punishment. The early Christians (before about AD 300) were on the other side of death than many

Robert Tarver | Robert Coe | Ronald Boyd | Christina Riggs | Tommy Jackson | William Kitchens

Christians today. By that I mean that they weren't the ones wielding the "sword," but the ones facing its wrath. They weren't the executioners, but the executed. Capital punishment was not an issue to debate; it was a threat to their lives. John the Baptist (Jesus's cousin) was beheaded. Jesus crucified. Stephen stoned. Peter crucified upside down. Almost all the apostles were executed in some fashion.

No doubt when all your friends are getting executed, that shapes the way you think about the death penalty.

But even more than that, Jesus radically reoriented how they thought about death. His death and resurrection caused their moral GPS to recalculate.

Death Was So BC

Like our world today, the world of the early Christians was very familiar with violence and death; also as in our world, there was widespread acceptance of capital punishment. Violence was epidemic; capital punishment was a regular occurrence. To oppose capital punishment was not just unpopular, it was dangerous, because it meant opposing the state.

It is in that world of imperial crosses, gladiatorial games, and Roman military conquests that the early Christians developed their own consciousness—and their witness was a remarkable ethic committed to life and to denouncing death in all its ugly forms.

To be a follower of Jesus necessarily meant standing on the side of life. Back then "pro-life" didn't just mean anti-abortion (though the early Christians were consistently against abortion too). Being a follower of Jesus meant standing against death in *all* forms, including capital punishment.

Across the board, those early Christians denounced the death penalty. In the words of David Neff of *Christianity Today*, they "found it unthinkable that a follower of Christ could take a life, even legally."[1]

My friend Ron Sider recently penned a stellar, comprehensive book on what the early Christians had to say about death: *The Early Church on Killing*.[2] In it he points out that the early Christians had a consistent ethic of life when it came to abortion, capital punishment, military service, and other issues. For the early Christians, people were created by God, made in the image of God, and no mortal had the right to kill another person; not even Caesar had the right to take life.

Sider also shows that while there were nuanced and conflicting views on some issues (such as military service), on the issue of capital punishment the early Christians were crystal clear: it is wrong for Christians to kill, or even to participate in the apparatus of state-sanctioned death. Just because a killing is legal doesn't mean that it's right; and just because the state kills doesn't mean that Christians should participate in that killing.

I have yet to learn of a single Christian leader in the first three centuries of Christianity who argued for capital punishment (or killing in general, for that matter). Nine different Christian writers in sixteen different treatises said that killing is wrong. No Christian writing before Constantine in the fourth century argued that there is any circumstance under which a Christian may kill.

The early church's ban against killing included capital punishment. I need to drive this home a little more, because until I started researching for this book, I had no idea how passionate the early Christians were about the death penalty.

The early Christian apologist Tertullian insisted that God "puts his prohibition on every sort of man-killing." Jesus, in rebuking the sword of Peter, said Tertullian, "cursed for ever the works of the sword" (Sider, 169).

Minucius Felix, a second-century lawyer in Rome, said that it is not lawful either to see or to hear of human slaughter. "So much do we shrink from human blood," he said, "that we do not use blood even of eatable animals in our food" (Sider, 64).

Origen, a third-century theologian, unequivocally condemned killing: "We must use the sword against no one. . . . The Christian lawgiver, Jesus, completely forbid putting people to death. . . . Christ nowhere teaches that it is right for his own disciples to offer violence to anyone, however wicked" (Sider, 72).

Cyprian, a North African bishop, called killing "a mortal crime" and said that the hand that carries the Eucharist dare not be "sullied by the blood-stained sword" (Sider, 87).

Wow.

Lactantius, writing slightly later, condemned death in six places in four books. He urged Christians to "keep away from human blood" and said that if Christians had their way there would be no need for prisons, rulers' swords, or punishments (Sider, 106).

No Christian was to participate in capital punishment. After his passionate condemnation of all killing, both legal and illegal, Lactantius concluded: "It is not permitted to commit homicide in any way" (Sider, 191).

But what those early Christian writers had to say went much deeper than just being against death. As I read their words, I began to recognize a few themes that kept surfacing. Let's check out a few of those themes.

From Death to Life

Moving from death to life, both symbolically and also socially, was one of the visible signs of the kingdom of God, one of the recognizable marks of the Christian witness. In the bloodstained Roman Empire, the Christians were, in the words of Clement of Alexandria, the "bloodless" people of peace (Sider, 35). Followers of Jesus were a contrast culture, a holy counterculture; they stood on the side of life.

Christians were to bear witness to love and grace. While *all* people love their friends, Christians were also called to love their enemies. In a culture of death, they were champions of life. In a culture of hatred, they were people of love. In a culture of fear, they were fearless. And that's why people paid attention to these renegade Jews.

The early Christian writers pointed toward the prophetic image of God's people beating their swords into plows (Isa. 2:4) as one of the key identifiers of the Christian life and witness. God's people were to beat their weapons into tools and turn instruments of death into instruments of life.

The Christians, according to church fathers such as Irenaeus, were to live in such a way that their witness would transform nations so that swords were turned into farm tools, hatred was turned to love, enemies became friends (Sider, 29). Justin Martyr, one of the earliest Christian writers, argued that Jesus and the church were the fulfillment of the messianic prophecy of turning death to life:

Shaka Sankofa (Gary Graham) | Bert Hunter | Jessy San Miguel | Michael Clagett | Orien Joiner

We ourselves were well conversant with war, murder and
everything evil, but all of us throughout the whole wide earth
have traded in our weapons of war. We have exchanged our
swords for plowshares, our spears for farm tools[;] ... now
we cultivate the fear of God, justice, kindness, faith, and the
expectation of the future given us by the Father through the
crucified one.... [T]he more we are persecuted and martyred, the
more do others in ever increasing numbers become believers.[3]
(Arnold, 81)

We often see the swords-to-plows metaphor used when it comes to weapons of war, but the early Christians also used it with other forms of violence. After all, that is exactly what Christ did on the cross as he made a spectacle of death: he turned something evil, the cross, into something beautiful. In Christ one of the ugliest symbols of death was transformed into an icon of hope.

Tertullian called on early Christians to follow that example:

"And they shall beat swords into plows..." [I]n other words, they
shall change dispositions of injurious minds, and hostile tongues,
and all kinds of evil, and blasphemy into pursuits of moderation
and peace. Christ is promised not as powerful in war, but in
pursuing peace. (Sider, 174)

It does make you wonder if we couldn't melt down an electric chair and make something better out of it—like a shovel.

No More Blood

One of the truths that we explored in an earlier chapter is that Christ's sacrifice meant no more blood, an end to the sacrificial system. The early Christians passionately believed this truth. In their view, what Jesus did on the cross changed the old logic of the sacrificial system, which in turn undermined the case for the death penalty.

The need for an end to sacrificial blood was a theme in the writings of many of the early Christians when it came to issues of violence, including capital punishment. In wording touched on earlier, Clement of Alexandria wrote, "By his blood he has gathered a bloodless host of peace" (Sider, 35).

This understanding of Christ's sacrifice meant an end not only to animal sacrifice, but also to the spilling of blood of other humans. Tertullian radically extended the prohibition against *consuming* blood in Acts 15:28–29 to include the *shedding* of human blood (Sider, 169).

Minucius Felix, after a radical conversion to the faith, was magnetized by an infectious love and ethic of life. Here's what he had to say: "Christians reject all homicide and cannot even watch a human person being killed. . . . To us it is not lawful either to see or to hear of human slaughter; and so much do we shrink from human blood that we do not use blood even of eatable animals in our food" (Sider, 64).

Arnobius wrote in the fourth century: "Evil ought not be repaid with evil. . . . It is better to suffer wrong than inflict it. . . . We should rather shed our own blood than stain our hands and our conscience with the blood of another" (Sider, 101).

In his writings on "public homicide," Lactantius raged against the ways we have glorified death—that we have a "thirst for blood" and "lose our humanity." Here are his powerful words insisting that it is wrong to kill, even legally:

> *It makes no difference whether you put a person to death by word or rather by sword, since it is the act of putting to death itself which is prohibited.... There ought to be no exception at all but that it is always unlawful to put to death a person who God willed to be a sacred creature.* (Sider, 110)

He goes on to say that when we kill, even legally execute, "the blood-shed stains the conscience."

A New Law

Like many of us today, the early Christians worked hard to reconcile the teachings of Jesus with the Old Testament. For some of them, just like some of us, it seemed as if something had radically shifted between the Old Testament and the New.

Opponents of Christianity mocked the glaring difference, as we see in this letter from Celsus to Origen, "Was it Moses or Jesus who teaches falsely? Did the Father, when he sent Jesus, forget the commands which he had given Moses? Or did he change his mind?" (Sider, 74).

As we discussed a bit earlier, one extreme view among the early Christians was a flat-out rejection of the Hebrew scriptures and the God of the Old Testament. Proponents of that view asserted that the Hebrew God was a separate and inferior entity to the all-forgiving, gracious God seen in Jesus. This view, known as Marcionism (after a second-century church leader, Marcion of Sinope), was deemed a heresy and rejected. Nonetheless, it was not easy to make sense of the contrast between law and gospel, and opinions differed widely. But one thing was accepted unilaterally: Christians were not to participate in the apparatus of death.

When it came to the "eye for an eye" Old Testament law, the early Christians had a view similar to the one I present in this book. (In fact, I took a lot of cues from them.) Their goal was not to encourage retaliation, but to put a limit on it.

Here's Tertullian's take on the matter:

> [God] required "eye for eye and tooth for tooth"—not indeed, for the purpose of permitting the repetition of the injury by retaliating it . . . but for the purpose of restraining the injury in the first instance; . . . for He knows how much more easy it is to repress violence by the prospect of retaliation than by the promise of indefinite vengeance. (Sider, 54)

The goal was clear: limit and end the patterns of violence. Tertullian went on to say that the aim of "turn the other cheek" was to "effectively extinguish all reprisals of an injury. . . . [W]hatever new provision Christ introduced, he did it not in opposition to the law, but rather the furtherance of it" (Sider, 54). Christ did not come to negate the law but to fulfill it—and that means trying to end all killing, including execution. We cannot kill to show that killing is wrong.

Like us, the early Christians wrestled to understand the few verses that might seem at first glance to justify capital punishment, among them Romans 13:1–5 and the Old Testament's "eye for an eye." Here are a few things Tertullian said about the latter:

Kevin Young | Donald Miller | Michael Sexton | Miguel Flores | Stacey Lawton | Tony Chambers

For people were of old accustomed to require "eye for eye, and
tooth for tooth" and to repay with usury "evil for evil"; . . . but after
[Christ] has supervened and has united the grace of faith with
patience, now it is no longer lawful to attack even with word, nor
to say "fool" even. . . . Anger has been prohibited. The law has
found more than it has lost. Evil-doing is not conceded even when
it is deserved. (Sider, 48)

Origen, too, had something to say about repaying violence with
violence: "For Christians could not slay their enemies, or condemn to
be burned or stoned, as Moses commands, those who had broken
the law, and were therefore condemned as deserving these punishments. . . . The letter killeth, but the Spirit giveth life" (Sider, 75).

Origen distinguished sharply between the "constitution" given to
the Jews by Moses and that given to the Christians by Christ. Under
Moses's law, Jews could kill enemies and use capital punishment.
But Christ's gospel is different: Christians cannot "slay their enemies,
or condemn [them] to be burned or stoned" (Sider, 76)—in other
words, Christians must not use capital punishment.

Lactantius went even further: a Christian dare not even *charge*
someone with a crime that could result in that person's execution,
much less participate in the execution (Sider, 110).

All these early writers looked at the law now as submitted to and
interpreted through Jesus. The result was a *new* law. Thou shalt not
kill was not enough—now we mustn't even *think* of killing. An eye
for an eye was hardly even relevant to folks "who count no man his
enemy but all his neighbors" (Irenaeus, 30).

Adamantius, a fourth-century physician and Christian, contended
that the old law's "eye for eye" prevented strife through fear (in what

he called a "precautionary manner") and that the gospel of Jesus prevented strife through persuasion and gentleness (Sider, 94). He also pointed out that Joshua had asked God to stop the sun from setting until he could finish killing, but now God says we are not even to let the sun go down on our anger (Eph. 4:26)!

Even the more "moderate" voices—like that of Irenaeus, who argued that Romans 13 (with its claim that governments "bear not the sword in vain") shows that God wants government to restrain evil but does not remotely imply that Christians should participate in the apparatus of death: "For no more shall the law say . . . thou shalt not kill, to him who has put away from himself all anger and enmity. . . . Nor an eye for an eye and a tooth for a tooth, to him who counts no man his enemy but all his neighbors, therefore cannot even put forth his hand to revenge" (Sider, 30).

According to Cyprian, we are to be like Christ: "For his murderers, Jesus did not ask for vengeance, but for forgiveness" (Sider, 87). Thus for the early Christians to retaliate, especially with things like capital punishment, would have been a betrayal of Christ.

The Wisdom of the Early Christians

When we take the time to listen to the wisdom of the earliest Christians—the ones who came after the apostles and before Christianity became culturally acceptable, if not mandated—we can hear many important principles that the church would do well to remember. We've encountered some of these principles in earlier chapters, but they're worth repeating here to show the connection with the early church.

Edward Castro | Claude Jones | David Johnson | Eddie Trice | Jack Clark | Wanda Allen

Just because it's legal doesn't make it right.

Many of the early Christians acknowledged that the laws of Rome don't trump the laws of God. We are accountable to a higher law than Caesar's. And God's law is about love.

They didn't want to *see* a person put to death, even justifiably and legally, much less *participate* in the executions of Rome. In the words of Athenagoras: "We cannot bear to see a man or woman put to death . . . even justly. . . . [T]o see a person put to death is much the same as killing them. . . . [H]ow then, can we put people to death?" (Sider, 31–32).

There is a new law, replacing the old law and justice.

Clement declared, "If you enroll as one of God's people, heaven is your country and God your lawgiver" (Sider, 35). You can see why many of these early Christians were accused of being enemies of the state. They answered to a new lawgiver, one who endangered the existing power structure. Origen spoke of God as the divine "lawgiver" who altogether forbids putting people to death and "nowhere teaches that it is right for His own disciples to offer violence to anyone, however wicked" (Sider, 72).

In the third century Cyprian pointed out the hypocrisy of killing to show that killing is wrong: "The world is soaked with mutual blood, and when individuals commit homicide, it is a crime; it is called a virtue when it is done in the name of the state" (Sider, 85). Stunning—he named the contradiction that when an individual kills it is a crime, but when we kill as a society we turn killing into a virtue. Cyprian is raising the fundamental question: How can we kill people who kill to show that killing is wrong? If he'd had a car, I'm sure he would have had that bumper sticker. When we execute others legally, crime is not only committed, it is also taught.

It's better to die than to kill.

The early Christians spoke of how they despised death in all its forms—and of how they would rather die themselves than take the life of another person. Tertullian wrote, "The Creator puts his prohibition on every sort of man-killing by that one summary precept 'Thou shalt not kill'" (Sider, 47).

They even insisted that the entire creation was made for life. When we use the things that God has created to destroy life, we sin. If these early Christians were alive today, they would look at things like the poisons used in lethal injection and say that they too are evil: "Iron and herbs are all created by God," said Tertullian. "Has the creator provided these things for people's destruction? No!" (Sider, 47).

Over and over the early Christians said, in effect, "For Christ we can die but we cannot kill." It was better to be killed than to kill (Sider, 179).

In fact, the early Christians were convinced by their own experience with the martyrs in their midst that the way that we die can be just as much a witness of grace as the manner in which we live. As Justin Martyr said, "For it is plain that, though beheaded, and crucified, and thrown to wild beasts, and chains, and fire, and all other kinds of torture, we do not give up our confession: but the more such things happen, the more do others in large numbers become faithful, and worshippers of God through the name of Jesus" (Sider, 26). They were fearless. They exemplified the biblical promise that love casts out fear: "There is no fear in love. But perfect love drives out fear" (1 John 4:18).

These are hard words for modern ears, and rightfully so, because they could easily be used to justify injustice or oppression. The early Christians were able to simultaneously call evil, evil—and at the same time expose that evil fearlessly, without mirroring it. This is why they willingly died. The martyrs' stories of scandalous grace convey their conviction.

Maximilian, as he was executed, nonchalantly asked his family to give his possessions to his executioner (Sider, 155).[4] James, prior to his execution, told his would-be executioner about Jesus and about God's love and grace—leading, as the legend goes, to the executioner's becoming a Christian. James and the new Christian (now an enemy of the state!) embraced one another enthusiastically as brothers—and then *both* of them were led to their execution. They died together.[5]

When it comes to punishing crime via the death penalty, the cure is as bad as the disease.

Tertullian writes, "Shall it be held lawful to make an occupation of the sword, when the Lord proclaims that he who uses the sword shall perish by the sword? . . . And shall he apply the chain, and the prison, and the torture, and the punishment, who is not an avenger even of his own wrongs?" (Sider, 60).

The early Christians believed that, in participating in killing those who have killed, we become as bad as the evil we want to rid the world of. Tertullian, for example, contended that if we retaliate, we become as bad as our offender: "If we are enjoined then to love our enemies, whom have we to hate? If injured, we are forbidden to retaliate lest we become as bad ourselves" (Sider, 45).

How often has vehemence been found worse than the causes that led to it? Just as Zechariah said, "Do not plot evil against each other" (Zech. 7:10, 8:17), the early Christians believed that they were not even to imagine evil or vengeance in their hearts.

Christians should wear evil down with love.

Thomas Akers | Robert Clayton | Dennis Dowthitt | Willie Fisher | Gerald Bivins | Robert Massie

The early Christians knew that grace dulls even the sharpest sword. The power of grace was to be their weapon of choice. Just as Christ forgave those who were nailing him to the cross, so Christians were to love even those who did them wrong. "Say to those that hate and curse you, You are our brothers!" wrote Theophilus of Antioch (Arnold, 295).

And Tertullian wrote, "Say to those who hate you, you are our brothers. For if those who are our enemies and hate us and speak evil of us and slander us are to be called brethren[,] . . . that is what it means to bless them that hate us and pray for those who slander us" (Sider, 53).

Knowing the dangers of the lust for revenge, the early Christians took a long view that included the restoration of all things and required revolutionary patience—and a trust that God's grace is bigger than we can imagine.

The love of God, and the early Christians' witness of that love, had the power to convert even the coldest heart. They were so convinced of that they were willing to bet their lives on it. And they did.

God's Holy Counterculture

You can be sure that the pro-life, anti-death views of the early Christians were not popular in the world in which they lived, as may be the case for some of us today.

They were accused of being idealists, dreamers, subversives, and even enemies of the state. One critic of early Christianity wrote a letter insisting that if all Romans followed the Christians, civilization would collapse: "If everyone were to act the same as you Christians, the national government would soon be left utterly deserted and without any help, and affairs on earth would soon pass into the hands of the most savage and wretched barbarians" (Arnold, 102).

Origen retorted that the world would not fall apart if it followed the teaching of Christ. That teaching would in fact disarm the world and win over the barbarians with love. It was Christ, after all, who said, "I have overcome the world" (John 16:33).

While these accusations of idealism and naiveté may sound familiar (and may even prove heartening to us today), it is essential to remember that the early Christians were *not* out of touch with evil. They knew it very well. The execution of Christ was a recent memory. Evil was very real to them. Nonetheless, they were convinced that in battling evil they did not have to *become* it.

There is a prophetic imagination in their faith. One of my favorite quotes is from Minucius Felix, who (you may remember) converted to Christ. You can hear his roots in the legal profession in this powerful declaration:

> What a beautiful sight it is for God when a Christian mocks
> at the clatter of the tools of death and the horror of the
> executioner; when he defends and upholds his liberty in the
> face of kings and princes, obeying God alone to whom he
> belongs. . . . Among us, boys and frail women laugh to scorn
> torture and the gallows cross and all the other horrors of
> execution! (Arnold, 127–28)

And one last benediction from the early Christians, this from Lactantius:

> *But if God only were worshipped, there would not be dissensions*
> *and wars, since people would know that they are the children of*
> *one God. . . . How happy and how golden would be the condition*
> *of human affairs, if throughout the world gentleness, and piety,*
> *and peace, and innocence, and equity, and temperance and faith,*
> *took up their abode[;] . . . nor would there be any need of prisons,*
> *or the swords of rulers or the terror of punishments, since the*
> *wholesomeness of the divine precepts infused into the breasts of*
> *people would of itself instruct them to works of justice.* (Sider, 106)

Hallelujah! We have a long way to go, but go we must.

Beyond the Early Christians

The more mainstream and popular Christianity became, the trickier it was to maintain a countercultural commitment to nonviolence and grace. As Christianity moved from a fringe movement to a more acceptable and accepted religion, new challenges arose. These hit a turning point in the fourth century with Constantine. He was the first Christian emperor, and he made Christianity the official religion of the Roman Empire. That meant a collision between the cross of Christ and the sword of Caesar.

Many issues got convoluted and confused during those years of transition.

One of those issues was the practice of the death penalty. Ironically, it was Constantine in 337 who abolished crucifixion, out of respect for Christ—but as we saw in the previous chapter, he did not abolish execution per se. One wonders what would have happened if Constantine had decided that all execution, not just crucifixion, was an offense to the executed and risen Christ. Apparently he did not see the paradox in his own imperial theology.

But the early Christians did.

One of the ways the young church began to respond was to try to codify some things, in a sense to institutionalize the radical commitment that Christ calls us to.

Evidence of that can be found in a text called the Apostolic Tradition. This is one of the earliest records in Christian history. In it church leaders laid out what was required for baptism—and what activities and careers were incompatible with the faith.

It would be sort of like saying today, "If you own a porn shop and become a Christian, you'll need to find a new job before you get baptized."

The Apostolic Tradition listed certain things that new converts needed to give up; if they failed to do so, they would be rejected. Over the process of three years, new Christians would reorient their lives in light of Christ, and then be baptized. Among the activities that were listed as unacceptable were prostitution, gladiatorial games, sculpting idols, and serving in a fighting capacity in the military. Also excluded, important for our purposes here, was "anyone who has the power of the sword" (Sider, 120).

Because it was perfectly acceptable in the larger society—even respectable—to be an official guard who oversaw executions, church leaders had to consider whether a Christian could hold an execution-related job. And it became as clear as if one were a prostitute or a gladiator: such workers needed to rethink their job.

This became such an important issue that it was actually written into the institutional requirements for baptism, as embodied in the

Apostolic Tradition: "The professions and trades of those who are going to be accepted into the community must be examined. The nature and type of each must be established" (Arnold, 113). Then it lists various professions that are in collision with the Christian faith, namely brothel-owners, gladiators, sculptors of idols, soldiers, and finally "a proconsul or magistrate who wears the purple robe or governs by the sword, shall give it up or be rejected" (Arnold, 113). Literally, those who worked within the empire's apparatus of death were ordered to find a new job or reconsider their baptism.

Another important collection of church orders, the Canons of Hippolytus, put it this way:

> *Whoever has received authority to kill, or else a soldier, they are not to kill in any case, even if they receive the order to kill. . . . He is not to burden himself with the sin of blood. But if he has shed blood, he is not to partake in the mysteries [for example, the Eucharist . . .], unless he is purified by punishment, tears, and wailing.* (Sider, 123)

All this to say, ensuring that Christians did not kill other human beings, including in the case of legally sanctioned capital punishment, was *very* important to the early church. Over the centuries, from that point on, things evolved dramatically. Not only did we diverge from the unequivocal conviction of the early church that capital punishment is wrong, but Christians became some of its biggest champions—even to this day.

I can't cover the remaining sixteen hundred years of Christianity, but let me offer a very disturbing quote from Martin Luther, one of Christianity's most famous figureheads. Luther, who has some fine

Clifton White | James Elledge | Jack Walker | Ronald Frye | James Knox | Michael Roberts things to say, and who pioneered some much-needed reforms in the church, had very disturbing ideas about capital punishment. Luther said, for example, that "the hand that wields the sword is . . . no longer man's hand but God's."[6] The result is what historian Joel Harrington has called "a celebrity endorsement" of execution.[7] And therein lies the struggle that has lasted to this day.

In the end, Christians in favor of the death penalty not only have the nagging problem of Jesus, but as we have seen, they are sharply at odds with the first three hundred years of Christianity.

FACES OF GRACE

Wounded Healer:

Defying Death Around the World

It's only a matter of time before Nyasha Manyau ends up on *CNN Heroes* or wins the Nobel Peace Prize. Her story is a reminder that there are grace stories all around the globe—stories of ordinary people challenging the logic of killing those who kill to show how wrong killing is. She's a shining light for grace. But her life has been anything but easy.[8]

Nyasha grew up in Zimbabwe. When she was eight years old her parents died in a terrible car crash. Bouncing from orphanages to foster homes, she never lost courage. Over the long days, long years, she worked jobs, made friends, charmed enemies, and

David Ward | Christopher Beck | Alvie Hale | Gerald Mitchell | Stephen Johns | Terry Mincey

Christians for the death penalty not only have the nagging problem of Jesus, but they are sharply at odds with the first three hundred years of Christianity.

managed to make it out of what could have been an impoverished destiny with very few choices.

Nyasha made her way into a solid, laudable job at a radio station, where her main responsibility was public relations with listeners. One day, as she was about to go on a break from the studio, a stubborn visitor insisted on seeing her. She tried to dodge him, but with no luck.

The man she met would forever alter the course of her life. He told her that he had to get something off his chest, to confess something that had long been haunting him.

He had killed her parents.

Anticipating her disbelief, he went on to explain that her parents had died in a car crash, yes—but that he had orchestrated it. Just to put to rest any lingering doubts, he had brought pictures of her parents after the crash. As if that news weren't traumatic enough, he went on to explain, in detail, that her mother had not been completely dead at the crash site; he'd had to track the ambulance to the hospital and unplug her from life support!

Coming out of the blue, it was a brutal, agonizing meeting that sent Nyasha's world spinning out of control.

Anger. Confusion. Hatred. Agonizing pain. Every unpleasant emotion she had ever known hit her. The man's motives in baring his soul to Nyasha were unclear, further complicating an already complicated situation. This was not an act of valiant repentance, a killer on his knees in a tearful confession begging for forgiveness from the one he had wronged. No, he seemed pretty egotistical and narcissistic. Yet he had become convinced that his terrible act was bringing a curse on him and his family, and he wanted to be done with it. He didn't seem to be overly concerned about Nyasha or her sister or her brother, much less her parents; he wanted his own situation to improve.

That meeting was an awful and awkward beginning, but soon things got even worse. The man would call Nyasha asking for help—for money, for rides. She is a generous person, but this was over the top. Eventually, as any sane person would, she started to cut him off. But then something happened to change their course: the man's son got terminally sick. This was not a manipulation or a dependency; this was a man who had done stupid and evil things, a man who had burned a lot of bridges and now found himself alone in the world (and with good reason). But his son was dying. Nyasha has a son of her own, so she felt his pain. Eventually she could no longer ignore him.

As she tells the story, she always feels the need to explain things with scripture, lest we believe she is an inherently good and generous person. She explains that God teaches us to love those who hurt us, to repay evil with good, to forgive seven times seventy times. So she did.

She began to accompany this man regularly on the hospital visits as his son struggled toward death. Sometimes the father would ask her to pray with him. She walked with him through the valley of the shadow of death, as he lost that beloved son. She held the man who had killed her parents as he wept over his dead son.

That next year they continued a polite friendship, with occasional phone calls and meet-ups. Then Father's Day rolled around. It was always a hard holiday for Nyasha, having lost her dad at such an early age. But she thought of that man, the killer of her parents. It must be hard for *him,* she thought: the first Father's Day without his son. So she prayed. Then she felt a whisper from heaven telling her that she should go spend Father's Day with him. Thinking that God had lost his mind, she talked to her son about it. She had committed to spending the day with him; they always spent Father's Day together. Without hesitation, he said confidently, "Go and be with him. Who are you to say no to God?" So off she went.

When she showed up at his house, he was delighted to see her. Nyasha, on the other hand, felt conflicted: the pain of her parents' death at the hands of this man was real and ever-present. But that did not stop her. This was the day. Believing that the time was right, she shared with him about Jesus, about her faith, about the God who had given her the strength to live, to forgive, to love someone like him who had done such a terrible thing. He asked her to pray that the God she worshipped would become his God. Later he confessed that he had never met anyone with such sincere and such courageous faith.[9]

It is no surprise that Father's Day was the beginning of a new life for him. He committed his life to Jesus, to the God who had borne such wonderful children as Nyasha.[10]

After Nyasha finished telling me her story, I asked if she still worked in the radio and media world. She laughed and laughed, then explained that her earlier employment had been just a job. Now she has found her vocation, she said. She does restorative justice. She helps people forgive. I asked her if Zimbabwe has the death penalty. Again she laughed. "Yes, as crazy as it may seem, we still do. But we are petitioning the government to end this practice." They have plenty of other problems. Zimbabwe is far from heaven. But she can proudly say with a smile, when it comes to execution, "We are getting there. Soon the death penalty will be dead in Zimbabwe."

As we closed our interview, held in Johannesburg, South Africa, she felt compelled to make sure I knew that South Africa had also abolished the death penalty. As the old apartheid system that the United States had condemned as inhumane and hideously unjust fell, a new South Africa emerged. When apartheid fell, the death penalty fell with it.[11] How beautiful is that!

CHAPTER SEVEN

Death on the Run

*From this day forward, I no longer shall
tinker with the machinery of death.*

—Justice Blackmun, the Supreme Court's
eighty-five-year-old senior member

We've looked at the Bible and seen how it subverts death and reverberates with grace. We took a blast back two thousand years to look at the significance of the execution of Christ. We saw the passionate opposition to the death penalty that marked the earliest days of Christianity. Now we're about to skip ahead to the more recent past. In this chapter, we will look at how the death penalty worked in that recent past and how it works today. At first glance it may look like death is alive and well—and often supported by followers of Jesus, the executed God.

Caution: Read slowly. I packed all the stats into one place.

There have been about 15,000 legal executions in the United States since our country's inception.[1]

Gerald Tigner | Tracy Housel | James Patterson | Daniel Zirkle | Jose Santellan | Paul Kreutzer

Methods have included burning, firing squad, hanging, gas chamber, electrocution, and lethal injection. By far the most widely used method in the first century of the United States was hanging, then the electric chair starting around the turn of the twentieth century, and now lethal injection (since the 1990s).

As you will see from a timeline later in this chapter, executions stopped for a decade following the end of the civil rights movement in the late 1960s, with a forced moratorium later issued by the Supreme Court. The death penalty was reinstated in 1976, and it took another decade for executions to really begin to pick up momentum again and happen in larger numbers.

Since the reinstatement of the death penalty in 1976 (through 2015), there have been 1,422 executions.[2]

Though lethal injection is now the current (very contestable) means of execution, the electric chair has still been used as recently as 2013, and in 2010 Utah executed someone by firing squad; in 1999 Arizona executed by gas chamber.[3]

Thirty-one states in the United States still have the death penalty, and there are around three thousand inmates awaiting execution.

One hundred fifty-six death row inmates in twenty-six states have so far been exonerated after being wrongly convicted since 1973.[4] And yet we would be naive to think that the courts had caught all the wrongful convictions. Certainly many innocent men and women who *should* have been exonerated have instead gone to an innocent death.[5]

Here are some other facts to consider:

- The U.S. federal government has approximately sixty-one people awaiting execution and has exonerated three since 1976.

William Burns | Gerald Casey | Alton Coleman | Rodolfo Hernandez | Richard Johnson

- There are approximately sixty women on death row in the United States. Sixteen women have been executed since 1976.

- In 2005, the Supreme Court ruled that the execution of juveniles is unconstitutional. (Specifically, the court decided that sixteen- to seventeen-year-olds are ineligible for execution.) Twenty-two juveniles were executed between 1976 and 2005.

- Compared to other nations, the United States ranks fifth in the number of executions per year. In 2014 China led the world (China's totals are not released), then Iran (with 289+ executions in 2014), Saudi Arabia (90+), and Iraq (61+).[6]

But check this out: 92.8 percent of U.S. executions have taken place in just fifteen of fifty states, and 98 percent if you bump it up to 20 states (since 1976).[7] Narrowing the perspective even more, of the approximately fourteen hundred executions carried out nationwide since 1976, nearly two-thirds have been performed in just five states, and Texas alone accounts for more than 37 percent of that total.[8]

One landmark study showed that over half of the death sentences since 1976 came from 2 percent of the counties in the United States. Eighty-five percent of U.S. counties have not executed a single person in forty-five years, and eighty percent of counties have no one on their states' death row.[9] That's a big deal. Read that one again. That means the death penalty is being driven by a very small minority of counties that use it very aggressively, while most of the United States doesn't use it at all.

We often say, "The United States practices the death penalty." But rather than referring to the country as a whole, it would be more accurate to say, "Texas has the death penalty. And Oklahoma, and

It all
raises the
fundamental
question . . .
Is there any
<u>good</u> way to
kill someone?

Missouri, and . . ." Or, to be even more precise (since only a few counties are involved), we might say just, "Harris County has the death penalty. And Dallas County, and Oklahoma County."[10] It's not that Arizona, say, has the death penalty, as much as Maricopa and Pima Counties have it. What initially feels insurmountable starts to feel manageable when you break it down in this way.

And even as the places where execution is still practiced have dwindled, much of the enthusiasm for death has also waned.

More than two-thirds of the United States is either not executing at all or virtually not participating (seventeen states have had zero executions in thirty-seven years, and another eleven have had three or fewer in thirty-seven years). Only seventeen states have executed anyone since 2010, and only nine states are executing with any regularity (Texas, Oklahoma, Missouri, Florida, Georgia, Alabama, Ohio, Arizona, and Mississippi).[11]

Death sentences have hit a forty-year low, and executions are at a twenty-year low. Executions continue to drop every year. And almost every year a new state adds its name to the abolition list.

Could it be that death is almost dead?

Death, Thou Art Dead (Almost)

Sometimes debate over the death penalty can sound like it's a clear-cut yes or no matter—either you are for the death penalty or against it. What this hides, though, is how much the practice of the death penalty has changed over time. If someone sees the death penalty as just and moral today, then one needs to explain how earlier generations of moral people justified the crueler methods of execution

Napoleon Beazley | Stanley Baker | Walter Mickens | Daniel Reneau | Robert Coulson that we find abhorrent today. We no longer allow punishments such as stoning, disemboweling, beheading, drawing, quartering, burning at the stake, crucifixion, breaking on the wheel, and the like. And that's a good thing!

Over the centuries, the way we execute people has evolved and changed.[12]

We've used wild beasts—crushing people with elephants, throwing people into snake pits, feeding people to lions and to alligators, even piranhas. In Latin, *damnatio ad bestias* ("condemnation to the beasts") was a common way to execute Christians. Even in the Bible, Daniel was thrown into a lion's den (but survived!).

The brazen bull was a device designed in ancient Greece where the victim was placed inside a hollow bull made of bronze and basically cooked to death.

We've burned people at the stake, a method of execution common for killing alleged witches and heretics. It also appears in the Bible in Genesis 38. Burning was legal even up until the 1800s, with famous executions in many countries like Denmark, Scotland, Britain, and Ireland. There are sixty-five documented executions by burning in the United States.[13]

The garotte used in Spain and other countries for hundreds of years was a cruel method of asphyxiation, where the person was placed in a chair or at a stake and a rope was slowly tightened with a rod, choking the person to death or even driving the rod into the spine.

We have boiled people to death in hot liquids like oil and water. It was made a legal means of execution in England by Henry VIII in 1532 and was used as recently as 2002 in Uzbekistan.

Sawing was common in Europe and other parts of the world, where the condemned was sawed in two, often while hanging upside down.

We've buried people alive, or walled them in and had them die of dehydration and hunger, a practice commonly called immurement.

Gibbeting was hanging people in cages, sometimes alive, sometimes not, by chains, humiliating them and their families as they dangled in public spaces.

We've crushed people with heavy stones, as in the famous U.S. execution of Giles Corey in the Salem witch trial.

Scaphism was when a person was stripped and fastened between two boats and forced to ingest materials that led to severe diarrhea. The diarrhea also attracted insects, which was exacerbated in some cases by pouring honey on the person, who would be stung by wasps and covered with other insects.

Then there's the breaking wheel, used in Europe in the Middle Ages but also in America. The condemned was strapped to a large wooden wheel that rotated slowly. The executioner struck the body with a hammer or iron bar as the wheel rotated.

Ling chi, also known as "death by a thousand cuts" was used in China for hundreds of years and was not outlawed until

1905. It involved the slow cutting away of flesh and eventually amputation.

Blowing from a gun—literally strapping someone to the mouth of a cannon—was used from the sixteenth to twentieth centuries. Among other places, it was used in the British Empire and by colonialists in areas like Sri Lanka, Mozambique, and Brazil.

The guillotine was used in France, Germany, and Sweden for beheading with a sharp metal blade. France used it up until 1977, and in 1996, lawmakers in Georgia attempted to replace the electric chair with the guillotine, but the bill was unsuccessful.

Hanging has been one of the most common means of execution over the years and has been used virtually all over the world. And in some parts of the world, the person is then "drawn and quartered" or cut into pieces. In 1606 this is how Guy Fawkes was to be killed after being sentenced to death for his involvement in the Gunpowder Plot (a plot to kill the kings of England and Scotland). Fawkes jumped from the scaffold, breaking his neck, but his body was quartered.

Stoning is an ancient form of execution seen in scripture, and it still exists in many parts of the world. There are many variations, but it often entails the victim being buried or lowered and a crowd of people hurling heavy stones at the person. It was the method used by Saul of Tarsus in the book of Acts to kill Stephen, who is recognized as the first martyr of the church. It is also the source of the adage from Jesus during another famous stoning of the woman caught in adultery, "Let the one who is without sin cast the first stone" (John 8:7).

These are just a few of the ways we have executed people over the centuries. In more recent years, in the United States we have used hanging, the firing squad, the electric chair, the gas chamber, and lethal injection.

It does all raise the question, Is there any "good"—or "decent"— way to kill anyone?

It's also helpful to see how we have evolved as we consider what crimes are worthy of death. As we noted previously, in the early colonies and in England, there were as many as two hundred crimes worthy of the death sentence. But these dwindled over time. After the mid-seventeenth century, there were no more executions for adultery, for example. After 1673, executions for bestiality came to an end in New England.[14] You get the point.

Now, in the United States, we execute only for murder, and even then only 0.1 percent of homicide cases end in execution.

The U.S. Supreme Court has said that the constitutional standard for acceptable punishment is an "evolving standard of decency" marked by the progress of a maturing society.[15] That's how the highest court in the nation says we must think about the Eighth Amendment banning cruel and unusual punishment—that there is an evolving standard of decency. Could it be that we will look back a generation from now and think of the death penalty like we now think of slavery?

Defenders of the death penalty must concede that there has been a moral arc to how we understand state executions over time. The question then becomes, Where is this moral arc taking us?

To answer that question, we need to take in what it means that we have progressed through several pivotal moments in U.S. death penalty history leading to what we have today. Besides narrowing the number of capital crimes, we stopped public executions. We made it illegal to kill minors and to execute the mentally challenged. We changed the legal methods of execution. We've seen states abolish the death penalty, and we've seen some of them reinstate it. We've seen the methods of execution change from mostly hanging, to mostly electrocution, to mostly lethal injection.

Let's take a little journey down the timeline of death to get a better grasp of where we've been, where we are, and where we're heading. Here's a chart of some of the key events in the evolution of the death penalty, especially for us here in the United States.

History of Death Timeline[16]

1608: The execution of Captain George Kendall is the first recorded in the new colonies.

1632: Jane Champion becomes the first woman executed in the new colonies.

Early 1800s: Many states reduce their number of capital crimes and build state penitentiaries.

1823–1837: Over 100 of the 222 crimes punishable by death in Britain are reclassified to a different punishment category.

1847: Michigan becomes the first state to abolish the death penalty for all crimes except treason.

1907–1917: Nine states abolish the death penalty for all crimes, or strictly limit it. By 1920, five of the nine reinstate it.

Aileen Wournos | William Putman | Mir Aimal Kasi | Craig Ogan | William Chappell

1930s: Executions reach the highest levels in American history, averaging 167 per year.

1950–1980: De facto abolition of the death penalty becomes the norm in Western Europe.

1966: Support of capital punishment reaches a record low in the United States. A Gallup poll shows support of the death penalty at only 42 percent.

June 1972: In *Furman v. Georgia,* the Supreme Court effectively voids forty death penalty statutes and suspends the death penalty.

1976: In *Gregg v. Georgia,* the death penalty is reinstated.

January 17, 1977: A ten-year moratorium on executions ends with the execution of Gary Gilmore by firing squad in Utah.

1977: Oklahoma becomes the first state to adopt lethal injection as a means of execution.

1984: Velma Barfield of North Carolina becomes the first woman executed since the reinstatement of the death penalty.

1986: In *Ford v. Wainwright,* the execution of insane persons is banned.

1988: In *Thompson v. Oklahoma,* the execution of offenders age fifteen and younger at the time of their crimes is declared unconstitutional.

1996: The last U.S. hanging takes place in Delaware.

William Jones | Leonard Rojas | Ernest Basden | Linroy Bottoson | Jerry McCracken

January 1999: Pope John Paul II visits St. Louis, Missouri, and calls for an end to the death penalty.

April 1999: The UN Human Rights Commission issues a resolution supporting a worldwide moratorium on executions.

June 1999: Russian President Boris Yeltsin signs a decree commuting the death sentences of all the convicts on Russia's death row.

January 31, 2000: Illinois Governor George Ryan declares a moratorium on executions. Since 1976, Illinois is the first state to block executions.

2002: In *Atkins v. Virginia*, the Supreme Court rules that execution of "mentally retarded" defendants violates the Eighth Amendment's ban on cruel and unusual punishment.

January 2003: Before leaving office, Governor George Ryan grants clemency to all the remaining 167 death row inmates in Illinois, because of the flawed process that led to their sentences.

June 2004: New York's death penalty law is declared unconstitutional by the state's high court.

December 2, 2005: The execution of Kenneth Lee Boyd in North Carolina marks the thousandth execution since the reinstatement of the death penalty in 1976.

February 2008: The Nebraska Supreme Court rules electrocution, the sole execution method in the state, to be cruel and unusual punishment, effectively freezing all executions in the state.

February 11, 2014: Washington Governor Jay Inslee suspends all executions.

November 21, 2014: Ricky Jackson is exonerated in Ohio, after thirty-nine years in prison. Then his two co-defendants, Wiley Bridgeman and Kwame Ajamu, are exonerated. This marked the 150th exoneration of innocence since 1973.

February 13, 2015: Governor Tom Wolf announces a moratorium on executions in Pennsylvania.

February 18, 2015: U.S. Attorney General Eric Holder voices his concern, calling for a nationwide moratorium on executions.

March 23, 2015: Pope Francis charges all Christians to abolish the death penalty.

March 31, 2015: The American Pharmacists Association releases a resolution declaring executions "fundamentally contrary" to the medical vocation, discouraging participation in executions.

April 10, 2015: The Tennessee Supreme Court suspends executions, challenging lethal injection. Prior to this, the Tennessee legislature voted to reinstate the electric chair as a backup method of execution.

April 18, 2015: As challenges to lethal injection escalate after botched executions, Oklahoma Governor Mary Fallin signs legislation to reinstate executions by lethal gas.

May 20, 2015: The Nebraska legislature repeals the death penalty, making it the first conservative-led state to abolish the death penalty in over forty years.

August 13, 2015: The Connecticut Supreme Court rules that the death penalty violates the U.S. Constitution and is cruel and unusual punishment.

So, here's where we are right now:

Most of the United States does not practice the death penalty—especially, as we saw earlier, if we break things down state by state, county by county. In 2014, only seven states carried out executions, and more than two-thirds of the executions that did take place happened in only three states (twenty-eight of thirty-six were in three states: Texas, Missouri, and Florida).[17] And in 2015, executions hit another record low—totaling twenty-seven. Only six states executed anyone in 2015, and Texas accounted for half of all executions (thirteen of twenty-seven).

Almost every year a new state abolishes the death penalty. In 2015 both Connecticut and Nebraska made the move. Nebraska, to accomplish that, rallied enough votes to override a governor's veto, becoming the first conservative-led state in forty years to abolish death; the historic vote was thirty-two to fifteen.[18] So death may be on its last breath.

The times, they are a-changin'. Polls show that opinion on the death penalty is shifting rapidly, here in the United States especially, but also around the globe. For the first time in many years, most Americans oppose the death penalty when they are presented with alternatives.

In 1996, 78 percent of Americans were in favor of the death penalty for people convicted of murder. By May 2001, support had dropped to 65 percent. A 2013 Pew study shows that that number had dropped farther, to 55 percent. The percentage of people openly opposed to the death penalty jumped from 18 percent in 1996 to 37 percent in 2013.[19] And those who are passionately for the death penalty have dropped in numbers, from 28 percent in 2011 to 18 percent in 2013. A recent study by the ABC television network shows that 52 percent of Americans oppose the death penalty when offered an alternative of life in prison. For the first time in many decades, a majority of Americans oppose the death penalty when presented with other options like life in prison. Indeed, death penalty support is at a new low.[20]

And it's not only public support that's gone down. The number of folks on death row has dropped to around three thousand, down almost 20 percent from 2001.[21] In addition, several more states have banned the death penalty in recent years; in fact, in six years, six states abolished it. Now a total of nineteen states (plus the District of Columbia) have banned execution, leaving (as we saw earlier) thirty-one states where it is legal. In 2014, Washington State Governor Jay Inslee announced that his state would not execute under his watch. Two other governors, Oregon's John Kitzhaber and Colorado's John Hickenlooper, issued executive orders halting upcoming executions, voicing serious concerns about whether the state should be in the business of killing. As Hickenlooper said, there is "a legitimate question whether we as a state should be taking lives."[22]

Interestingly, the 2011 Pew study found that the number of folks against the death penalty because they believe it is wrong (27 percent) was the same as the number of people against it because they think the system is very flawed and broken. (These were the top two reasons that folks were against the death penalty in Pew's research.)[23] For these reasons and others, many people are deciding that death has had its day and it is time for a new era.

Bobby Fields | Richard Williams | Amos King | Bobby Cook | Michael Thompson

Globally, we're also seeing some huge shifts. Japan is now the only other industrial democracy to practice the death penalty. With a population of 126 million people, Japan has 157 people on its death row. But Japan has nearly stopped executing. In 2013, Japan had eight executions; in 2014, zero.[24] In early 2014, Japan released the world's longest-serving death row inmate, seventy-eight-year-old Iwao Hakamada, after he had served forty-eight years in prison for a crime he is now believed to be innocent of.[25]

In the United States, the shift in death penalty attitudes and laws is embodied in the reflections of folks deeply embedded in the system. We've seen prosecutors and executioners, Supreme Court justices, and legislators make some courageous statements. Consider these words of a longtime death penalty proponent now converted to opposition:

> *For more than 20 years I have endeavored—indeed, I have struggled—along with a majority of this Court, to develop procedural and substantive rules that would lend more than the mere appearance of fairness to the death penalty endeavor. . . . I feel morally and intellectually obligated simply to concede that the death penalty experiment has failed.*
>
> **—William J. Brennan Jr., retired Supreme Court justice**[26]

> *I think this country would be much better off if we did not have capital punishment.*
>
> **—John Paul Stevens, retired Supreme Court justice**

Walanzo Robinson | Louis Jones | Keith Clay | Larry Moon | John Hooker | James Colburn

In the summer of 2015, a monumental case split the U.S. Supreme Court as it considered the legality of execution, in particular in regard to lethal injection. Even more significant than the one vote difference was this statement by Justice Antonin Scalia, one of the death penalty's biggest defenders, just after the decision. Justice Scalia said he "wouldn't be surprised" if the Supreme Court found the death penalty unconstitutional and got rid of it altogether (he said this at the University of Minnesota Law School on October 20, 2015).[27] That was one of his last public statements. On February 13, 2016, Justice Scalia passed away. The vacancy created by his reliable pro-death-penalty vote raises monumental new questions.

Death may very well be on its deathbed, at least in America. We have a little more work to do in Iran, Iraq, China, and Saudi Arabia.

FACES OF GRACE

A Brother's Lament

I got a call in the summer of 2014 about heading down to the U.S. Supreme Court for a week of protest. This is an annual event on the anniversary of the reinstatement of the death penalty. Every year some of the best and brightest voices for abolition meet up and fast from food, pray, and sometimes get arrested.

My wife, Katie, and I headed down. It was the first time I'd gotten to meet some of the people we had worked with virtually—family members of murdered victims, family members of executed

Scott Hain | Don Hawkins | Earl Bramblett | Larry Jackson | Juan Chavez | Gary Brown murderers, and some exonerated former death row inmates—and I was stoked to hear them share their stories.

I know they've shared those stories a thousand times. But for each speaker the telling seemed as raw as if it were the very first time. Hearing their stories felt a little like therapy, like attending a "Survivors Anonymous" meeting, but it was a lot more than that. It was also a family get-together. All the speakers had had their families ripped away from them. Their loved ones had been murdered, some as victims of vicious crime, and others killed by the state-sanctioned homicide of execution. But in common they had trauma, loss, outrage, and grief. They needed each other. And they reminded each other of the power of forgiveness, grace, and compassion, and the sacredness of life—every life.

The first to tell his story that day was Bill Babbitt.[28] Bill had seen his brother killed, murdered by the state of California. And though it had happened years earlier, the pain was still raw. No matter whether a loved one had been killed by a deranged gunman or by the government, the pain the members of this group felt was the same; the tears were the same; the trauma was the same.

With a big smile Bill talked about his younger brother, Manny. They'd grown up together, and you could tell he'd been a great brother. But at only eighteen years old, Manny had headed off to fight in Vietnam. He didn't just fight; he was on the front line of the Marines in one of the war's bloodiest battles, the long-running siege of Khe Sanh. Every month hundreds were killed there, and Manny remained at that front for seventy-seven horrific days. He sent word home of the bloodshed, the limbs scattered, the scorched bodies. At one point a piece of shrapnel pierced his skull, injuring him so badly that he was mistaken for dead, and his body was tossed into the cargo hold of a helicopter that was evacuating dead bodies out of the area. When he woke up in that cargo hold, he was the only living being on a pile of carnage. It's hard to even imagine.

He returned from the war a different person, Bill said. Manny was traumatized, devastated—and paranoid. Folks were not exactly supportive: after two tours of duty and five major campaigns, Manny found himself homeless, living on the streets of Providence, Rhode Island. His family fell apart. His life fell apart. On several occasions he was hospitalized for obvious mental problems. Eventually, he ended up in Bridgewater Hospital for the Criminally Insane—the kind of institution that inspired the novel *One Flew Over the Cuckoo's Nest*. It was a terrible place, where people were warehoused and heavily medicated, neglected, abused. Manny tried to take his own life.

After three years at Bridgewater, despite pleas from his doctors, Manny was released. He got a one-way ticket to Sacramento, knowing that his big brother would take care of him. Manny showed up at Bill's job at the railroad one day. Bill had not been warned about Manny's hearing voices, or his nightmares, or his fears and delusions. But, like a good brother, Bill gladly took him in. And he did his best. But Manny was handed over without medications, no referral—just that one-way ticket to California.

Manny was in terrible shape, hardly resembling the brother Bill had known. Police spoke of having seen Manny hide behind bushes, sneak around corners, and hunker down as if the Viet Cong were around the corner. He was clearly not well.

And yet, Bill told us, his desperate frustration still audible, his brother was not "sick enough." He couldn't be forced into a hospital

Robert Knighton | Kenneth Charm | Kia Johnson | Joseph Trueblood | Ernest Martin unless he threatened his own life or the life of someone else. And that hadn't happened, yet.

Six weeks passed.

One day Bill was reading the newspaper and came across an article about an elderly woman whose apartment had been broken into. She herself had been assaulted. Though she didn't die during the break-in, she did eventually die in the hospital of a heart attack. That story, along with something that Bill found among his brother's belongings, made him suspect that Manny might have been responsible for the crime.

Cautiously, he contacted the authorities about his concern. He was careful to explain that Manny was not well, that he was not a monster but he did need help. The police assured Bill that he didn't need to worry about his brother facing execution and that they would see to it that Manny got the help he needed. "They *promised*," Bill said, tears in his eyes after three decades of sharing this story.

And yet, after eighteen years of appeals, Manny faced execution.

During his initial trial, he'd had a state-appointed attorney who showed up drunk to court every day—and who had never tried a criminal case. He had an all-white jury. As an African-American, Bill mentioned this concern to Manny's lawyer at one point. The attorney responded that he hadn't had good experiences with black jurors, and that Manny stood a better chance with "educated," "intelligent" folks on the jury.

Given Manny's inadequate representation, the all-white jury heard little of Manny's mental illness and next to nothing about his service to the country and the trauma that followed. All they heard about was a "thug" who took an elderly woman's life.[29]

Manny was sentenced to death.

The governor, also a Vietnam veteran, showed no mercy and denied clemency.

To make things even more troubling, one year before his death, Manny was awarded the Purple Heart for his service in Khe Sanh. He was honored in uniform, saluted, and given one of the highest honors this country bestows. And a year later, the same country that had given him the award for his wounds in Vietnam took his life.

Even more heartbreaking, they killed him on a day special to his family.

On Bill's fiftieth birthday, May 3, 1999, he watched Manny die at the hands of the state of California. Manny refused his last meal and asked that the fifty dollars it would have cost be donated to homeless Vietnam veterans. Manny Babbitt's last words were "I forgive all of you."[30]

Bill went on to talk about his own grief and how much it has meant to be with other victims who have experienced similar trauma. He had a very hard time forgiving himself initially. Even though his brother's last, forgiving words were offered as a general benediction—"I forgive all of you"—Bill had a hard time accepting that forgiveness. "I felt so guilty. I felt like I'd murdered my own brother," he said. He started drinking, and he contemplated suicide.

Bill Babbitt finished his story by talking about how he became friends with David Kaczynski, the brother of "the Unabomber," Ted Kaczynski.[31] They shared many things in common—namely, the trauma of turning in a brother whom they loved but feared was mentally ill and dangerous. The differences between Manny and Ted, though, are striking. Ted was a white, well-educated professor who graduated from Harvard and held a PhD—and who could afford good legal counsel. Manny could not. Ted was responsible for killing three and injuring twenty-three others, but he got life in prison. Manny assaulted someone who later died of a heart attack, and he got the death penalty. Ted Kaczynski is still alive at seventy-four years old, and Manny is not.

CHAPTER EIGHT

Race, the Death Penalty, and Lynching

The 13 states that comprised the Confederacy have carried out more than 75 percent of the nation's executions over the last four decades.

—from the Connecticut Supreme Court treatise that declared the death penalty unconstitutional in 2015

One of the most powerful arguments against the death penalty is the simple fact of how disproportionately it is applied based on race. Even if you think the death penalty is just in theory, it is hard to support when we see how often its application is distorted in practice. And if we are going to talk about race and the death penalty, then we must also talk about the suppressed history of lynching in the United States.

It would be irresponsible to talk about the death penalty in the context of the United States and not mention lynching—especially since we've seen the powerful parallels between the lynching of black folks in America and Jesus as the first lynchee.[1]

Edward Hartman | John Smith | James Brown | Joseph Keel | John Daniels | Robert Henry

Lynching is defined as the killing of a person, often by hanging, for an alleged offense, usually without a legal trial. It is what Bryan Stevenson, quoted in earlier chapters, has called "racialized terror." Lynchings claimed the lives of thousands of men, women, and children in the United States, especially in the late 1800s and early 1900s.

I want to be careful not to equate lynchings with current-day executions. Not even the most ardent supporter of capital punishment is advocating the legitimacy of lynching. Still, the relationship between the death penalty and lynching is nonetheless eerie and haunting. Understanding what was behind lynchings can shed light on what is behind public support of the death penalty today. And what we see is that it has a lot to do with race.

It turns out that the decline of lynching relied heavily on the increased use of capital punishment. The roots of the death penalty are sunk deep in the legacy of lynching; as lynchings decreased, legal executions increased.

Of course, there is one key difference between lynching and capital punishment: capital punishment is administered by the state, whereas lynchings are "vigilante justice" (though in their U.S. heyday they were often underwritten tacitly or explicitly by police, judges, and other agents of the state). But despite that difference, the parallels between lynching and the death penalty are startling.

Eight in ten lynchings that occurred in the United States from 1889 to 1918 occurred in the South. Now (since 1976) eight in ten executions are in the South. In other words, the places that were most inclined to unofficial execution by lynching a hundred years ago are drawn to official execution today.[2] It is fair to say, as Bryan Stevenson and the other esteemed lawyers of the Equal Justice Initiative assert,

Eight in ten lynchings occurred in the South. Now eight in ten executions are in the South. The states that lynched are the ones that are still executing today.

"Capital punishment remains rooted in racial terror—a direct descendent of lynching."[3]

A Suppressed History

I didn't hear much about lynchings growing up in Tennessee, even though historically they had taken place all over that region and the KKK was founded in my state. I can't remember hearing much about lynching in my high school history classes or even in my college political science classes. In fact, I can't remember anyone mentioning it at all when I was growing up.[4]

And that's part of the problem. The horrific history of lynching is buried deep down in the consciousness of black folks and is dangerously on the verge of being forgotten by white folks. Just hours from where I grew up, in Dyersburg, Tennessee, a mob tortured a man named Lation Scott with a blazing-hot poker iron; they gouged out his eyes, shoved the hot poker iron down his throat, and pressed the poker iron all over his body before castrating him and then burning him alive over a fire. This was not ISIS today; this was the Bible Belt—the *Bible Belt!*—in 1917.

I'm convinced that Jesus was right when he said, "The truth will set you free" (John 8:32). The first step toward a better future is telling the truth about our past. It was Holocaust survivor Elie Wiesel who said, "Without memory, our existence would be barren and opaque, like a prison cell into which no light penetrates; like a tomb which rejects the living. . . . If anything can, it is memory that will save humanity. For me, hope without memory is like memory without hope."[5]

As Americans, we *need* to hear the story of lynchings.

Until recently, it was estimated that nearly 3,500 African Americans and 1,300 whites were lynched in the United States between 1882 and 1968, mostly from 1882 to 1920.[6] However, in 2015 the most thorough study of lynching to date revealed that the extent of the killing was worse than we'd imagined.

According to that new information, in the twelve most active lynching states—Alabama, Arkansas, Florida, Georgia, Kentucky, Louisiana, Mississippi, North Carolina, South Carolina, Tennessee, Texas, and Virginia—there were over 3,959 documented lynchings of African Americans alone between the years 1877 and 1950.[7] (Future studies may reveal even more.)

The circumstances leading up to these murders varied. Some of the lynched resisted mistreatment or refused to work for free. Many tried to intervene when another person was being falsely accused or abused. Others were said to have looked at a white person the wrong way, spoken inappropriately, or sat where they were not allowed to sit. Nearly a quarter of lynchings were sexual in origin—for example, a black person accused of sexually assaulting, or even consensually dating, a white person.

In 1889 in Aberdeen, Mississippi, Keith Bowen allegedly tried to enter a room where three white women were sitting. He was lynched by the entire neighborhood.

In 1904 in Reevesville, South Carolina, General Lee, a black man, was lynched by a white mob for knocking on the door of a white woman.

In 1912 in Shreveport, Louisiana, Thomas Miles was lynched for inviting a white woman to have a cold drink with him.

In 1940 in Luverne, Alabama, Jesse Thornton was lynched for referring to a police officer by his name without the title of "mister."

In 1919 in Blakely, Georgia, William Little, a soldier in uniform returning from World War I, was lynched for refusing to take off his Army uniform.

In 1916 in Cedarbluff, Mississippi, a man was lynched for accidentally bumping into a white girl as he rushed to catch his train.[8]

Though now, one hundred years later, we are so ashamed of this part of our history that it is rarely talked about, in its heyday the lynching of black Americans wasn't something hidden away. On the contrary, lynchings were often public spectacles, announced in advance in newspapers and over radios. Thousands showed up to watch these public displays.[9]

Looking back, the lynching scene seems surreal, more like a circus or carnival than a murder. Ambitious business folks would set up merchandise, postcards, souvenirs. Vendors set up food stands. Kids were dismissed from school so they could watch. Cameras clicked everywhere.

There is no other word but *evil* to describe the mind-set that not only justified lynching but made it entertainment. Children were often given the chance to cut off pieces of flesh—fingers, toes, ears, even genitals—to take home as souvenirs.[10]

Postcards were made on the spot and sold. Spectators could get their picture taken with the body of the lynched, to be used on the front of their cards. To this day, there are still postcards preserved with smiling white folks beside charred black bodies with a text that reads: "This is the barbeque we had last night."[11]

This description of the lynching of Thomas Brooks in Fayette County, Tennessee, just a few hours away from where I grew up, is an on-the-spot report of the party atmosphere that prevailed:

> *Hundreds of Kodaks clicked all morning at the scene of the lynching. People in automobiles and carriages came from miles*

around to view the corpse dangling from the end of a rope. . . .
Picture card photographers installed a portable printing plant at
the bridge and reaped a harvest in selling the postcard showing a
photograph of the lynched Negro. Women and children were there
by the score. At a number of country schools the day's routine was
delayed until boy and girl pupils could get back from viewing the
lynched man.[12]

It may seem crazy to us now, but it must have seemed normal to us back then. What's even more disturbing is this: while some of the folks who participated in the lynchings were hate-filled racists, hooded KKK members, many of the tens of thousands of folks who participated in and celebrated lynchings were well-respected white folks who sat in church pews every Sunday morning. The practice of lynching cannot be blamed on a small cohort of fanatics. That would be too simple.

For many, lynching was seen as necessary. It was a way that some individuals tried to protect themselves from a category of people they deemed threatening. As such—that is, as a form of public protection—it was sanctioned by the community and carried out by members of the community. It was a form of "extralegal justice," if you will.

It's important to note that lynching was a normative part of society at the time, not the action of a frowned-upon, rogue mob as we might be prone to think of it. And it didn't happen only in the South. Whites lynched people in nearly every state (including New York and California). And even though the victims were primarily African Americans, lynching was not used only against black folks. It was also used against Native Americans, Chinese Americans, and white Americans. The word "lynching" came to include all sorts of public humiliation and torture, often involving whipping, shooting, stabbing, and hanging.

By the 1890s, lynching had reached a feverish pitch in the South, and burning the victim slowly for many hours was a chief method of torture. That treatment did not always mean death, but it usually did.

Not only did radios and newspapers celebrate the lynchings, but so did judges, governors, and senators. Cole Blease, a two-time governor and U.S. senator from South Carolina, proclaimed that lynching was "a divine right of the Caucasian race to dispose of the offending blackamoor without the benefit of a jury."[13]

As I read the stories of lynchings, I realized that they contained some of the most evil stuff I've ever heard. What some deemed "justice" looked more evil than any crime the alleged lynchee could have done. In these pages I have often said of the death penalty, "The cure is as bad as the disease"; but with lynching, the disease was racism, and the "cure" spiraled into some of the most vicious stuff humans can do to each other.

Consider this story. A mob in Valdosta, Georgia, in 1918 set out to lynch Sidney Johnson, who had been accused of murdering his boss, Hampton Smith. Failing to find Johnson, they decided to lynch another black man, Haynes Turner, who was known to dislike Smith. Turner's wife, Mary, who was eight months pregnant, protested vehemently and vowed to seek justice for her husband's lynching. The sheriff, in turn, arrested her and then gave *her* up to the mob. In the presence of a crowd that included women and children, Mary Turner was "stripped, hung upside down by the ankles, soaked with gasoline, and roasted to death. In the midst of this torment, a white man opened her swollen belly with a hunting knife and her infant fell to the ground and was stomped to death."[14]

In a Doddsville, Mississippi, case in 1904, lynching victim Luther Holbert was still alive, along with a black woman, as spectators methodically chopped off their fingers and gave them out as keepsakes. Then their ears were cut off. Eventually, Mr. Holbert was beaten so severely that his skull was fractured and one of his eyes hung from the socket. Members of the mob used a corkscrew to bore holes into the bodies and pull out chunks of flesh. Both bodies were burned as white men, women, and children watched over their lunches of deviled eggs and lemonade.[15]

In the 3,959 lynchings studied by the Equal Justice Initiative, not a single white person was convicted of murder—and of all the lynchings after 1900, only 1 percent resulted in the lyncher being convicted of a criminal offense.[16]

Eventually lynchings lost favor, but as I noted earlier, when illegal lynchings decreased in number, "legal" lynchings increased in the form of public executions. "Perhaps the most important reason that lynching declined is that it was replaced by a more palatable form of violence," says the Equal Justice Initiative report.[17] By 1915, court-ordered executions outnumbered lynchings in the former slave states for the first time.

But those executions looked a lot like the old lynchings. For example, two-thirds of those executed in the 1930s were black. As African Americans fell to 22 percent of the South's population (by 1950), they still made up 75 percent of the executions. To this day, even though African Americans make up only 13 percent of the nation's population, 42 percent of death row inmates are black, and 34 percent of those executed since 1976 have been black.[18]

We have not exorcised the demons of racism from our land—or from our courts. Take the 1987 case of *McCleskey v. Kemp*. In this case, the U.S. Supreme Court considered statistical evidence that demonstrated that Georgia decision-makers were four times as likely to impose death for the killing of a white person as for a black person. Interestingly and sadly, the court accepted the data as accurate and described racial bias as "an inevitable part of our criminal justice system."[19] Essentially, the justices said, racial bias is expected and acceptable.

It is not that the death penalty *replaced* lynching, mind you; we had the death penalty *during* lynching. But as lynchings began to come to an end, executions increased dramatically—especially among people of color with white victims, and especially involving accusations of rape.

The primary victims of lynching were black folks accused of raping white victims. Theodore Roosevelt said this: "The greatest existing cause of lynching is the perpetration, especially by black men, of the hideous crime of rape—the most abominable in all the category of crimes, even worse than murder."[20]

Sexual intercourse between black men and white women, even when consensual, was seen as an intolerable crime. People spoke with disgust of "race-mixing" or even more crudely of "mongrelization." And it's important to see a parallel today: over 80 percent of executions involve white victims, though white folks make up only 50 percent of the victims of murder.

This part of our history is not over and certainly has not been healed. It still leaves a residue. Even as recently as 2014, on the anniversary of the horrific Mississippi lynching of fourteen-year-old Emmett Till (after he allegedly flirted with a white woman), a young black man in North Carolina was found hanging from a tree. There are still many questions about his death, which his family has called

To this day, even though African Americans make up only 13 percent of the nation's population, 42 percent of death row inmates are black, and 34 percent of those executed since 1976 have been black.

a "lynching." It turns out his only possible "crime" was dating a white woman.

It's easy to see why so many black folks over the years have felt deeply, mystically connected to Jesus on the cross, even as the KKK and white Christians used the Bible in terribly distorted ways. Jesus, black folks proclaimed, knew their pain, understood their suffering. As noted earlier, he was the first "lynchee."

As we look back, it's hard to understand how so many Americans could have been so cruel. But they were; *we* were. And it's hard to understand how so many American Christians backed their cruelty up with the Bible, but we did.

We can still see the residue from lynchings in the out-of-proportion execution of people of color killed when their victims are white, and the travesty of justice that often results when defendants are poor, black or brown, or found guilty by all-white juries. If our history of lynching is what's behind some people's passion for the death penalty today, then the only moral response possible is to end the death penalty as quickly as possible.

Racial Bias

Even without reference to lynchings, it's not hard to make the case that our legal system, especially when it comes to the use of the death penalty, has a clear racial bias. Racism was written into the law itself long before (and independent of) the expediency of lynching.

In North Carolina the law code of 1855 said, "Any slave, or free Negro, or person of color, convicted of . . . an assault with intent to rape, upon the body of a white female, shall suffer death." Some legal codes went so far as to give one penalty to black defendants and a different, lesser sentence—or no sentence at all—to white defendants. In Mississippi as late as 1860 it was still not a crime to rape a black woman over twelve years old, but of course a capital crime to rape a white woman. In Georgia, the law explicitly sentenced a black person to death for rape, but a white person got as little as two years. In Louisiana it was a capital crime to print or distribute material that might spread discontent among the free black population or insubordination among slaves. Virginia explicitly provided the death penalty for slaves who committed any crime for which free white people would serve a sentence of three years or more.[21]

And we're not talking only about ancient history here. In the prominent 1958 case of Jimmy Wilson, the defendant, an African American accused of robbing a white woman of $1.95, was sentenced to death.[22]

This is the racial backdrop of the death penalty in America.

Still to this day, there are recent cases where judges, lawyers, jurors, and even *defense attorneys* have referred to the defendant as a "nigger." And I'm talking in the past few years, not decades ago. Even in the past *year* there have been cases of African Americans sentenced to death by all-white juries. Many studies have shown that blacks are over four times more likely to get a death sentence than whites (which Dale Recinella compares to the fate of smokers, who are less than two times more likely to get coronary disease than nonsmokers).[23]

In the case of Walter McMillian, his only "crime" was falling in love with a white woman in Alabama. Despite dozens of black witnesses who verified Mr. McMillian's alibi, he was convicted and sentenced to death. Bryan Stevenson, who handled the case for the defense, writes about it in *Just Mercy*. In a coincidental moment of luck or a miracle (or maybe both), Bryan found an audiotape that was not part of the known evidence. As he was listening to recorded sessions of the interrogation of the defendant, his dysfunctional tape player flipped the tape over accidentally at just the right moment, when the key witness denied McMillian's involvement in the crime. As a result of that crucial testimony, McMillian was the first man to be freed from death row and released in Alabama. Bryan says it's a miracle that the prosecutor recorded the exculpatory statement, and an even greater miracle that no one had destroyed that evidence. The district attorney now says he doesn't think McMillian was even at the scene of the crime. And Stevenson says McMillian is no guiltier than you or I, but was targeted only because of the color of his skin.[24]

As noted earlier, in one of the central court cases on race, *McCleskey v. Kemp,* the sharply divided Supreme Court issued a five-to-four ruling accepting the racial disparities in the imposition of the death penalty as "inevitable."[25] The justices basically said racial bias exists in the system as a whole but must be proved on a case-by-case basis. A certain amount of racial bias is inevitable?! Even though the death penalty system reeks of racial bias, the justices pointed out that if we were to do away with it, what would we do with other areas of justice where that same racial bias exists? Wow. It's like an airline saying, "We know our planes keep crashing, but we need each plane to be looked at individually. Meanwhile, keep trusting us to get you where you need to go."

Justice Lewis Powell rightfully said of the decision: accepting the argument that race plays a significant role in the administration of the death penalty would call into "serious question the principles that underlie our entire criminal justice system." Sadly, the court refused to address the deep racial injustice in our justice system. Justice William Brennan, representing the dissent, said that the court feared "too much justice."[26]

One of the other areas we can see the ugly residue of racism persist is in jury selection. We still have black defendants regularly found guilty by all-white juries, even in death penalty cases. My friends at the Equal Justice Initiative have done a thorough report entitled, "Illegal Racial Discrimination in Jury Selection: A Continuing Legacy."[27] In it EJI director Bryan Stevenson says: "Nearly 135 years after Congress enacted the 1875 Civil Rights Act to eliminate racially discriminatory jury selection, the practice continues, especially in serious criminal and capital cases." The report goes on to show that there are counties where 80 percent of African Americans qualified for jury service were excluded. In majority-black counties, defendants face all-white juries. The researchers found that some prosecutors employed by state and local governments were trained in how to exclude people of color and still find "race-neutral reasons"[28] for striking jurors, concealing their racial bias. In documented cases, African Americans have been excluded because they appeared to have "low intelligence"; wore eyeglasses; were single; were married; were separated; were too old at forty-three years and too young at twenty-eight. African Americans were barred for being associated with historically black colleges and for the way they walk, for chewing gum and for the neighborhoods they live in. A Georgia prosecutor struck a juror because he was black and had a son in an interracial marriage. In South Carolina, a prosecutor struck a black juror because he "shucked and jived" as he walked. A Louisiana court allowed the prosecutor to strike a black juror who he thought "looked like a drug dealer." When asked to explain why he removed so many African Americans, one district attorney in Alabama said he believed many of the people removed were of "generally low intelligence" despite the lack of any evidence suggesting that could be true. Each of these justifications was upheld by the court as legitimate "race-neutral" reasons for striking potential jurors of color. For this reason it is not unusual for a defendant who is African American or Latino to face an all-white courtroom—white lawyers, white judges, white juries. In the words of one exonerated death row prisoner, "I looked around the courtroom. The judge was white. The prosecutor was white. The jury was white. Even though I was innocent, I knew I had no chance."[29] He, like many defendants, was guilty until proven innocent. And sometimes that means decades on death row before being able to prove your innocence.

Dale Recinella has said that the legal system is the institution in the United States that has been the least affected by the civil rights movement. Approximately 98 percent of district attorneys in death penalty states are white. Nationwide, of over 12,000 state and federal judges, 90 percent are white, even though the population is more than 25 percent minorities.[30] With predominately white judges, white jurors, and white lawyers, it is not uncommon, especially in parts of the South, for the only person of color in the room to be the defendant.[31] Corporations would be sued if they looked like some of our courts.

One of my favorite stories, on a lighter note but still related to race, is from Bryan Stevenson. I've mentioned that he's an attorney, but I should add that he's an African American attorney down in Alabama. One day when he showed up to court, a judge unknown to him told Bryan that he needed to leave because defendants weren't allowed in the courtroom without an attorney present. He explained to the judge that he was an attorney. What made it even better is that his client was a young white man!

Hector and Susie Black

I first heard about Hector Black from a wild, charismatic brother named David, who joins my community for morning prayer on occasion.[32] David is an eccentric fusion of faith: part Pentecostal, part Catholic, and always armed with a guitar. With a story for every occasion, he has more morning energy than most of my community combined. One morning, brother David told me about Hector Black.

When David first told me about Hector I almost missed it, partly because it was 8:00 A.M. (not my prime hour). With his usual fire, David told us after morning prayer about this tall, lanky, Amish-looking mountain man with overalls and a smile who was a legend in the movement to abolish the death penalty. Honestly, I didn't think too much of it until I went to visit the men on Tennessee's death row and saw a tall, lanky, Amish-looking mountain man with overalls and a smile. I thought to myself—that's the guy David told me about. (Seeing Hector with the men on death row was a little like the old *Sesame Street* tune that goes, "One of these . . . is not like the others.") Hector had been visiting the men before I got there and, unfortunately, had to leave when I arrived. But when I got

Donald Wallace | William Powell | Jimmy Slaughter | Stanley Hall | Glen Ocha home I asked David to tell me about Hector again (this time in the afternoon rather than at 8:00 A.M.).

Hector grew up fairly wealthy and graduated from Harvard. He's a concert pianist. He served in World War II but came out of it a conscientious objector and a passionate pacifist. Eventually, back in the States, he encountered the Bruderhof, a community of Christians known for their radical faith and their commitment to nonviolence. (Having been kicked out of Germany because they were against the Nazis and against the war, the Bruderhof ended up in Paraguay and then moved to the States.)

That community is where Hector met his wife, Susie. She was raised Amish but then joined the Bruderhof. Her roots as a strong farmer with calluses and a German accent are still apparent. After the two fell in love and got married during the civil rights movement, they ended up leaving the rural life of the Bruderhof in favor of a life together in inner-city Atlanta, where they could join the momentum of Martin Luther King Jr. and others.

As they settled into their new home, they were among the only white folks in the segregated world of Georgia. Jokes about the "white Blacks" came and went as the neighborhood became home, and they became family. Before long, they had brought a girl from the neighborhood into their home, rescuing her from a troubling family situation—a youngster named Patricia. Susie taught Patricia all sorts of skills, like sewing and cooking (stuff the Amish are famous for). As a result, Patricia grew up with a wild fusion of African American, Amish, urban, and farming in her background.

When Patricia's mother and sister died, Susie and Hector became her only family. With their encouragement, Patricia went to college and became a social worker. Her dream was to return to the neighborhood and give back. She used the skills passed on to her to teach others how to cook and sew. She created a whole business of stitching bridal dresses.

One night someone broke into Patricia's house while she was home alone. The man who broke in was deeply troubled mentally: he told Patricia about the spirits that were at war in his mind and in his soul. The conflict mediation and anti-violence skills that she'd learned from her pacifist godparents came in handy. She disarmed the perpetrator and ended up having a conversation with him— and cooking him a meal. She cooked dinner for the man who had come to rob her!

I wish I could say that the story ends with his conversion and changed heart, but it doesn't. He did end up robbing her. And he tied her up, went out and got high, came back, and demanded sex. She said, "You would have to kill me first." And he did.

That's how Hector got involved with the death penalty, or the death penalty got involved with Hector. He insisted that he did not want to hate this man, but he did want to understand him. Why would someone do something so evil?

As Hector learned more about the killer, whose name was Ivan Simpson, he discovered that the man had been born in the psych ward of a mental hospital. Not the best of beginnings. Then, as an eleven-year-old, Ivan had watched his mother drown his sister in front of him.

When Hector finally met Ivan, his heart broke. The more he heard, the more he became convinced that execution was not the best ending to an already tragic story. In the end the court agreed, handing down a sentence of life without parole.

Lonnie Pursley | Earl Richmond | George Miller | Michael Ross | Vernon Brown | Bryan Wolfe

Hector still ached for Patricia, and yet he knew that attempting to prevent Ivan's execution is exactly what she would have been doing if she were still alive, for she was a woman of grace. Hector and Susie were two of the most outspoken people against the execution of Ivan Simpson, and Hector and Ivan later struck up a correspondence. Eventually the Blacks ended up adopting him. He was their first visit to death row. Now he is their son. To this day the Blacks say that they've learned more about God and Jesus and grace from Ivan than any book or sermon has ever taught them.

I hope to visit Ivan one day, and I have his address here on my desk so I can write to him. And I'm already making plans to visit Susie and Hector on their farm. I might need to borrow some overalls for that visit.

CHAPTER NINE

The Death Penalty's Hall of Shame

I do not think that God approves the death penalty for any crime, rape and murder included. Capital punishment is against the better judgment of modern criminology, and, above all, against the highest expression of love in the nature of God.

—Martin Luther King Jr.[1]

We have come a long way so far in this book. Let's take a minute, collect our breath, and see where we have traveled. We first heard from victims of crime who gave compelling reasons why they are against the death penalty. Then we discovered how neither the Bible, nor God, nor Jesus can be used to support the death penalty. We also witnessed how the early church was amazingly unified against the idea that Christians should have anything to do with death. We have seen how Western culture and the United States in particular have evolved when it comes to how we execute

Michael Pennington | Kevin Conner | David Martinez | George Sibley | Gary Sterling and what we execute people for, to the point today that the majority of the country no longer practices execution in the state justice systems. We have also seen how race has played an uncomfortable and unjust role in who it is we execute, whether by lynching or by official execution.

In this chapter we will tackle less lofty statistics and issues and deal with the sheer messiness endemic in our practice of the death penalty. I call these matters the death penalty Hall of Shame. They will give you a glimpse into the disturbingly dysfunctional system we have.

Botched Executions

I should warn you that this section deserves to be rated R. It does not paint a pretty picture. The sad truth is that executions often do not go smoothly. There have been reports of people writhing in pain for over an hour, people's heads catching on fire, even some people surviving their own execution.

In the case of Stephen McCoy, who was executed in Texas in 1989, the scene was so horrific that folks fainted watching him die. Randy Woolls and Billy Wayne White, also executed in Texas, were both poked and prodded with needles so long that eventually the needles and not just the lethal injections contributed to their death. Then there was the bizarre case of Brandon Rhode, who was executed in Georgia in 2010; while facing execution he attempted suicide, but the prison system decided to treat him and bring him back to health before proceeding with his execution.[2]

Here are a few more stories of executions[3] that did not go according to plan:

Kenneth Turrentine | Robert Shields | Timothy Johnston | Frances Newton | John Peoples

- In 1983 John Evans caught on fire during his Alabama execution by electric chair. After his initial electrocution, two doctors pronounced him still alive, so the executioners reattached all the electrodes and did it again. And again. It took fourteen minutes to kill Mr. Evans, his body charred and smoldering by the end.

- In Mississippi in 1983 Jimmy Lee Gray faced the gas chamber. He gasped for air so desperately that officials had to clear the witness room. He died banging his head against a steel pole behind him. Later it was revealed that the executioner, Barry Bruce, was drunk at the time.

- In the 1988 Texas execution of Raymond Landry, two minutes into the execution by lethal injection the syringe came out of his vein, spraying chemicals across the room. A spokesperson winsomely called it "a blowout."

- In 1992 Donald Harding faced the gas chamber in Arizona, but he turned purple and thrashed about so violently that one witness said, "We put animals to death more humanely."

- In Texas Joseph Cannon made his final public statement before his 1998 death by lethal injection. As the execution was started, the vein collapsed and the needle popped out. He told them, "It's come undone." Officials pulled the curtain closed, only to reopen it fifteen minutes later to reveal a weeping Mr. Cannon. He made another statement before facing death again.

- In 2009 Romell Broom was poked and prodded for over an hour in Ohio. The process was so distressing that he began to weep. Eventually, Governor Strickland called off the execution. Mr. Broom is still alive, one of the few people to survive his own execution.[4]

You'd think botched executions would have ended over time as we refined the art of killing, but that's not the case. With sickening regularity, botched executions are making the news. On July 23, 2014, Joseph Wood gasped for nearly two hours, during which time his attorneys made an emergency appeal to Supreme Court Justice Anthony Kennedy. One witness counted a horrifying 640 gasps before he died. The Arizona Department of Corrections released a report that revealed he had been injected with over fifteen consecutive doses of poison (midazolam and hydromorphone). Arizona's protocol explicitly states that a prisoner will be executed with 50 milligrams of each drug; Woods received 750 milligrams.

Also in 2014 there was Clayton Lockett in Oklahoma. Amid controversy over the secrecy of lethal injection drugs and despite warnings about experimental new cocktails, Oklahoma went forward with the execution. As the execution proceeded, with Mr. Lockett panting, clenching his teeth, and straining to rise off the gurney, prison staff closed the blinds and asked the witnesses to leave. Mr. Lockett was later said to have died of a heart attack rather than from lethal injection. There was a second execution scheduled that same evening, a man named Charles Warner. His execution was temporarily stayed. Nine months later, Mr. Warner lost the fight for his life and was led again to his execution. His last words as he died were, "My body is on fire." An autopsy report later revealed the wrong drugs were used for his execution.

I can't leave out the case of Richard Glossip, also in Oklahoma (which is a troubling case on many counts as he is believed by many to be innocent). The state ordered the wrong drugs. Instead of potassium chloride, which stops the heart, they had acquired potassium acetate, a food preservative. His execution was halted hours before he was set to die. With her usual relentless hope and charm, Sister Helen Prejean, who was with Richard, said this: "Potassium acetate is a food preservative, but today it was a Richard Glossip preservative because he is still alive!" Mr. Glossip continues to fight to prevent his execution and to prove his innocence.[5] And, at least for now, all executions in Oklahoma (and several other states) have been stopped.

Even if we believe that these men are guilty of the things they are being executed for, it is hard to miss the sickening reality that what's being done to them is the very thing we are trying to rid the world of. Once again, the cure is as bad as the disease.

When people do eventually die at the hands of the state, the cause of death is often listed as "legal homicide." It seems they get that part right.

Wrongful Convictions

In chapter 11 we will talk more fully about the 156 people who, since 1973, have been released from death row after it was discovered they were not guilty of the crime they were sentenced to die for. Their stories should make us rethink the wisdom of any punishment that is irreversible. But that number does not include those who have been executed despite serious doubts and, in some cases, even concrete evidence of their innocence.[6] That is what we will talk about here. It is now impossible to put those cases right.

Robert Rowell | Shannon Thomas | Elias Syriani | Eric Nance | John Hicks | Kenneth Boyd

Having the power over life and death is an overwhelming responsibility. Have our systems of justice and our politicians lived up to this level of responsibility? Could *anyone* do so in a way that guarantees that the innocent are never executed?

The stories below might help us answer those questions.

Cameron Todd Willingham was executed by lethal injection in Texas in 2004 for setting fire to his home, killing his three children. Experts have recently said that the arson theories used in the investigation were scientifically invalid. Many people now believe that the fire was accidental. So not only did Mr. Willingham face the traumatic loss of his children, but he was accused of deliberately killing them. And he was executed for it.[7]

In the case of Lionel Herrera,[8] who was awaiting execution on death row, another man confessed to the crime for which Herrera had been convicted. A former Texas judge was among those who submitted an affidavit of this new confession. The Supreme Court ruled that such evidence was irrelevant. Despite this confession and other new evidence, Herrera was executed in 1993. These were Mr. Herrera's last words: "I am innocent, innocent, innocent. I am an innocent man, and something very wrong is taking place tonight."[9]

One dissenting Supreme Court justice said this: "Of one thing, however, I am certain. Just as an execution without adequate safeguards is unacceptable, so too is an execution when the condemned prisoner can prove he is innocent. The execution of a person who can prove he is innocent comes perilously close to simple murder."[10]

Troy Davis was executed in Georgia in 2011 for the murder of police officer Mark Allen MacPhail. No physical evidence ever tied him to the crime. His conviction was based on the testimony of nine witnesses—seven of whom later recanted or changed their testimony. Some of them said that they had selected Davis's image in the lineup of suspects because they had seen it on the news. Of the two who stood by their testimony, one has long been suspected of committing the murder himself. The Davis execution triggered widespread national outrage, and the movement to end the death penalty gained thousands of new supporters almost overnight.[11]

Frank Lee Smith was sentenced to death in Florida on the testimony of a single witness. No physical evidence tied him to the crime. Four years later, the same witness saw a photo of a different man and realized she had made a mistake. DNA tests later confirmed that Smith was innocent, but by then it was too late. After fourteen years on death row—and nearly a decade of attempting to reverse the original conviction—Mr. Smith had already died in prison of pancreatic cancer. Less than a year after his death, Mr. Smith was further exonerated by DNA evidence that identified another man as the killer.[12]

We need to stop and think through the implications of what former U.S. Supreme Court Justice John Paul Stevens once said: "I think, beyond a shadow of a doubt, that there is a Texas case in which they executed the wrong defendant, and that the person they executed did not in fact commit the crime for which he was punished." Justice Stevens was not talking about any case in particular, which makes his statement even more haunting. Add to that the fact that he is speaking from Texas, which is responsible for half of all executions. When it comes to execution, there is no way to undo a mistake.

Mental Illness and the Death Penalty

Then there's the mentally impaired. Consider a current case, a man named Scott Panetti, who faces execution in Texas. If ever there was a clear case of mental illness, this is it. Scott Panetti suffers from

Perrie Simpson | Marion Dudley | Marvin Bieghler | Jaime Elizalde | Glenn Benner paranoid schizophrenia and was hospitalized a dozen times prior to the crime he's on death row for. He's been sick for over thirty years and was pronounced "disabled" six years prior to his incarceration.

Mr. Panetti was allowed to represent himself during his 1995 trial, with his life on the line. He wore a cowboy costume and attempted to subpoena the pope, John F. Kennedy, and Jesus Christ. His case exposes deep flaws in our criminal justice system, especially when it comes to the practice of the death penalty for those with mental illness.

During the years he's been in prison, his lawyers have been fighting to have the death sentence commuted to a lesser sentence, on the basis of mental illness. And they seem to have good grounds. To be considered competent for execution, says the law, Mr. Panetti is supposed to understand the reason for his execution. Yet he believes that he is being put to death for preaching the gospel, not for the murder of his wife's parents.

Most countries in the world refuse to execute the mentally ill. So does the United States, at least on paper. The U.S. Supreme Court, in *Ford v. Wainwright,* established that the mentally ill should not be executed. And yet Mr. Panetti is still facing death. In December 2014, less than twelve hours before his scheduled execution, he was granted a stay. His lawyers continue to fight for his life.[13]

Another disturbing case involving a mentally ill person is that of Thomas Provenzano. He believed he was Jesus. A fed-up lawmaker suggested "that if he thinks he is Jesus Christ, why don't we crucify him? I'd make him a cross, and we could take it out there and nail him up." Well, Florida didn't crucify Mr. Provenzano, but they did execute him in 2000.[14]

Then there's the case of Larry Robison. He was a veteran, honorably discharged from the Air Force, who returned home mentally ill.

Despite a diagnosis of paranoid schizophrenia, he was unable to obtain psychiatric treatment. His mother's attempts to help were unsuccessful, as he was too old to be covered under her health insurance policy. Eventually, Mr. Robison had a psychotic breakdown—the first time he had ever been violent—and he was convicted of the murders of five people. In a sad irony, the state of Texas paid $2.3 million to execute him, undoubtedly much more than it would have cost to treat his illness. At the time Texas ranked forty-eighth out of the fifty states in the money it invested in mental health. Mr. Robison was executed on January 21, 2000.[15]

Judicial Override and the Death Penalty

Did you know that in some states[16] a judge can impose a death sentence even after a jury has recommended a life sentence? That can and does happen regularly in the state of Alabama. Since 1976, judges have overridden jury verdicts 107 times. Judicial override is so widespread that it accounts for one-fifth of death row prisoners in the state—21 percent of the 199 folks on Alabama's death row were sentenced to death through judicial override.[17]

Consider the case of Courtney Lockhart, who was convicted of capital murder in 2010. The Alabama jury found that his post-traumatic stress disorder, developed after military service in Iraq, warranted a sentence of life without parole. In fact, they voted *unanimously* against the death penalty. However, the presiding judge overrode this recommendation and sentenced Mr. Lockhart to death.[18] He's still fighting for his life.

What's more—the exercise of this judicial override has been shown to elevate during election years, when judges run on the

Richard Thornburg | Willie Brown | Daryl Mack | Dexter Vinson | Joseph Clark | Jackie Wilson

Did you know a judge can impose a death sentence even after a jury recommends a life sentence?

basis of being "tough on crime." This surely has also contributed to Alabama's having one of the highest per-capita death-sentencing rates in the country. So Alabama makes the death penalty Hall of Shame.

Alabama is also the only state not to guarantee a lawyer—at one point, 40 of the 185 folks on death row did not have representation.[19] (I'm sure that's changed now that Bryan Stevenson and the Equal Justice Initiative are shaking things up down there!)

Economic Bias and the Death Penalty

Along with the race of the victim, one of the most consistent determinants of execution is economics. As the old saying goes, "Whoever doesn't have the capital gets the punishment." Sister Helen Prejean talks about the world of contrast between the "O.J.s of the world and the No J.'s."[20]

U.S. Supreme Court Justice William O. Douglas said this in *Furman v. Georgia:* "One searches our chronicles in vain for the execution of any member of the affluent strata in this society."[21] Bryan Stevenson, in an indictment of how the death penalty is applied in the United States, may very well be right: "You are better off being rich and guilty than poor and innocent."[22] It is clear that the imposition of the death penalty is not so much a result of the heinousness of the crime as of the income of the defendant and the quality of the legal counsel which that affords him or her.

I've heard tell of a legendary sleeping defense attorney, infamous for representing poor clients in Texas and falling asleep during trial. He was the court-appointed defense attorney for three men executed during one study of inadequate counsel. The same study showed that prosecuting attorneys were making $150 an hour, $150,000 a year.[23]

In a most bizarre case in 2013, a sixteen-year-old in Texas killed four people as he drove under the influence of alcohol. During the trial, his attorneys argued that his family's wealth was to blame: he was a victim of "affluenza," they asserted. Ethan Couch and his friends stole alcohol from Walmart, piled into a car, and struck and killed four pedestrians. Couch was driving seventy miles an hour in a zone marked for forty. In addition to the fatalities, nine others were injured. Couch's blood alcohol was .24 at the time of the crash, and he had Valium in his system.

This all happened in the state of Texas, the most deadly state in the country when it comes to legal executions, and yet the young, wealthy, white man responsible for taking the lives of four people and injuring nine others got probation. He was sentenced to an elite recovery center that costs nearly half a million dollars a year. Not only did his wealth buy his freedom, but it was allegedly responsible for his guilt. Affluenza.[24]

Other Entries in the Hall of Shame

We could go on a long time about the routine mistakes made in our justice system involving the death penalty.

Roger Keith Coleman was convicted in Virginia of raping and murdering his sister-in-law, but the trial and appeal were plagued by errors and inadequate counsel. The worst mistake was filing the appeal one day too late, which may have cost Coleman his life. He and his lawyer were told that filing one day late was the same as not filing at all. In a final attempt to save his life, the governor considered intervening if Mr. Coleman could pass a lie detector test. He was given the test, designed to measure stress and anxiety, on the day of his execution. Needless to say, he failed it. He was executed in 1992.[25]

Here's one of the most bizarre cases I've ever heard of: Joseph Amrine in Missouri. After his conviction, new evidence surfaced, including DNA evidence, that conclusively proved Mr. Amrine's innocence, but the push for his execution continued. The prosecutor argued before the Missouri Supreme Court that the court's concern is not innocence but constitutionality—since the court needs a constitutional violation to stop an execution. One judge asked the prosecutor, "Is it not cruel and unusual punishment to execute an innocent man?" To which he responded, "If there is no underlying constitutional violation, there is no right to relief." The court rejected that argument—but only by one vote; the court was split four to three. Unbelievable![26] The court was one vote away from killing Mr. Amrine on the basis that it's okay to kill an innocent person as long as his constitutional rights are not violated. Amrine was eventually released.[27]

This has been a brief tour of the Hall of Shame, some of the dark—and all too common—realities of capital punishment in America.[28] And while some of these stories sound like a comedy of errors, the results are not. They are lethal and irreversible. We need to ask ourselves a hard question: Are we good enough to oversee the use of the death penalty?

It's time to put an end to this madness of execution.

Mauriceo Brown | Brandon Hedrick | Robert Anderson | Michael Lenz | William Wyatt

Learning to Love a Terrorist

Back in the 1990s, after the first Gulf War, there was a veteran from the front lines who came home troubled and traumatized. I remember hearing about newspapers that had released some excerpts from letters he'd written home from the war. I poured over everything I could find in the press. I remember reading his words, telling his family how hard it was to kill. He told them he felt like he was turning from a human being into an animal, as day by day he became more tolerant and accustomed to the bloodshed of war, as it got easier to kill.

That man was Timothy McVeigh. He was responsible for the 1995 Oklahoma City bombing, which killed 168 people—making it the worst act of domestic terrorism in U.S. history. He came home from serving in the Army Special Forces horrified, crazy, dehumanized, and then he became the worst domestic terrorist our country has ever seen. In an essay written after his conviction, he cried out against the bloodshed he'd seen and helped create in Iraq:

> *Do people think that government workers in Iraq are any less human than those in Oklahoma City? Do they think that Iraqis don't have families who will grieve and mourn the loss of their loved ones? Do people believe that the killing of foreigners is somehow different than the killing of Americans?*[29]

In his deranged plan, it was the *killing* that he wanted to stop: he wanted people to see the bloodshed in Iraq and in Texas and stop the evil of killing. He bombed the federal building in Oklahoma City in hopes that complacent Americans could see what "collateral damage" looks like and, in response, cry out against bloodshed everywhere, even in Iraq. Instead, the government that had trained him to kill called for the death penalty. After training McVeigh to kill and sending him off to war to kill, we were now going to kill him to show that killing is wrong.

But there was a wonderful interruption to the pattern of death—a man named Bud Welch. His twenty-three-year-old daughter, Julie Marie, was one of the lives ripped away in the Oklahoma City bombing. Initially, Bud Welch felt what any father would: rage. "I wanted him to fry," Bud says. "I'd have killed him myself if I'd had the chance."[30]

As the dust settled, his emotions didn't. He began to think about Julie—and her passion for life and for grace. "Execution teaches hatred," she used to say. Before long Bud's heart began to change.

"It was hatred and revenge that made me want to see him dead, and those two things were the very reason that Julie and 167 others were dead," he says.

He decided to steer his anger and grief in a new direction. He arranged a visit with Timothy McVeigh's dad and family. Bud had remembered seeing an image of Bill McVeigh on the news that stuck with him because he recognized the crippling pain in the older McVeigh's eyes. "I recognized that pain, because I felt it too." So they arranged to meet.

When they met, Bud says there was an immediate connection— one that still endures. He has come to love the McVeighs dearly, and to this day says that he "has never felt closer to God" than when he met them.

Here's how Bud remembers it:

Eric Patton | James Malicoat | Derrick Frazier | Farley Matchett | Clarence Hill | Arthur Rutherford

Bill had asked me, "Bud, are you able to cry?" I'd told him, "I don't usually have a problem crying." His reply was, "I can't cry, even though I've got a lot to cry about." But now, sitting at the kitchen table looking at Tim's photo, a big tear rolled down his face. It was the love of a father for a son.

Timothy's life was eventually taken. But Bud Welch held the hands of the McVeigh family as they lost their son. They had done the same for him as Bud continued to work through his own grief over the loss of his daughter. As he befriended the McVeigh family, Bud says he felt that "a tremendous weight had lifted" from his shoulders.

As he thinks back on it, one of the things he laments is that the McVeigh family will always be stigmatized by what Timothy did. Bud has the delight of remembering all the good his daughter Julie did in the world, even up to the moment she died. But Timothy will be remembered as a monster by most. It is all the more reason for Bud Welch to become a part of the McVeigh family. They carry the weight of death together.

Bud has become one of the most courageous, credible, and grace-full voices in the movement to end the death penalty and all violence. His life is a wonderful interruption of the cycle of violence.[31]

CHAPTER TEN

Putting a Face on the Issue

*The whole system is fatally flawed. . . . I think the
number of people exonerated since '72 should say
something. . . . If I were going to fly on a plane and
went up and bought a ticket and asked, "How is your
safety record?" and they said, "We had 142 crashes since
1972, but don't worry about it," I don't think I'm going
to get on that plane. . . . The bottom line is, the death
penalty does not encompass justice. . . . It's little more
than state-assisted revenge. And I don't think revenge
falls within any definition of justice which I know.*

—Marty Stroud, former Louisiana prosecutor[1]

We're going to switch gears a little bit. We've done some history. We've done some Bible study. We've heard the facts
and stats. But I have to tell you that these were not what
changed my mind about the death penalty. It was the people I met

Donell Jackson | Willie Shannon | John Schmitt | Angel Diaz | Corey Hamilton | Carlos Granados and their stories that changed my mind. The faces. The names. The people behind the numbers.

Ultimately, we are not talking about an "issue." We are talking about people. The people caught in the system of violence—victims, prisoners, guards, and families of the dead and of the scheduled to die. These people have names and faces. They bleed and cry and sneeze and laugh and get the hiccups. They are people made in the image of God just like you and me—no matter how much this world has managed to quash that divine image.

It is the *people* I met who changed my mind on this "issue." They put a face on stale rhetoric and heartless debates and tiring biblical exegesis.

It was meeting folks on death row who were guilty of murder but were different people now than when they did the crime twenty years ago.

It was meeting men who had been condemned to death, only to later be found innocent and set free—after losing up to thirty years of their life.

It was meeting women who were victims of violent crime who found a better way forward than execution.

It was talking with executioners who were haunted by their work of ending a human life.

It was listening to prosecutors and judges and governors who were trying to sleep at night after realizing they had contributed to an innocent person being put to death—and still others who couldn't sleep at night after putting someone to death even when they knew they were guilty.

It was spending time with people on death row who were counting the days until their life would be ended.

In the end it wasn't the facts or the debates that convinced me. It was the stories that changed my mind on the death penalty. And that's where we're going to turn now. We're going to put names and faces on this issue.

Let's start with those who have been condemned to death. The names of those who have been executed in the United States since 1976 have been listed on the bottom of every page in the book. Every name a child of God. Many of them did terrible things. Many of them were different people when they did those terrible things than they were decades later when they were executed. And many others were likely innocent of the crimes for which they were executed. Their names remind us of all the new victims we have created as we continue the cycle of killing to show that killing is wrong, or as Dr. Martin Luther King Jr. said: "Capital punishment is society's final assertion that it will not forgive."[2]

A Sinner Set Free by Grace

Now let me introduce you to one of the men who was condemned to die but is still alive. And I thank God he is.

Billy Neal Moore grew up in Columbus, Ohio.[3] You can tell the minute you talk to him that he has a soft heart and has had a hard life. His dad went to jail early on. His mom had multiple sclerosis and died young. He was a bit mischievous as a youngster, but not malicious. He admits to dressing up for weddings he wasn't invited to and attending the receptions to get some fancy free food. It helped that he lived across the street from a Pentecostal church. But he didn't really hear much about God there, just enjoyed crashing parties.

He was sent off to Catholic school, but he didn't feel God there much either. In fact, Billy decided that if God was anything like the nuns he met in school, he didn't want much to do with God. Life got harder for him after his mom died and his dad was sent to prison, and he felt sort of lost. So, without anywhere else to go, he headed to the military. He went to the Army recruiting office and told them, as he recalls it, that he wanted to kill people. "They were glad to take me!" he says, laughing but sincere. So he headed to Vietnam. And then, he adds, laughing even harder, "Of all things, they made me the military police! They gave me a badge and a gun."

When he returned, he was pretty desperate for money. A friend he'd met in the military had a solution. That friend knew someone who kept a large amount of cash in the house—Billy didn't know it at the time, but it was this guy's uncle—and suggested that they rob that house. His friend assured him nothing could go wrong.

But it did.

"When you do something unnatural, you do unnatural things to get you in that state of mind," Billy recalls. He and his buddy smoked some pot, drank a bunch of Jack Daniels, then beer, then wine, and headed to the house.

As they were robbing the house, the owner showed up and startled them.

At twenty-two years old, Billy took the life of this seventy-seven-year-old man, something he says he will regret for the rest of his life.

He was horrified by what he had done, and fully confessed to the crime. Once arrested and in jail, he was so tormented by his actions that he decided to kill himself. In his cell, he managed to rip a sheet into strips and weave a rope together to end his life. After all, he concluded, it's what he deserved. But then he heard a voice from God.

He smiles as he tells the story. He barely believed in God, much less heard God speak. But what he heard was loud and clear: "If you are so upset about committing one murder, why are you going to commit another one?"

And with that, the suicide was interrupted. He wouldn't kill himself. But he decided that if the state wanted to kill him, he would let it. He had very little reason to live.

Death might have been easier than what Billy did next. Much to the chagrin of his lawyer, Billy confessed everything to the authorities. "God wouldn't let me shut my mouth," he says. He told the entire story of what had happened in a two-and-a-half-hour confession, returning the money, the gun, and laying everything on the table. Billy discovered the sacrament of confession, as it were. He didn't care what happened next; he just knew that he had to tell the truth. And the more he shared, the more he felt healing in his soul. The truth was setting him free. Unfortunately, the state wasn't.

When the trial was over, the judge applauded Billy's honesty and then sentenced him to death. To be precise, the judge said, "Mr. Moore, you have done a good and honorable thing. However, on Friday, September 13, 1974, you will be executed between the hours of ten and two."

"I didn't even know God at this point," Billy said, "but I started calling on him then."

It wasn't that he had never heard about God. It was that he had never *felt* God's grace, never *felt* God's love—even in church, even in Catholic school, even among Christians.

Just before his scheduled execution he got a letter from his cousin, candidly asking him if he "knew Jesus." Billy shot a sarcastic letter back telling his cousin it was a little late in the game. He was about to be killed, and it didn't feel like Jesus cared a whole lot.

But then two things happened that changed everything. He had an encounter with a pastor. And he had an encounter with the victim's family. Both of these led him to Jesus.

Billy got a visit from a pastor and his wife, who had driven 250 miles to spend time with him. The pastor said, "I know you killed a man. And you are sentenced to death. But there is another judge named Jesus." They went on to tell him about God's love and grace and shared with him one of the central passages of the gospel, John 3:16–17: "God so loved the world that he gave his one and only Son. . . . God did not send his Son into the world to condemn the world, but to save the world through him."

As Billy tells the story, he is quick to point out that it wasn't just the words; this time he could *feel* God's love and grace. "I could feel the Holy Spirit loving me—through them. This is what I had been looking for my whole life. I felt *loved*."

He wanted to be baptized, and being a good pastoral couple, his visitors were eager to baptize him. But that was not an easy task inside the walls of a maximum-security prison, especially when one has a theology of full immersion (not just sprinkling some water on the head). This pastoral couple were not a timid bunch, however, and so they convinced the warden to get them a tub. Even that turned out to be insufficient for Billy's tall frame, especially given his bad knee from the war. So they devised a plan: they'd drag him through the little tub, head first, baptizing the top half and then submerging the bottom half. God would have a little grace on this one. And so it went.

Then came the second encounter—with the victim's family. After his baptism, the next step in his journey seemed clear: he needed to ask forgiveness from the people he had hurt. In Billy's words, "God said, 'You need to write them and apologize.'" So he did. He wrote a letter that simply said, "I am truly sorry. If you can find it in your heart to forgive me, I appreciate it. . . . And if you can't, I understand." They wrote him a letter back, telling him they were Christians, and that meant grace, forgiveness, life, love.

Not only did they forgive him, but their exchange launched a restorative friendship that continues to this day. While Billy was in prison, they wrote each other every week. When Billy tells this story, he always says, "It was the family of the person I killed that helped me get to the point that I could forgive myself." They taught him that if Jesus forgives you, and the people you wronged forgive you, who are you not to forgive yourself?

His first execution date, the one originally set by the judge, came and went. Billy laughs about the fact that his less-than-helpful lawyer forgot to tell him that the first execution date had been postponed. "No one came to my cell on the day of execution, and I wasn't going to ask them if they forgot."

That was the first in all sorts of wild events. One might even call them miracles. (Billy does.)

Because Billy pleaded guilty from the get-go, the many appeals of his lawyers didn't stand much of a chance. It's as if the court simply resolved, "There is no question he did it. He's guilty. He knows it; we know it. Execute."

He was assigned over thirteen execution dates over a period of ten years, each one canceled due to an appeal or a motion or a postponement. But on May 24, 1984, it was the real deal. He was ordered to pack up all his stuff. He was presented with the execution warrant and asked what he wanted done with his body after the execution. Prison staff took him to "death watch"—that peculiar place where everyone makes sure you don't kill yourself so they can do it for you.

As he was going through the motions, his mind began to mess with him. As Billy says, "Satan was attacking my mind." He had read about what he was about to experience, and his mind kept replaying it—2,600 volts of electricity. For sixty seconds. Then a thirty-second pause. Then another 2,600-volt surge. He had heard the gory stories of eyes popping out, skin catching on fire, teeth shattering. But then "God spoke," Billy says with a smile.

I'll admit that I have reservations sometimes when folks say God told them something, because sometimes the things they say next are troubling. But there's no doubt in my mind that Billy heard from God.

He says the Lord gave him a verse: Psalm 118:17. He could hear it as clearly as if someone were reading it to him. "I shall not die, but live, and declare the works of the Lord" (KJV). He felt God tell him to say these words himself. The message was so powerful that he started saying the verse out loud. And it was so clear to him that the message came from God that he was determined to say nothing else.

He laughs at the fact that folks thought he'd gone crazy. Guards came to give him a final hug, and he recited the verse: "I shall not die, but live." Folks came to see what he needed in his last moments on earth, and he hit them with the verse as they stared in confusion or pity. When the time came for someone to shave his head in preparation for the helmet of the electric chair, he said, "I shall not die, but live."

Just before the scheduled execution, he was escorted past the captain's office. Astonishingly, the captain stopped the guards; the execution had been called off, he said. To this day, Billy calls it a miracle.

Prison staffers put him back in his cell. And he just kept whispering to himself the words of Psalm 118:17. His fellow prisoners were ecstatic. People didn't come back from death watch; it just didn't happen. And yet it did.

Six years later (just to show you how exhaustingly dysfunctional and traumatizing our system is), he was given another execution date: August 22, 1990. But on August 21, he got another thirty-day stay of execution.

In a surprising move, the parole board decided to reconsider his case. They decided to bring in the victim's family, which by then had become Billy's family. They were some of his greatest advocates, pleading with everyone to cancel the execution. In fact, they didn't just want him not to be killed, they wanted him to be released, claiming that he was a different man than he'd been sixteen years before.

And those family members didn't hold back. They got everyone from Jesse Jackson to Mother Teresa behind him! They brought a bus—the *victim's* family, mind you—filled with their friends and loved ones to plead for Billy's release. The pastor who had baptized him in the bathtub was there too. It was a surreal scene before the parole board. Everyone there was begging for Billy's life to be spared.

The victim's family said, "We have been writing letters for sixteen years. He is now our brother. You cannot kill him." And then something spectacular happened. Folks on the parole board spoke on the phone with Mother Teresa. Her request was characteristically simple and direct. She said to them: "Do what Jesus would have you do."

At the conclusion of their deliberations, they commuted the death sentence to life, a move seldom seen in Georgia. Billy laughs, telling this, since he didn't know about the commutation until he heard it announced on television. Even more hilarious, they had "found" a new picture of Billy that flashed all over the television announcement. Prior to this the media had repeatedly shown Billy's mug shot, taken when he'd been abruptly pulled out of his cell at 2:30 A.M. Now

William Lynd | Earl Berry | Kevin Green | Curtis Osborne | David Hill | Karl Chamberlain they had a dignified photo of Billy when he was eighteen years old in his military uniform, with the U.S. flag behind him; that's the photo they showed now as they announced his commuted sentence.

But it wasn't over yet. Georgia had a law that required folks whose death sentence was commuted to life to do twenty-five years before they were eligible for parole. Somehow the miracles continued to unfold. On November 8, 1991, after about seventeen years in prison, Billy was freed. He is one of only seven people to have had their sentence commuted by the Georgia State Board of Pardons and Parole, and the only one to have been released.

To this day Billy remains friends with the victim's family. And today he is a pastor. He knows the meaning of the promise, "God will make a way when there seems to be no way." Every time I hear him preach, he recites the old King James Version of that verse in Psalm 118, which he heard whispered to him from heaven: "I shall not die, but live, and declare the works of the Lord." He is doing just that. And Rev. Billy Neal Moore knows the power of grace. Not surprisingly, he has become an abolitionist, for he knows all too well that "the death penalty is the state carrying out revenge—nothing more, nothing less."

Billy Neal Moore's story is not just a good story. It is a gospel story. It is a resurrection story. In his own words, "There is no reason for me to be standing here—but Jesus Christ." And his message is simple: "God doesn't love me any more than God loves you. But watch this [he says with a huge smile] . . . I killed a man, and God doesn't love me any less than he loves you either. God is love. All God can do is love."

On Texas's Death Row

I first heard about Duane Buck right after Troy Davis was executed in Georgia. You may recall that I mentioned Troy Davis in the previous chapter as someone who was most likely innocent of the crime he was executed for, which garnered some media attention. This may be one of the main reasons Duane's story made national news. But unlike Troy Davis's case, Duane's guilt is not in question. He admits to having killed two people in 1995, and he says he will regret those murders for the rest of his life.[4]

But his case raised other questions. For starters, race played a major role in why he was sentenced to death rather than life in prison. In Texas, where Duane is, one of the things considered during sentencing is "future dangerousness." In order to sentence someone to death, the state has to convince a jury that the defendant is a future danger to society. As you might suspect, this measure is riddled with problems. For starters, there are much better ways to protect innocent people from truly dangerous individuals than killing the people who pose a threat. This argument is what led Pope John Paul II to revise the Catholic stance on the death penalty to say even more strongly that in contemporary society we have sufficient ways to render someone "inoffensive" without executing that person and "without depriving him definitively of the possibility of redeeming himself."[5] In short, there is no place for the death penalty in contemporary, industrialized society.

Dale Bishop | Derrick Sonnier | Christopher Emmett | Larry Davis | Jose Medellin | Heliberto Chi

But this "future dangerousness" thing tends to get complicated. In Duane's case, in that Texas courtroom, race was considered a contributing factor when determining future dangerousness. An expert witness argued that black folks are more likely to be violent than white folks, and men more likely to be violent than women. That same expert witness testified in five other trials that were later granted new sentencing hearings because of the racial bias. But not in Duane's case; his sentence stood.[6]

Duane Buck had a marvelous conversion in prison. Since that time he has worked hard to heal what wounds can be healed from what he did. The surviving victim in this case has been an outspoken opponent of the death penalty for Duane. Duane has become a bridge-builder inside the walls, creating opportunities for reconciliation to happen between inmates and guards. Inside the walls, he has become a pastoral figure, well loved by his fellow inmates and guards alike. He is known as "Preacher Buck."

In eighteen years he has not been written up for a single violation (which is saying something, when you can be written up for things as trivial as having too many postage stamps). And yet he faces execution because he was deemed a danger to society by an all-white jury who heard an expert witness for the state claim that because he's black he's more likely to be violent. (Nobody pointed out the flip side of these statistics at the time: that he is also more likely to be executed by the state because he's black.)

I felt moral outrage when I heard his story. Why could Duane not get a new sentencing hearing? And why should this powerful pastor, doing God's work inside our prisons, die instead of continuing to work among his congregation? When it comes to the death penalty, one of the central questions we must ask is this:

No one is beyond redemption. Not Moses. Not David. Not Saul of Tarsus. Not you. Not me. Not Billy Neal Moore. Not Duane Buck. No one.

Is *anyone* beyond redemption? I think I know the answer, at least in Duane's case.

Let us begin to make a refrain of it, like the chorus of a good song:

No one is beyond redemption.

Not Moses. Not David. Not Saul of Tarsus. Not you. Not me. Not
Billy Neal Moore. Not Duane Buck.

No one.

CHAPTER ELEVEN

Putting a Face on the Innocent

*More often than we want to recognize, some innocent
defendants have been convicted and sentenced to death.*

—Supreme Court Justice Sandra Day O'Connor[1]

O n July 2, 2001, U.S. Supreme Court Justice Sandra Day
O'Connor, a known defender of the use of the death penalty, declared that "serious questions were being raised
about whether the death penalty is being fairly administered." She
attributed much of the problem to disparities in legal counsel between those who have resources and those who don't. "If statistics
are any indication, the system may well be allowing some innocent
defendants to be executed." Later, she said even more assuredly in
Nebraska, "More often than we want to recognize, some innocent
defendants have been convicted and sentenced to death."[2]

And there is the heart of the matter: sometimes innocent people
are sentenced to death. Worse yet, as we saw earlier, sometimes innocent people are *executed*. How can we call this justice?

Gregory Wright | Elkie Taylor | George Whitaker | Denard Manns | Gregory Bryant-Bey

As I noted earlier, there have been over 156 death row inmates exonerated in twenty-six different states since 1973. Given the nearly 1,450 executions that have taken place since the reinstatement of the death penalty in 1976, that means about one person for every nine executed has been proven to be wrongfully convicted, sentenced to death, and later exonerated and released from death row. Every wrongful conviction means that an innocent person has been robbed of decades of life, millions of tax dollars have been wasted, and the family of the victim has been repeatedly retraumatized— all this while the person *actually* responsible for the crime remains at large and unaccountable. And remember: 156 is the number of death row prisoners who have been able to *prove* their innocence (a process, by the way, that has taken, on average, about fifteen years).

Innocence raises so many questions. And these statistics have names.

Watching Friends Die

Let me introduce you to one of the 156 exonerated individuals. His name is Curtis McCarty.[3]

I was invited to speak in Nebraska a couple of years ago at an anti–death penalty event. I tag-teamed that event with Curtis.

I will never forget his opening line: "My name is Curtis, and I spent my entire adult life in prison for a crime I had nothing to do with."

Curtis was convicted based on faulty evidence—which was later conveniently "lost." The forensic scientist in his case was Joyce Gilchrist, known as "Black Magic"[4] for her ability to work magic with evidence that didn't match the facts. She testified in his case and thousands of others in her twenty-year career. She helped send twenty-three people to death row, and nearly a dozen of them have been executed. Joyce Gilchrist was eventually fired.

The prosecutor in Curtis's case was Robert H. Macy. With the help of Ms. Gilchrist, Robert Macy sent seventy-three people to death row during his twenty-one-year career. Keep in mind, other than Texas, Oklahoma is the most deadly death penalty state in the country (with 112 executions since 1976). Twenty of those seventy-three prosecuted by Robert Macy have been executed. And two were exonerated—Curtis and another man named Robert Lee Miller.

While we were together in Nebraska, Curtis described what it was like to spend two decades of his adult life on Oklahoma's death row, watching the only friends he had die, one after another. As I listened to him, I had a hard time imagining what it must have been like to be accused, much less convicted, of a crime you didn't even know about before your arrest.

Nineteen long years. Wondering when it would be your turn to die. And so desperate to believe the system would work, that there was no way you would actually be found guilty by a jury, but then having it happen not once but twice.

I *can* imagine the joy he must have felt when he was publicly exonerated and freed in 2007.

Since my time with Curtis I've gotten to know many of the "exonerees," those condemned to die and later set free—"mistakes" of the system that were recognized as such and "fixed."[5] They remind us of the many *unrecognized* mistakes that surely exist: folks whose innocence we did *not* discover in time, not before their execution, those awaiting execution for crimes they're innocent of, and those still serving life sentences for crimes they didn't do but nonetheless pleaded guilty to (in many cases accepting a plea bargain to avoid execution).

A recent study estimates one in twenty-five folks on death row has been wrongly convicted and is likely innocent, reminding us undoubtedly that innocent people have also been killed.[6] And other innocent people still sit behind bars, hoping, praying, waiting for the truth to set them free.

So for every nine executions there has been one exoneration. And for every hundred people condemned to die, four are likely innocent. What if other institutions had that same track record? Would we drive a car if we knew one in twenty-five was faulty? What if an airline crashed four or five planes for every hundred flights? You'd want to find a new airline.

We have a crisis on our hands.

It is a regular occasion these days to hear about another wrongfully condemned person who has been set free. In 2014 Louisiana's longest-serving death row inmate, Glenn Ford, a black man found guilty by an all-white jury, was released.[7] Ford had been convicted of murder and sentenced to die by electric chair. There were no eyewitnesses. No murder weapon found. His two court-appointed attorneys had never tried a case before a jury. He was released twenty-nine years, three months, and five days later. Innocent. Even though the prosecutor, Marty Stroud III, admitted to a debacle of errors, saying, "Glenn Ford was an innocent man. . . . They would not have even been able to arrest Glenn Ford, let alone try him for the crime," Ford was denied any compensation after those three decades on death row. He died of cancer a year after his release.[8]

Then Ricky Jackson in Ohio was released after thirty-nine years on death row, along with his two co-defendants, Wiley Bridgeman and Kwame Ajamu. These three had spent a total of 117 years in prison for a crime they had nothing to do with.[9]

Mr. Bridgeman came within three weeks of his execution.

I remember seeing Ricky on the news as he walked out of prison a free man. He had tears in his eyes, and an ear-to-ear smile lit up his face. "The English language doesn't even fit what I'm feeling," he said.[10]

I realized that Ricky went to jail the year I was born. He had been in jail the entire time I have been alive, and I'm getting old. Thirty-nine years of his life were spent behind bars for a crime he had nothing to do with. He was convicted on the basis of a twelve-year-old child's testimony—a child we now know didn't even see the crime.

Richard Dieter, the executive director of the Death Penalty Information Center, said, "If the country needed any more reminders of the risks inherent in the death penalty, the release this year of five more inmates who had been sentenced to death should be the final wake-up call."[11]

A Reluctant Repentance

These are only the folks who have been able to prove their innocence. And in some cases, they have proved their innocence despite all attempts of the state to stop them.

Take James Richardson of Florida, who was wrongfully convicted in the poisoning deaths of his seven children. Can you imagine losing your seven children and then being falsely accused of deliberately killing them? And then being convicted and sentenced to death?

Edward Bell | Luke Williams | Willie Pondexter | Kenneth Morris | James Martinez

Even if you believe the death penalty is just, knowing that <u>innocent</u> people are being sentenced and sometimes executed should give you pause.

The only reason he was freed was because a key piece of evidence undermining the state's case was stolen from the prosecutor's office by a man dating a secretary there. This suppressed evidence showed that the star witness, a babysitter who had accused James of killing the kids to collect insurance money, had later recanted. And it turns out there were no life insurance policies on the children!

Richardson was freed in 1989, after serving twenty-one years on Florida's death row.[12]

One of the things that makes it so difficult for the wrongfully convicted to prove their innocence is that states often place a time limit on introducing new evidence of innocence. In some states that time limit can be a matter of months or as little as three weeks after the initial trial.

Peter Neufeld, co-director of the Innocence Project, said, "If a man can demonstrate to the court that new evidence has been discovered five years after the conviction that proves his innocence, to keep him behind bars for any reason is irrational and unjust."[13] Amen to that.

When it comes to innocence, there is a conundrum. On the one hand, we want prompt justice; on the other hand, it usually takes at least ten years to prove innocence after a guilty verdict, especially when the defendant is working with limited finances and the (often inexperienced) legal counsel he or she can afford. It is typically difficult for the defense to find resources for DNA and other tests that could prove innocence—expenses covered by the state when testing serves the purposes of the prosecution. So while no one wants a trial to last ten or twenty years, to speed up the death penalty and execution process would mean the death of more innocent people. Remember that in some of the cases described above it took over thirty years for defendants to prove their innocence. If we take all the 156 exonerees and add up all the years they cumulatively spent in prison, it is 1,779 years.

That's lot of years stolen from innocent people's lives.

Retired Florida Supreme Court Chief Justice Gerald Kogan (a homicide detective and then prosecutor before rising to his state Supreme Court post) has expressed his doubts about our current system:

> There are several cases where I had grave doubts as to the guilt of a particular person.... I estimate that, in the last 40 years, I have participated either as a prosecutor, as a defense attorney or a trial judge or as an appellate judge on the Supreme Court in the disposition of more than 1,200 capital cases. I don't know of anyone else in the State of Florida who has that kind of experience.... So when I speak to you, I speak to you based upon what, I hope, has been those things I have learned in the last 40 years.... There is no question in my mind, and I can tell you this having seen the dynamics of our criminal justice system over the many years that I have been associated with it[,] ... we certainly have, in the past, executed those people who either didn't fit the criteria for execution ... or who, in fact, were, factually, not guilty of the crime for which they have been executed.[14]

Here is the point. Even if you believe that the death penalty is right in principle, knowing that innocent people are being sentenced and sometimes executed should give you pause. There is no redress once someone has been executed. Why should we have a system in which irreversible injustice is inevitable?

CHAPTER TWELVE

The Haunted Executioners

Those of us who have lived through an execution know just what the death penalty does to those who must perform it. In my tenure as warden, I helped perform three electrocutions in Florida and oversaw five lethal injections in Texas. In both places, I saw staff traumatized by the duties they were asked to perform. Officers who had never even met the condemned fought tears, cowering in corners so as not to be seen. Some of my colleagues turned to drugs and to alcohol to numb the pain of knowing that a man had died by their hands. I myself was haunted by the men I was asked to execute in the name of the state of Florida. I would wake up in the middle of the night to find them lurking at the foot of my bed. One of them had been cooked to death in a botched electrocution. I stood just four feet away watching the flames rise out of his head, hearing the electrician ask me, "Is that enough? Or should I continue?"

—Ron McAndrew, former prison warden [1]

Daniel Wilson | Jack Trawick | Michael DeLozier | John Fautenberry | Marvallous Keene

I remember a woman at a speaking event who came up to me and told me with tears in her eyes that she had been part of an execution team, a "death team" as it was called in her state. She told me she had worked for years in corrections but the "death team" was something completely different. She just could not take the life of another person. I could see the agony in her face. Clearly there was a lot of pain behind her tears.

When we discuss the death penalty, we talk a lot about "victims" and "offenders." It's easy to forget the folks who are responsible for carrying out the executions. How does the death penalty affect *them*?

There are countless executioners, wardens, corrections officers, and administrators who have described the agonizing burden of being a part of the machinery of death. Over and over I have heard those people assert that "we are just not meant to have that kind of power" over life and death.

When we take away someone's life, it can feel like something in us dies. As a veteran once told me (but it's just as true with executioners), "Killing someone, even a murderer, also kills some of the good in you."

No one knows that better than Ron McAndrew.[2]

The Good Warden

Ron is a North Carolina boy, and even though he's in his seventies now, you can still hear the twang in his voice. He's a tough dude—

"Killing someone, even a murderer, also kills some of the good in you."

frank, matter-of-fact. Honestly, when I talked with him on the phone I could tell that I'd never mess with him. I could tell he's a man who worked inside the system for decades; he's not wearing tie-dye and listening to Bob Marley. But there's so much more to him than his experience in that system. It's been said that we need to hold justice in one hand and compassion in the other. I heard both those traits when I talked to Ron. And his experience as prison warden, overseeing executions, made his compassion feel all the more authentic.

Ron grew up down south and joined the military. After serving in the Air Force and some subsequent overseas adventures, he ended up in Florida and was desperate for work. Taking what he could find, he started out as a bottom-rung corrections officer. Following a slow climb through the ranks, he ended up as warden—his dream job.

He was a believer in the system: if you do the crime, you'll do the time. And most importantly for his new position in Florida, where overseeing executions would be part of his job, he was a strong supporter of the death penalty. He had been raised by his grandparents in the heart of the Bible Belt. "An eye for an eye" was a part of his criminal justice philosophy. His family had been victims of violence, and he had no mercy for those who had killed them. When one of the killers committed suicide in prison, Ron felt no remorse. In fact, at the time, he would have been glad to step up to the plate and supervise that execution himself.

But the time came when he actually had to *do* it. In 1996, he oversaw his first execution, that of a man named John Earl Bush. Then there was another. And another. Gradually something happened to Ron, something distinctly unsettling.

He describes the discomfort he began to feel, or at least to recognize. There were subtle moments, like one day when he took the death team out to eat after an execution, a tradition that had developed among them. In a greasy diner in that small town, every-one knew what his team did, and Ron found it harder and harder to be proud of it. He remembers staring into his grits that day, in-creasingly conflicted, wondering how they could take a life and just go out to eat afterward. He brought an end to the post-execution outings to the diner; they just didn't feel right. But the executions did not stop coming his way.

During one of the executions, that of a young man named Pedro Medina, things went terribly wrong. As Pedro sat in the electric chair, flames shot from his head, and smoke came from his eyes, nose, and ears. The room was filled with the haunting odor of burned flesh. Ron was caught in a nightmare; faced with the horror of it all, he had to decide whether to stop the execution or keep going. The dam-age already done was unthinkable, and despite the malfunctioning electric chair, it felt to Ron as if there were no other choice than to finish the job. He continued the execution, allowing another surge of electricity into Pedro's body. It took nearly half an hour to complete the job. As McAndrew recalls the incident, he says, "We burned him to death."

He was tormented by the experience. "I'll never forget the mus-cles in his body, the twisting, the clenching of his fists, his toes turn-ing apart like they were being pried apart by a wrench. It was the most ghastly thing I've ever seen, and I've seen a lot of dead people in my time."[3]

What he had seen haunted him. Literally. "I started to have some horrible nightmares," he said. "It was the faces of the men that I ex-ecuted. I woke up and saw them literally sitting on the edge of my bed. I'd move over to make room for them. They didn't say anything to me. They just looked."

Drinking a bottle of whiskey a day, his attempt at drowning

unwanted images, wasn't making a difference. Taking sleeping pills sometimes helped him sleep, but they didn't bring rest to his soul.

Finally, he went on a soul-searching journey—to rethink his life, his purpose, his calling, and to find God.

And he took time to think about this business of execution.

During that time, he headed to Texas to shadow a number of lethal injection executions, hoping to bring a more humane way of execution to Florida and pioneer a new way of killing in this country.

But even as he oversaw executions less brutal than the electric chair, it never felt right. Even though he was "doing his job," he wasn't sure any person was meant to have that kind of job.

Now he speaks of his faith and his new vocation: he is an abolitionist. He is an expert witness, and rightfully so. He has participated in over 125 cases, testifying to what he knows: that it is wrong to kill. And it is wrong to kill those who kill.

No more sleeping pills. No more bottles of whiskey, although we did have a fun little conversation about Tennessee moonshine. He is a new man, and part of the reason is because he left a line of work that no one should ever have to do: supervise death.

It's still unclear to me whether Ron's transformation happened all of a sudden or was a gradual awakening. Nonetheless, it happened. In Ron's words:

> *It was not a bolt of lightning. I didn't have a light in the sky. It was just a dull awakening one day, when I had this wonderful feeling of relief. It was the feeling that the death penalty was wrong, that I should have known it was wrong, and that I would pull up my bootstraps and I'd do something about it. No matter who disagreed, no matter who it pissed off. I knew it was wrong. I knew the right thing to do was to fight it.*

Matthew Wrinkles | Vernon Smith | Kenneth Mosley | Gerald Bordelon | Gary Johnson

The problem is, no matter how hard you try, people are human beings. Even the best ones have their flaws, and even the worst ones have a glimmer of goodness.

When he speaks, Ron talks about what happens when a "number becomes a human." He says that as a warden it's fairly easy to see each death row inmate as just another convict in a cell. Until the warrant arrives. "Then everything changes," Ron says. The warden visits the convicted man every day from then on, spending time with him the month before the execution. Through that acquaintance the warden realizes, in Ron's own words, that "he's a person. He's not a number. He suddenly becomes human."

The "System" of Death

It's easier to kill people if you don't know them. That's why the system creates carefully designed barriers between executioners and those they are being asked to kill. But sometimes there is a glitch in the system. These words were spoken by prisoner Connie Ray Evans to prison warden Donald Cabana, with whom he had become good friends. At the time, the warden was about to execute Evans, a man he believed to be innocent.

> *Yeah, it's good to have someone else to blame. Ya'll always accuse us of blaming our parents, schoolteachers—anybody but ourselves for ending up in the joint. Hell, Warden, ya'll do it too. You didn't commit the crime, Earl did. You didn't convict him, the jury did. You didn't sentence him to die, the judge or jury or some damn body else did. And when you kill him, it ain't really you that's doin' that, either. It's the state, the folks out there doin' it.*[4]

Julius Young | Mark Brown | Martin Grossman | Michael Sigala | Joshua Maxwell

As we look at the "system" we have, or survey the "machinery of death," as it's often called, one of the disturbing things we learn is that we have a deadly system without any real killers. The burden of death is carefully divided among so many different people in the hopes that no one carries its full weight—at least that's the intention. But on lonely nights, perhaps everyone carries the weight of taking someone's life away.

It's striking that this was the case for Jesus as well. He was executed not just by some Roman soldiers, but also by a host of other contributors, none of whom wanted to carry the shame and burden of the execution—Judas, and the Sanhedrin, and Caiaphas, and Herod, and the angry mob, and Pontius Pilate washing the blood from his hands.

And so it goes.

We have attorneys who open the door to death.

We have a jury that finds someone guilty.

A judge (or judges) who sentences the convicted prisoner to death.

A governor who nods in approval or signs a warrant.

A clemency board that removes all obstacles.

A warden who oversees the execution.

Prison guards who prepare the person to die.

A "death team" that performs the execution.

A physician who inserts the needle.

And a coroner who pronounces the defendant dead.

We have a system that kills but that has no killers. We have a system that has mastered the sterilization of state-sanctioned, legal homicide.

To help sterilize the horrors of execution, the death chamber itself has been remodeled to look like a hospital room. As is protocol in many states, the IV for administering the lethal injection is placed in the defendant's arm and covered before the curtain is opened to witnesses. And if there is any problem, that curtain is drawn again to protect witnesses from seeing any pain or mishap. Barring a botched execution, the typical lethal injection process looks like a clean medical procedure, one in which witnesses don't see even a needle. After the convicted person gives a final statement, the warden gives the nod: the death team members push their buttons to release the cocktail of drugs. There is no one person responsible. No one wants to carry the full weight of taking away a human life. Which raises the question: So why do we do it?

During executions by firing squad, it is common practice for there to be a blank cartridge given to one of the shooters, to help with the diffusion of responsibility, to allow all the shooters to at least believe that they themselves may not have killed the person. Even in the 2010 firing squad execution in Utah of Ronnie Lee Gardner, a new and improved dummy cartridge was used that fired wax instead of a bullet, allowing for an even more realistic recoil.[5] It allows each member of the firing squad to believe afterward that he may not have fired that fatal shot. For this reason it is sometimes called "the conscience round." We work so hard to protect our conscience as we do unconscionable things.

That's why we build these bureaucratic walls. We devise ways to create distance between the killers and the killed; we work hard to ensure that they cannot see each other as human. Guards are part of the machinery of death, "just doing their job." Inmates are numbers, not names. They are statistics, not people.

The scriptures speak of those we are up against as "principalities and powers" (Eph. 6:12, KJV), not flesh and blood. It is not the people themselves but the system of killing that we are fighting as we seek

Samuel Bustamante | Kevin Varga | Billy Galloway | Michael Beuke | Rogelio Cannady to abolish the death penalty. And people are bound up in the cogs of that system all along the way.

It is our duty, our shared responsibility, to become the monkey wrench that stops the wheels of death from turning.

An Anonymous Death

I learned a lot about the importance of anonymity and secrecy when I visited Nebraska's death row. I was in Nebraska for a speaking engagement but then got the chance to run off and visit with several of Nebraska's eleven men on death row. I was escorted by my friend Stacy, an anti–death penalty activist who helped lead the way as Nebraska abolished the death penalty. She told me all about how anonymity works in Nebraska.

In Nebraska, death row is housed about fifty miles from where the executions happen. This, Stacy explained, is to be sure no one who works directly with the death row inmates in Tecumseh has to be anywhere near their execution in Lincoln. The inmate facing execution is moved to Lincoln the week before the execution for "death watch." Death watch must be one of the world's saddest ironies: folks facing execution are carefully supervised to make sure they don't kill themselves and rob the state of the opportunity.

Death team members are pulled out of the general prison staff and taught in a vacuum. Even though Nebraska has not executed anyone since 1997, and has fewer than a dozen people on death row, the training procedures for the death team happen regularly—it's a very eerie form of deprogramming in which emotions are tamed and consciences are numbed so that these people are prepared to take a life when called upon.

The completely anonymous death team goes through mock execution trainings every six months, perhaps in part to keep the process sharp in their minds, but certainly also to keep their consciences desensitized to the task before them. If an execution is actually scheduled, these drills become a weekly affair. Members of the team perform the execution ritually, with one guard acting as the one to be executed as the others strap him down, carefully following protocol. And, as with most forms of execution, it is not one person but several who carry the burden of responsibility. There are even "subs" (alternate death team members) trained, as it is common for team members to call in sick on the day of execution.[6]

Even the other guards, let alone the public, are not to know the members of the death teams. The entire process is a covert operation. They are trained in secret, told not to discuss their role in the execution with colleagues, and even asked to sign a statement of confidentiality, guaranteeing that they will not reveal the identity of other death team members or those who train them.

Think of the old image of the executioner with a mask over his head. Legal execution still happens that way in many countries. Even in the United States, we protect the identity of those who do the grim bidding of the state. I remember one prison warden describing how he escorted the executioner into the death chamber with a hood over his head so that no one could see who he was.[7] These are ways that we hide the identity of folks who kill. We justify it by saying that we're protecting them from others, but we may just be protecting them from their own shame and conscience.

Perhaps it makes sense why some scholars and political scientists would argue that if we are going to execute, then we should do it in a way that is public and unsanitized, perhaps even require that people serve on execution teams as they do on juries—just so we can't ignore the gruesome reality we support as citizens. Then there would be no place to hide from the horror of execution, no way to escape or mask the reality of what we, with the help of the executioner, are doing. There should be no way to pull the curtain (either literally or figuratively) as wardens do on the executions that go wrong. If, as states and as a country, we are going to be in favor of killing, then we should know what that really means. If we are for the death penalty, we should be willing to push the button.

I'm convinced that if we had to look in the mirror, we would make some radically different choices about how we do justice. This is especially true when we take the long view and look back at where we have come—the lynching, the electric chair, and so on—and when we look ahead at countries like South Africa that are pioneering new models of justice.

One of the tasks before us is "ripping away the veil" that separates people from each other. We have to show the humanity at stake when it comes to the business of killing. That's why you see names and stories packed into this book.

It's hard to kill people we are called to love. And it's hard to demonize folks we know.

"I Might Could've Been Your Friend"

There's one other man you need to know before we move on from this section on the executioners. A man named Donald Cabana, mentioned briefly earlier in this chapter. He wrote that book called *Death at Midnight: The Confession of an Executioner*. A dear friend of former warden Ron McAndrew, profiled above, he died just a few years back.

William Garner | Derrick Jackson | Joseph Burns | Roderick Davie | Michael Land | Peter Cantu

When Ron told me about Donald Cabana, he spoke of him as you hear someone speak of a friend from AA. They were both in recovery—from death. They had similar stories as folks who had been responsible for overseeing executions. They fought the same monsters at night.

Cabana's book is a collection of stories and memories. He tells about the men he came to know, and even to love. But he also tells of the toll that death takes on those who perform it. "In the abstract," he says, "the death penalty is quickly endorsed and facilely supported by an increasingly vocal populace. *For those few, however, who are actually authorized by the state to kill another human being, the death penalty becomes a chilling exposé of the darkest emotions of the citizenry.*"[8]

Cabana began his twenty-five years of service in corrections convinced of the need for capital punishment. Then he actually *did* it. He executed Edward Earl Johnson, Connie Ray Evans—men with names. He had heard their life stories by then. He had held them as they cried. Before they were executed, they asked him to pray with them, for they loved the same Jesus he loved.

As you can imagine, after all those years in the system, Donald Cabana, like Ron McAndrew, was done with killing: "Capital punishment exacts a toll on those who must carry it out," he cautions. "There is nothing commonplace about walking a healthy young man to a room, strapping him into a chair, and coldly, methodically killing him."[9]

He speaks of the struggle to run the prison with his head instead of his heart, a distinction that became nearly impossible. That's because he *had* a heart and a head.

There were subtle moments, like when a man about to be executed told Cabana that he'd heard that people go to the bathroom

Holly Wood | Cal Brown | Teresa Lewis | Brandon Rhode | Michael Benge | Donald Wackerly

"Capital punishment exacts a toll on those who must carry it out. . . . There is nothing commonplace about walking a healthy young man to a room, strapping him into a chair, and coldly, methodically killing him."

in their pants and asked if the warden would just make sure he died with dignity. And then there were the obvious ones, a mother grabbing his hand before an execution and pleading desperately: "Please sir, don't kill my baby. Don't take my child away from me. You don't have to do this, do you?"

These are Cabana's words describing his emotions as he ordered the door closed on the gas chamber of a man named Connie Ray Evans, whom he had grown to love:

> I ordered it sealed, even while realizing that some of my self remained inside. There is a part of the warden that dies with the prisoner. . . . Both are victims, unwilling captives of a human tragedy that is presented on a stage shrouded by mystery. It is played before a small, invited audience that is hidden from public view. Acted out in the darkness of night, as if to shield the citizenry from the awful reality of it all, an execution is a drama that panders to public fear and to a lust for vengeance, which is otherwise disguised as justice. Executions strip away the veneer of life for both warden and prisoner. Connie Ray Evans and I transcended our environment and the roles in which we had been cast. The two of us had somehow managed to become real people to each other. There were no more titles or social barriers behind which either of us could hide—I was no longer a prison warden, and he had become someone other than a condemned prisoner. We were just two ordinary human beings caught up in a vortex of events that neither of us could control.[10]

And these were some of the last words of Connie Ray Evans before his execution, spoken to Cabana before the warden executed his friend:

Larry Wooten | Jeffrey Landrigan | Phillip Hallford | John Duty | Billy Alverson | Jeffrey Matthews

I know you have a job to do. I don't blame you, Mr. Cabana. I wish we could have known each other outside the prison. Who knows, under different circumstances, I might could've been your friend. God knows, you've been one to me.[11]

They prayed the Lord's Prayer together. And then Connie Ray Evans was executed. And Donald Cabana quit his job.

Execution's Expert Witness

For over a decade, Michelle Lyons's job was to observe executions. According to a wonderful profile by Pamela Colloff that ran in *Texas Monthly,* Michelle watched 278 people die.[12] One of the requirements of her job as the public face of the Texas Department of Criminal Justice was, after dropping her daughter off at school, to watch people be killed by the state. She worked in the iconic Huntsville penitentiary, home of the most active death chamber in the country. Over the years she sat side by side with family members of victims and family members of the executed. It took a toll on her. She can still remember the 276 men and 2 women she watched die—the tears, the final breaths, then more tears.

One of her colleagues—actually, the man who had recruited her to be a public information officer for the Texas prison system— eventually shared with her that he was tormented. Formerly the system's director of public information, he now mentioned having "dreams." He had always been a refuge of sorts for Lyons; he would try to ease the pain of an execution by inviting her to go out for a margarita afterward.

Now the memories forced themselves onto her, too. She remembered, for example, an elderly woman, dressed in floral and pearls, who came to watch the execution of her son. Rising from her wheelchair, she placed her old, wrinkled hands on the pane of glass that separated her from her boy.

Lyons received this letter from Robert Coulson, who was later executed:

> Ms. Lyons,
>
> Hi, if you are reading this then they killed me. I wanted to tell you that I enjoyed talking to you, you seem like a really great lady. I'm sorry we didn't meet under different circumstances. . . . Thank you for your kindness. Have a wonderful day.

Michelle Lyons eventually left that job and no longer is called upon to witness executions, but she remains haunted by the 278 she was present at. Her greatest concern today is what she will tell her daughter when she grows up and is old enough to understand what her mother used to do: "I don't want her to think badly of me for having been there. Not because I was doing something wrong. It's just that when you look at that number, it's a lot of death. I hate that someday she'll have to know that about me."

FACES OF GRACE

I remembered hearing about Mr. Hinton's moving release from prison on the news, but I recently had the privilege of meeting him and hearing him tell his story.

One day in 1985, Mr. Hinton was at his mother's house, helping

Ms. Lyons,

Hi, if you are reading
this then they killed me.
I wanted to tell you
that I enjoyed talking
to you, you seem like
a really great lady.
I'm sorry we didn't
meet under different
circumstances. . . . Thank
you for your kindness.
Have a wonderful day.

—Robert Coulson

her around the house and in the yard, and two officers came and told him he was under arrest. They took him to jail and began interrogating him, asking him if he had a gun. He said no. They asked if his mother had a gun, and he told them she did. They went back to her house and got the gun, using it as a key piece of evidence to convict him of a crime he had nothing to do with. Mr. Hinton later found out he was arrested for the murders of two restaurant managers in Birmingham. The "expert" witness in the case had eyesight problems and admitted he had trouble operating the microscope. Despite passing a lie detector test, no incriminating evidence, and a verifiable alibi, Anthony Ray Hinton was found guilty and sentenced to death.

Several years later, as he prayed "for God's best," he met Bryan Stevenson—who he had no money to pay but offered to cover his gas. With his characteristic humility, Bryan agreed to take the case. Mr. Hinton laughs as he explains that in order to convincingly prove his innocence and counter the earlier ballistics expert, they needed a white, Southern, pro–death penalty expert . . . who would tell the truth. They found three good fits—two from Texas and one from Virginia. All three agreed without hesitation that the bullets from the victims did not fit the gun belonging to Mr. Hinton's mother. That's not surprising. But what is surprising is that after proving his innocence, Mr. Hinton spent another sixteen years in prison.

He lost one appeal after another, taking the case all the way to the Supreme Court, which eventually ruled for a retrial in a rare unanimous decision. It was obvious the state did not have a case. Prosecutors admitted they could not match the bullets from the crime scene to Mrs. Hinton's gun, which was their only evidence in the original trial. On April 3, 2015, some thirty years after his arrest, Mr. Hinton was released.

Benny Stevens | Daniel Bedford | Rodney Gray | Jason Williams | Donald Beaty | Gayland Bradford

Tragically, his beloved mother had died while he was in jail.

It's hard to imagine. Living thirty years in a five-by-seven cell for a crime you had nothing to do with. Even now, Mr. Hinton spoke about what it is like to be a free man and still wake up every morning at three because that's what you did for thirty years. He's a tall guy, and he laughs as he tells the story of getting a bed when he was released . . . not just any bed, but a "big bed . . . a California King bed." But then he goes on to describe how he still sleeps in one little section of the bed, curled in a fetal position, because that is how he slept for thirty years.

The state stole years of his life, but they did not steal his soul. They did not steal his joy. He told us about what it was like to use his imagination to escape the long loneliness of prison life. "I had tea with the Queen of England," he said laughing. Even as he laughed, tears rolled down his face. He described what it was like to feel the rain fall on his body as he left prison, the first rain he had felt in thirty years. He was welcomed out with a royal celebration of friends and family with a big "Free at Last" cake. Before he cut the cake, he made an announcement. Since he was fresh out of prison after three decades, the cake was five dollars a slice.

"They couldn't take my joy," he said, laughing, even as tears welled up in his eyes. His pain and frustration were real. "What kind of human being puts a man in a cage like that, as though my life didn't matter?" But then he went on, "When God is for you, who can be against you?" Mr. Hinton described how near God was to him all those years and how scripture was his "coffee in the morning," giving him fuel for hope and endurance.

He finished off one of the most moving testimonies I have ever heard by talking about forgiveness and grace. "I do not hold any hatred for the people who put me there," he said. "I have seen what hatred can do. What would it profit me to hate? . . . I forgive them. I forgive them without them asking."

And it is not just for them, he said. "I did not forgive them so they can sleep good at night. . . . I forgive them so that I can sleep good at night."

Anthony Ray Hinton is one of the most incredible faces of grace I have ever met. And what happened to him is one of the most disgraceful things I have ever seen. Bryan Stevenson said this upon Mr. Hinton's release from prison: "Race, poverty, inadequate legal assistance, and prosecutorial indifference to innocence conspired to create a textbook example of injustice. . . . I can't think of a case that more urgently dramatizes the need for reform than what has happened to Anthony Ray Hinton."[13]

CHAPTER THIRTEEN

A New Vision of Justice

It is never too late to do justice.

—Bryan Stevenson[1]

A t the end of the day, this book is about awakening our moral imagination. Let's imagine what justice could look like in a post–death penalty world.

The word "justice" gets abused and misused. People demand "justice" all the time but have very different things in mind as they call for it. It has been so misrepresented that justice itself might do well to find some new lawyers; it needs better representation.

For starters, the word for "justice" in the Bible is the same word as "righteousness." This overlap shows that the central concern of biblical justice was not "getting what you deserve"; rather, it was making right what was done wrong, restoring what had been destroyed, healing the wounds of an offensive act. It was about bringing balance and wholeness back to the community, which is why you often see scales as an icon for justice.

But the scales can be misleading, since it is not just about balance or even "eye for an eye" justice. Real justice goes much deeper. One of my friends who is a biblical scholar says the best contemporary translation for the ancient notion of "justice/righteousness" is "restorative justice."

There is a powerful movement for death penalty abolition (and prison reform) growing on the foundation of this same concept: restorative justice. The vision for restorative justice is having an impact around the world, even right here in the States.

As I wrap things up in this discussion, it makes sense to spend a little time thinking about alternative forms of justice. I don't want to be just about denouncing execution. I also want to at least scratch the surface of thinking what the alternatives might be. What are better forms of justice than killing to show that killing is wrong? The best critique of the justice we have now is the demonstration of something better.

Restorative justice can be a way forward after even the most violent crimes. In fact, it is in these deserts of desperation that many of the models of restorative justice have been born. Some of those models, often called Truth and Reconciliation Commissions, include structures where victims and offenders are able to name harms done and identify responsible ways to heal those harms—beginning with truth-telling. Such commissions have emerged from some of the most horrific events, including South Africa's apartheid and Rwanda's genocide. They provide space for repentance and reconciliation, for the possibility of restoring the breach created between victim and perpetrator.

Especially after events such as the Rwandan genocide, as the dust starts to settle and people begin asking, "What does justice look like?" they begin to realize that more blood is not the answer. Trying to kill all the killers would only exacerbate the problems and aggravate the wounds. To heal from those wounds, they cannot fight fire with fire but must put out fire with water.

So when I was in Rwanda, I saw on the hillsides clusters of men in pink uniforms carrying shovels, hoes, and other tools. They were the people who had been responsible for the genocide; their punishment was to help rebuild the country they had helped destroy. There are more stories of hope and forgiveness, and real "restorative justice," in Rwanda than anywhere else I've been. I met folks who had adopted the children of those responsible for killing their own family members. I stayed with a family where the matriarch had become a caretaker for folks who'd lost their family in the genocide. It's very likely that members of her tribe were responsible for murdering the family members of the children she now took into her home.

Everywhere I looked I saw restoration. There were countless stories of grace. That did not mean turning a blind eye to evil, mind you. Just the opposite—everywhere I went we saw memorials to the genocide. Forgiving did not mean forgetting. And it also was not cheap grace. Those who were responsible for the genocide were spending their lives healing the wounds they had created. They knew evil better than anyone in the world: they had stared it in the face. But they also now knew that God is a God who heals, and shedding more blood will not stop the shedding of blood. Their wounds show us how to heal from atrocity.[2]

It is no surprise that many places traumatized by violence—places like Rwanda and South Africa—no longer have the death penalty. Apartheid was a relic of the old world of injustice and had no place in the hopeful new world the survivors were building. Thus places like Rwanda and South Africa have become the classrooms for new models of restorative justice.

Paul Rhoades | Gary Welch | Rodrigo Hernandez | Edwin Turner | Robert Waterhouse

Likewise, after the Holocaust, Germany and most of Europe abolished the death penalty. Jews were some of the most vocal opponents to capital punishment for perpetrators of wartime atrocities there. Death was not the solution; it was the problem.

Ethicist David Gushee makes a stunning observation about Europe in the middle of the twentieth century. After decades of lynching, the Holocaust, and back-to-back wars, Gushee says that Europe had "death fatigue." Gushee observes: "A human family that had adequately absorbed the lessons of the years from 1914 to 1945 probably would have abolished the power of any nation-state to kill its own citizens." He goes on to point out that all western European countries on whose soil much of the blood was spilled abolished the death penalty. "Europe had lost its taste for blood."[3]

Even the new post–World War II state of Israel, with plenty of moral ammo to kill the ones responsible for the atrocities of the Holocaust, decided at the outset that there was no place for the death penalty.[4] Wearied by all the bloodshed, the Israelis concluded that state-sanctioned killing had no place in the future that they envisioned.

This "death fatigue" may also explain why it is so common to see victims speak out against the death penalty after traumatic incidents like the Boston Marathon bombing, the Sandy Hook school shooting, or September 11. Those who have seen a lot of death often don't want to see another life taken, creating even more victims and more trauma.

Could it be—after the more than ten thousand people murdered in gun violence each year at home and all the killing of ISIS and other terrorist groups abroad—that Americans are experiencing "death fatigue" and losing our taste for blood? I hope so.

Robert Moorman | George Rivas | Keith Thurmond | Robert Towery | Timothy Stemple

A Crash Course in Restorative Justice

Simply defined by one of its gurus, Howard Zehr, restorative justice is "a process to involve, to the extent possible, those who have a stake in a specific offense and to collectively identify and address harms, needs, and obligations, in order to heal and put things as right as possible."[5]

There are a few distinctive contrasts between the dominant criminal justice system and restorative justice. Books have been written on how to fully remodel our justice system to benefit from these contrasts, but this is restorative justice 101, so we'll just scratch the surface:

Two Different Views of Justice

Criminal Justice

- Crime is a violation of the law and the state.

- Violations create guilt.

- Justice requires the state to determine blame (guilt) and impose pain (punishment).

- **Central focus:** offenders getting what they deserve.

Restorative Justice

- Crime is a violation of people and relationships.

- Violations create obligations.

Larry Puckett | William Mitchell | Jesse Hernandez | David Gore | Mark Wiles | Shannon Johnson

- Justice involves victims, offenders, and community members in an effort to put things right.

- **Central focus:** victim needs and offender responsibilities for repairing harm.

Three questions, unique to each system, highlight the differences between criminal justice and restorative justice:

- **Criminal justice:** What laws have been broken? Who did it? What does the offender deserve?

- **Restorative justice:** Who has been hurt? What are the victim's needs? Whose obligations are these?

One of the things I like about restorative justice is that it avoids the conflict model of defendant versus prosecution. It asks, Who is the offender? And often it finds that the offender was once a victim too. This helps track the harm to its roots, while criminal justice rips the weed and leaves the roots to fester. If the offender has been a victim, that earlier hurt does not absolve responsibility, but it does help create a broader lens for what harm might need to be identified and healed. Trauma specialists such as psychiatrist Sandra Bloom point out that speaking of "trauma" rather than "victimization" may be a helpful step. Unresolved trauma tends to repeat itself. If not dealt with, trauma gets reenacted and creates more trauma. We can see this not only in personal trauma but in the trauma of war as well. Some of those who were traumatized in wars overseas have come home to create more trauma: mass killings (the Oklahoma City bombing, for example) and other PTSD-related crimes such as that committed by Vietnam vet Manny Babbitt (introduced in chapter 7).

The focus of restorative justice is first on harm—identifying what harm has been done to people and the community. Then it moves toward the obligations that grow out of the wrong or the harm done—looking at what it means to take responsibility and be accountable for the harm done. And finally, it moves toward action—engaging and participating in the concrete work of healing the harm done. The offender has a major responsibility in this process, especially in healing the harm done, but the community and the victim may also identify roles that they need to play.

Restorative justice goes back directly to the ideas of at-one-ment and shalom that we looked at in chapter 5, encompassed in the vision of living in a sense of "all-rightness" with each other, God, and society. Stated another way, in the South African philosophy of *ubuntu*, "People are people through other people." We are all connected. Crime wounds the community. Alienation is both a cause and an effect of crime. The work of real justice is to restore people to the interwoven fabric of society again, or in some extreme cases to confine them from doing damage to the community.

The U.S. legal system is designed as an adversarial one, as noted above: prosecution versus defendant. The model seen in scripture and attempted in many communities throughout history and around the world is, in contrast, communal. Similarly, rather than professionals who represent the offender and the state, and a mediating judge, many models of restorative justice offer a collaborative, dynamic, inclusive process whereby outcomes are mutually agreed upon rather than imposed. Victims, community members, and offenders are included, rather than being alienated or being "represented" by professionals.

In our current justice system in the United States, the *state* often replaces the *victim* (*Furman v. Georgia,* for example). This has a way of alienating people from each other. When the state steps in, it undermines community. At the heart of biblical justice and restorative justice is not alienation, but "at-one-ment" and reconciliation. We are not talking about sentimental, let's-just-hug-and-make-up justice. Genuine restorative justice work is the hardest work in the world—and it takes the most courageous people in the world to do it. Thus it has to be a choice.

What else can we say about restorative justice? It is about respect. In fact, Zehr says that it all comes down to that one word, *respect:* a balanced concern for all parties.[6]

Restorative justice is also about real people—people who have harmed and been harmed. It's about humanizing harm rather than systematizing punishment. It is about being concerned for all people—victim, offender, and community. It is about revealing truth rather than concealing it, tearing down the bureaucratic legal walls that alienate and systematize.

Restorative justice is about telling the truth—the truth that can set us free. It is about sharing access to information rather than having information brokered through legal professionals only. Restorative justice is about transparency rather than secrecy. Truth-telling is the beginning of healing. Yet often our current justice system conceals or compromises truth, or releases information only as needed through professionals. Often it even encourages defendants to lie or compromise the truth to get a plea bargain.

Restorative justice is about accountability—trying to put right what was made wrong. Real accountability is different than punishment: it is better for victims, for society, and for the offenders themselves.

Restorative justice is about empowerment, because it takes everyone seriously. It takes evil and pain seriously. It takes victims seriously. And it takes people who have committed crimes seriously. Rather than simply figuring out the legal punishment for a particular crime, it asks victims and offenders to name and recognize the harm done. It also reminds all parties that there are consequences to crime. Those consequences should be about restoring what one has damaged, which requires understanding both the harm and the humanity of the harmed. In the best cases, the victim and the offender are able to agree on an appropriate punishment for the harm done. It is empowering for the victim *and* the offender to have a say in the consequences of a crime, rather than simply to have a punishment dictated objectively.

As we think beyond the confines of the current criminal justice system, restorative justice allows us to consider what is truly best for the victim, and for all. Questions raised by restorative justice about who the stakeholders are and what their needs are lead, by their very nature, to new approaches in death penalty cases. As we've seen, the criminal justice model has silenced and disempowered many victims' families when the state stepped in as prosecutor. We've heard in this book about victims being silenced by gag orders or threatened with obstruction of justice for suggesting punishments other than execution. But many attorneys, convinced of the validity of restorative justice, are now asking questions about what it looks like to include the victims in the process of sentencing and to incorporate the needs and concerns and desired outcomes of the survivors. Plea agreements that are based on victims' needs and that allow offenders to accept responsibility for their actions are becoming more common.

Donald Moeller | Donnie Roberts | Garry Allen | Mario Swain | Brett Hartman | Ramon Hernandez

So we address the harms, yes—but we also need to address the causes of the crime. What are steps we can take to keep this from happening again?

I was speaking at a Quaker school in Pennsylvania a while back, where I got a little lesson in restorative justice. (Quakers tend to be really good at it.) That day a kid had been caught dealing drugs at school. It was amazing to see the response. The entire community came together, because the offense had affected the entire community. The conversation that ensued (which I did not stay for but was later told about) reflected both a deep, genuine concern for this young man and a deep, genuine concern for the community and the environment that they all felt responsible to protect. The questions that were being asked were not just, Should he go to jail? Students were asking things like: Are you in need of money? Are you, or are any of us, struggling with addiction (since obviously this student had buyers)? What harm has been done? What is an appropriate response to the harm done? And these were fifteen-year-old kids!

This event illuminates the ways in which restorative justice humanizes both those who have harmed and those who have been harmed. Desmond Tutu always likes to say: "God's justice set the oppressed free from being oppressed and the oppressors free from oppressing."[7]

Quakers have been instrumental in casting a vision for restorative justice. Right here in my hometown of Philadelphia we have one of the oldest prisons in the United States, and it was founded by Quakers. But their vision was far from the prison system we have today.

The Quakers modeled the prison after monasteries, where monks and nuns referred to their private chambers of prayer as *cells*. In another religious overlay, the word *penitentiary* shares the same root as *repentance.* The original intention of imprisonment was not to create a dead-end trap for criminals or a business of incarceration, but to give hurting and hurtful people the space to repent, to re-think their lives, and ultimately to be restored to society.

Various countries, including New Zealand, are now reimagining and restructuring their criminal justice system to reflect a more re-storative model. In 1989, the reforms in New Zealand included a re-vamped juvenile justice system to focus on restorative justice.[8] Many communities in the United States are pursuing models of restorative justice in schools and neighborhoods, alongside new (and old) models of community policing. I met the chaplain of one European prison who had integrated the ancient monastic spiritual disciplines and prayer into the life of the prison. "We turned the prison into a monastery—and turned that unholy place into something much more holy." His goal was to see men and women healed and able to live a life outside of those bars.[9]

What Real Justice Looks Like

One way to think of restorative justice is to remember that one per-son's mistake has the power to prevent many other people from making the same mistake. One person's scar can prevent another person from getting cut in the same way. We are wounded healers.

Consider this: a man chooses to drink and drive and kills a young girl. The story could end there, with the man's execution or with life in prison. That's what punitive justice looks like. But imagine if that man did the hard work of restorative justice and joined hands with

Andrew Cook | Carl Blue | Frederick Treesh | Ray Thacker | Rickey Lewis | Larry Mann the victim's family to speak out about the horrors caused by drinking and driving.

That's exactly what happened in the case of Joe Avila, and it required much more courage from both the victim and the offender than a lengthy prison sentence would have. In this case, jail was the easy option. But it was also the empty, lifeless, dead-end option.

Joe Avila was well respected in the community, had two daughters of his own, a good job, and a drinking problem. Joe had been arrested seven times for drinking and driving before doing it one last time in 1992. He hit the car of seventeen-year-old Amy Wall, who was killed. Joe was uninjured and managed to drive home, park the car, and go to bed.[10]

When he woke up the next morning, he was full of regret, haunted by what he had done. Beyond devastated, he considered taking his own life. But the day after the accident, police came to his home and arrested him. While in jail, he got a visit from a prison chaplain. He told Joe about Jesus, and how Jesus had died to heal and forgive all the wrong we do, a message that resonated in the troubled man's soul. Joe also met with my friend Elaine Enns, a pioneer in the field of restorative justice, who talked to him about God's justice and how it differs from much of what gets dubbed "justice" in our world. They imagined together what restorative justice might look like in this situation, what could help heal the wounds he had caused.

By this point the trial was well under way. Joe's defense had tried some desperate measures, such as blaming a tree for Amy's death, but now Joe's new revelation meant a change of tactics. He saw all the pain the trial was causing the already traumatized family, and so he switched gears. He changed his plea to guilty in the middle of the trial. He decided to own up to his terrible mistake and take responsibility for the harm he had caused. But he also hoped for healing, help, and redemption.

He was given twelve years in prison, the maximum sentence. His wife and children visited him over the years, and he continued to seek God's healing and guidance and to meet with my restorative justice friend Elaine. He did a lot of internal work and realized that God had forgiven him. But he wanted to do something meaningful with his life and with his past—not to earn God's grace (which had been freely given), but in *response* to it. He began organizing restorative justice meetings in prison, trying to help others learn from their mistakes and from his own.

After nearly eight years in prison, Joe was released. One of the first things he wanted to do was meet with Amy's family, but they were not willing. Joe understood and respected that. But something in him still ached for reconciliation, for what one might call closure.

Joe found work washing windows, but he always felt that part of his purpose—his *primary* purpose—was to participate in God's work of restorative justice. He told his story every chance he got, eventually ending up on the radio. In a show that aired before the holidays, Joe talked about the costly mistake of drinking and driving. Amy's father was flipping through the channels and could find only one with good reception. Yep, it was Joe.

He listened to Joe, and he was moved. He quickly called his son and told him to listen too. Amy's father tried to call in to the radio show and talk to Joe, but he couldn't get through. And perhaps that was just as well, because it meant they would end up meeting in person—Joe's hope fulfilled.

Soon after the radio program, Joe met with Amy's family. He sat down with her father and her brother, and later with her mother.

Elroy Chester | William Van Poyck | James DeRosa | Brian Davis | Kimberly McCarthy

Tears flowed. A deep wound began to heal just a little that day. Amy's mother gave him a videotape of the girl whose life he had taken.

The story doesn't end perfectly, but it does end well. Eventually, Joe and Derek Wall, Amy's brother, spoke together at a conference. The power of their voices together was unbelievable. Oh, and both of Amy's parents came.

This is what restorative justice can look like.

After twenty-five years of restorative justice work with victim and offender reconciliation, this is what Elaine Enns has concluded: "We need a hospital, not a prison. Not a place where we create more anger, more wounds. No one is beyond redemption. There are people who are sick and they need help. They need a hospital, not a prison."[11]

Here's a little summary from Howard Zehr and Harry Mika on the principles of restorative models, or what they call the "signposts for restorative justice":

1. Focus on the harms of the crime rather than on the rules that have been broken.

2. Show equal concern and commitment to victims and offenders, involving both in the process of justice.

3. Work toward the restoration of victims, empowering them and responding to their needs as they see them.

4. Support offenders, while encouraging them to understand, accept, and carry out their obligations.

5. Recognize that while obligations may be difficult for offenders, those obligations should not be intended as harms, and they must be achievable.

"We need a hospital, not a prison. Not a place where we create more anger, more wounds. No one is beyond redemption. There are people who are sick and they need help. They need a hospital, not a prison."

6. Provide opportunities for dialogue, direct or indirect, between victim and offender as appropriate.

7. Find meaningful ways to involve the community and to respond to the community bases of crime.

8. Encourage collaboration and reintegration of both victims and offenders, rather than coercion and isolation.

9. Give attention to the unintended consequences of your actions and program.

10. Show respect to all parties—victims, offenders, and justice colleagues.[12]

John F. Kennedy had a great line about what it will take to bring an end to war: "War will exist until that distant day when the conscientious objector enjoys the same reputation and prestige that the warrior does today."[13]

It may also be true of the death penalty and our punitive justice system. Until we have alternative models of restorative justice that enjoy the same reputation and prestige as the punitive, death-dealing models of "justice" we have now, death will continue to prevail.

God, give us the courage to imagine a future where the death penalty is history.

A Word About Forgiveness

A book about the death penalty and grace would be incomplete if we didn't talk a little bit about forgiveness. It's helpful to distinguish between restorative justice and forgiveness, because they are related but not the same thing.

As prominent black intellectual and public theologian Cornel West has said, "Justice is what love looks like in public."[14] And I'll add, for our purposes, "Restorative justice is what forgiveness looks like in public."

Forgiveness is at the heart of God. Inasmuch as we forgive we shall be forgiven, Jesus said.

Forgiveness heals the world. It also heals our own hearts. It frees us from the poison of resentment. I heard once that when we refuse to forgive someone, it is like eating poison and hoping that someone else will die. We think that by not forgiving we are hurting the other person, but we end up stalling our own healing.

Aba Gayle, a mother whose nineteen-year-old daughter was murdered, knows both the poison of anger and the power of forgiveness:

> I knew that I didn't need the State of California to murder another human being so I could be healed. . . . It's time to stop teaching people hate and start teaching people to love. The whole execution as closure idea is not realistic. . . . Anger is just a horrible thing to do to your body. Not to mention what it does to your soul and spirit. Forgiveness is not saying what he did was right—it's taking back your power.

Desmond Tutu is a genius on forgiveness. I've taken a lot of cues from him. One of the things he suggests in his *Book of Forgiving* (written with his daughter Mpho, an Episcopal priest) is a stone exercise.[15] Carry around a stone the size of your palm for a day. Hold it in your nondominant hand. Don't set it down all day. This exercise is a way of thinking about the burden of holding on to a grudge, or even to a legitimate wrong that has been done to us. The stone in our hand is a reminder of the weight we carry when we choose not to forgive—a weight that keeps getting heavier as time passes.

One of my friends in college had an amazing senior project. He's an incredible artist, and one of his art installations involved transforming an entire house into a piece of art. When you entered the space, you walked through a hallway that had hundreds of rocks hanging from the ceiling. Each rock had a negative word on it: *faggot, stupid, bitch, mistake, fat, whore.* It was impossible for a person to walk through the hallway without running into those rocks and causing them to swing. They clanked together and bumped into you as you walked. When you made it through the gauntlet of stones, the room opened up, and there was a cross with a pile of rocks at the foot of it. The experience was moving: you still heard the clanking of the stones behind you, contrasted with a certain peacefulness as you looked at the cross that had disarmed so many.

My friend's installation inspired us to create a pile of stones in our little chapel here in Philadelphia. In it we have some rocks that people can write on, to remember the things we are laying down at the cross. It is a constant reminder of the things we have forgiven people for and the things for which we have sought forgiveness.

Forgiveness is not forgetting. "Forgive and forget" is a misnomer. We *must* remember. We need to remember the wrong done to us, even as we forgive. A friend once reminded me that even Jesus still had the scars from the nails when he rose from the dead. In fact, it was the scars that convinced would-be doubters like Thomas that Jesus was who he said he was. Our own scars remind us of the power of grace. They remind us of what we have been able to survive.

Forgiveness does not undermine or subvert justice. It creates the possibility for real justice to happen. It casts out the toxic residue of resentment and the desire for revenge. It frees us from the inside out.

When we deem others unforgivable or we label them monsters, we take away their accountability. It can be too easy to "write them off," which makes it impossible to heal the wounds they caused. No one is better off when we shut the door of our heart to the possibilities that forgiveness can open up. To truly heal the wounds of injustice is to invite a person who has harmed us to do something to restore the damage that person has done.

Archbishop Tutu gives some good, practical tips on forgiveness. He suggests that it may be helpful to first "practice" telling the story of our pain and "practice" forgiving with someone we trust and who loves us, before we talk with the person who has hurt us.

As we tell the story to those we trust and then eventually to the person who caused harm, we can name the hurt. We can identify the feelings with the facts, remembering that no feeling is wrong or invalid. Then we can grant forgiveness. The power to forgive always lies in the hand of the one who has been betrayed.

"Forgiving is how we move from victim to hero," says Tutu.[16] We know that we are beginning to heal when the hurt is not the end of the story. We can begin a new chapter. That leaves room for all sorts of possibilities.

FACES OF GRACE

A Story of Two Mothers . . . Moving from Death to Life[17]

On February 12, 1993, Mary Johnson's only son was murdered. He was only twenty years old. Devastated beyond words, filled

Askari Muhammad | Michael Wilson | Dennis McGuire | Edgar Tamayo | Kenneth Hogan with rage, even hatred, Mary was paralyzed with the anguish of it all.

The perpetrator was sixteen-year-old Oshea Israel, who eventually received a twenty-five-year sentence for second-degree murder.

But something spectacular, one might even venture to call miraculous, happened. Mary was reading a poem entitled "Two Mothers," which to this day she only knows to be written by "Anonymous" (who, apparently, has written lots of great hits).

The poem is about two angelic figures meeting in the heavens. As they meet on the streets of gold, they can tell by the stars in each other's crowns that they were both mothers on earth. And they can also tell by their blue-tinted halos that they have both known the deep sorrow and despair of losing their sons. As they describe their boys to each other with deep joy and motherly affection, the one mother realizes that she is talking with Mary, the blessed mother of Jesus. Mary describes the cruel death of her son, and how she would have gladly died in his place. The other mother falls to her knees, but Mary raises her back up, kisses her on the cheek, wipes away her tears, and says, "Tell me the name of the son you love so . . ."

The other mother, looking straight into her eyes, says, "He was Judas Iscariot. I am his mother."

When Mary read that poem she was moved, compelled, to meet with Oshea, the man who killed her son, and eventually his mother . . . and the healing began. As she first met Oshea, she laid it all out there. "You don't know me, and I don't know you. You didn't know my son and he didn't know you . . . so we need to lay down a foundation to get to know one another." They talked for hours.

Oshea couldn't believe Mary could forgive him, the power of that forgiveness beyond words. He asked for a hug. And they did. Mary knows the power of her story, and she knows how scandalous it seems to our unforgiving world. When he left the room, she says she cried in disbelief, "I've just hugged the man who killed my son." But as she got up, she felt her soul begin to heal.

Years later, in March of 2010, Oshea was released after seventeen years in prison. And Mary helped throw him a welcome home party. In fact, they ended up living next door to each other on the north side of Minneapolis.

As he returned home, Oshea said he was blessed to have "two moms." Those two moms now claim each other as sisters and share the role of motherhood to Oshea. Mary Johnson went on to start an organization, called From Death to Life, to support moms who have lost their children, and moms whose children were responsible for taking life.[18] When I went to visit Minneapolis I stayed in the house where they all meet, a holy little place called the St. Jane House, with photos of reconciliation and healing plastered all over the walls. And Mary came over for dinner. She explained that now they have two support groups that meet regularly each month—the moms whose kids were killed, and the moms whose kids have killed—and both groups meet together whenever they can. They know all too well their healing is bound up together—they need each other. As Mary hugged me with her warm, contagious smile, I thought to myself with a profound awe, "These same courageous arms embraced the man who killed her son." I felt like I had been hugged by an angel—with a blue-tinted halo.

Robert Henry | Jeffrey Ferguson | Anthony Doyle | Tommy Sells | Ramiro Hernandez

CHAPTER FOURTEEN

Making Death Penalty History

There is no humane way to kill another person.... It is impossible to imagine that states today cannot make use of another means than capital punishment to defend peoples' lives from an unjust aggressor.... All Christians and people of good will are thus called today to struggle not only for abolition of the death penalty, whether it be legal or illegal and in all its forms, but also to improve prison conditions, out of respect for the human dignity of persons deprived of their liberty.

—Pope Francis[1]

Often folks will ask me how close we are to really ending the death penalty once and for all.

The short answer: as close as you and I want to be. (The long answer is this book!)

In this book I have pointed to several signs that death is on its deathbed: In 2014 death sentences hit a forty-year low, and executions

Jose Villegas | William Rousan | Robert Hendrix | Clayton Lockett | Marcus Wellons

A 2014 poll showed nearly 80 percent of millennial Christians are against the death penalty, and only 5 percent of Americans believe Jesus would be in favor of the death penalty.

hit a twenty-year low. Of the scheduled executions, nearly two-thirds have been stopped. Recent polls show for the first time in many years that a majority of Americans are against the death penalty when given other alternatives, like life in prison.

Maybe we have the death fatigue that we talked about in chapter 13. As we lament another execution by ISIS, it becomes harder and harder to cheer one on in Texas.

Across the board there are monkey wrenches messing up the machinery of death. As we will see later in this chapter, a group of doctors in North Carolina refused to participate in execution, insisting that it is a violation of their medical oath. And their stance wasn't just grandstanding; it made a real difference.

Legal matters associated with the secrecy of lethal injection poison are a major issue stalling executions around the country. At the heart of that issue is the fact that companies don't want to be associated with making medicine that kills people.[2]

And of course there are the botched executions, like that of Clayton Lockett (mentioned in chapter 9), who writhed in pain for forty-three minutes before dying of a heart attack, with the Oklahoma prison warden calling it "a bloody mess."[3]

On top of that, there is the question of innocence. Many people who agree with the death penalty in principle can't bear thinking of executing an innocent person. As we have seen, there has been a continual stream of exonerations making the national news in recent years. The danger of wrongly executing the innocent is real.

It might be that folks are also getting tired of the massive resources spent on death penalty cases. It is a well-established fact that it costs more to kill someone than to keep someone in prison for life. Check out the sites I list in the back for facts on ways the death penalty is taking its toll on us. If you remain unconvinced, consider this article from *Forbes* magazine[4] breaking down the dollars and cents. Political conservatives are now blasting the money wasted on the death penalty, money that could be used to support victims, prevent crime, and repair broken schools and neighborhoods. In some states, like Nebraska, conservatives have led the way to abolition. We may see the same happen in states like Kansas, Montana, and maybe even my home state of Tennessee.

Then of course—and this excites me—there is the faith factor. The pope has been speaking out boldly for the abolition of executions. Echoing the pleas of his predecessors Benedict XVI and John Paul II, Pope Francis said, "All Christians and people of good will are called today to struggle not only for abolition of the death penalty, whether legal or illegal, and in all its forms, but also to improve prison conditions, out of respect for the human dignity of persons deprived of their liberty."[5]

And it's not just the pope.

Young Christians are overwhelmingly against the death penalty. A 2014 Barna poll,[6] for example, showed that not even a quarter (23 percent) of millennial Christians committed to their faith agreed with the statement: "The government should have the option to execute the worst criminals." Roxanne Stone, the vice president of publishing at Barna, said, "This parallels a growing trend in the pro-life conversation among Christians to include torture and the death penalty as well as abortion. For many younger Christians, the death penalty is not a political dividing point but a human rights issue."

I am inspired by this new generation of Christians who are suspicious of death. They want a more consistent ethic of life. For this generation, pro-life doesn't just mean anti-abortion. It means being for life; being anti-death. Every human holds God's image, and every time we take a life we delete a part of God's image in the world.

It's not just young people and not just Christians who are looking at things differently either. Only 5 percent of Americans in the general public believe that Jesus would be in favor of the death penalty.[7] And despite the fact that six of the nine Supreme Court justices are Catholic,[8] only 2 percent of Catholics believe Jesus would support the death penalty.[9] These are all good signs that times are a-changin'.

One of the largest evangelical associations in the United States, the National Latino Evangelical Coalition, issued a statement against the death penalty with the unanimous support of their board. As I was finishing this book, the National Association of Evangelicals, representing over ten million Christians from forty-five thousand congregations in forty denominations, issued a new resolution on capital punishment. Their pro–death penalty statement had not changed since it was written in 1973—until now. The new statement flags many of the social and theological concerns raised in this book and recognizes the work that people of faith are doing to create alternatives to the death penalty. That's a big deal. In addition to being distinguished by a personal relationship with Jesus and a high view of scripture, evangelicals have provided an unwavering political base and a solid theological backbone for the death penalty in America—until now. With the statement of the NAE, I believe we got one step closer to the end of the death penalty. Grace has a foot in the door of evangelicalism. The new resolution is one small step for the NAE, but it is one giant leap for abolition.

And the Southern Baptists . . . well, we'll keep working on them.

Hundreds of pastors and clergy in the heart of Texas have joined forces to stop executions in our deadliest state. I am proud of the faith community for standing on the side of life and fighting hard for an end to the death penalty. It's happening!

But the death penalty is not yet dead—not quite.

Even with the surge of abolitionist energy sweeping the country, there is a small but vigilant pro-death minority. Even in Nebraska, the newest abolitionist state, millions of dollars are being spent to try and bring the death penalty back by popular vote. In 2014 seven states accounted for 100 percent of the executions, and nearly 80 percent of those executions were in only three states. And the same trend continues in 2015, with only twenty-eight executions in 2015. Nearly half of them were in Texas (thirteen of the twenty-eight executions). And 85 percent of all executions in 2015 were in just three states (all but four were in Texas, Georgia, and Missouri). Nonetheless, bucking the trend toward life in this country, some of these states are renewing their charge to continue to kill: Tennessee voted to bring back the electric chair, Utah voted to bring back the firing squad, and Oklahoma the gas chamber.

So I want to end this book with a pro-life charge. I want to invite you to join me and the heroic people I've introduced you to, along with hundreds of other murder victims' families against execution, and let's kill the death penalty once and for all.

Let me offer a few ideas that can keep us moving.

Let's Put Life into the Death Debate

One of the things I've tried to do in this book is show the toll execution takes on all of us—executioners, victims, the condemned, the exonerated, even the taxpayers who fund it. Execution is doing great damage to our collective psyche.

It's been incredible to see prison wardens, prosecutors, judges, and governors come out against the death penalty in recent years. And when you ask them why, they usually tell you a story about someone, or offer up a name. Even just this week I have a pile of letters from folks who are rethinking the death penalty—including governors, senators, and parole board members. What has moved them is often their faith. But there is almost always a specific individual story involved as well.

That's why we need to keep making the issue of the death penalty *personal*.

My friend John Dear, a wild Catholic activist, once told me about his friendship with Mother Teresa. Like John, she was very concerned about the death penalty. So they got to conspiring and came up with a plan. When there was an imminent execution on the horizon, John would get the phone numbers for key decision-makers and stakeholders and pass them on to Mother Teresa, and she would give them a buzz. After all, she had some street cred that could go a long way, even with the toughest politician.

Obviously, the incoming phone calls put these decision-makers in an awkward position: the elected official or clemency board chair (or whoever) would have to either say he didn't care to talk to Mother Teresa or take the call and deal with the "sermon." Either choice proved tricky.

On one occasion she called a governor. And he accepted the call. Mother Teresa talked to him, only to find out later that the scheduled execution they had talked about had been halted. John said to me, "The next time Mother Teresa and I saw each other, she grabbed me by the arms, swinging me in a ballroom dance, smiling and laughing and singing out loud, 'We saved a life! We saved a life!'"

Later, John got curious. He asked her what exactly she'd said to that particular governor. Mother Teresa answered plainly: "I told him to do what Jesus would do." Fantastic.

But check this out. There's more.

Shortly after John told me the story about Mother Teresa, I went on a trip to Tennessee to visit with some of the men on death row. On my way I stopped by a Christian conference where that state's governor was speaking, and I ended up getting to talk with him for a minute. I knew he was a man of faith, a Presbyterian, but I also knew that he had not been very courageous on this issue; in fact, his state had recently voted to reinstate the electric chair. We had exchanged some e-mails already, and so I wasn't sure what to say. Then I remembered the advice Mother Teresa had given: "Do what Jesus would do." Before I knew it, those words were rolling off my lips. I'm no Mother Teresa, but I can only hope that *this* governor does the same thing her governor friend did.

After the meet-up with the governor, I headed off to meet the men at Riverbend, Tennessee's maximum-security prison. Joined by a few friends, I sat down for several hours with a bunch of the men on death row, five of whom had scheduled execution dates before them. I told them about my brief encounter with the state's top official an hour earlier, and then I asked them what they would say if *they* had a few minutes with the governor who planned to execute them.

I sat on the edge of my seat, anticipating the possible responses— perhaps a few choice, unrepeatable words. Then one of the guys said, "We'd invite him to join us for our prayer meeting on Friday—to come pray with us, worship with us, and get to know us." I saw enthusiastic nods around the room and heard a few grunts of affirmation. I was stunned. Men scheduled to die had just invited the man who would sign their death warrant to come and pray with them!

Every time I remember those men and their invitation, I am reminded that part of our work as grace-filled revolutionaries is to see the humanity in everyone. That has been my hope for this book—to humanize an "issue."

That's what moves us all—stories, like hearing of folks walking to their death who ask if they could take off their shoes and walk in the grass one last time, barefoot. It's hard to kill people when you know them.

Let's Make It Personal

There's another lesson I've been learning recently. There is power in a name. Injustice needs a name and a face.

All through this book are names. Names of victims. Names of the executed. Names of executioners.

We can't make death penalty history until we make death penalty *personal*.

Naming injustice—putting a name and a face to injustice—is what's happening around the hashtags related to racial justice in our country: #MichaelBrown, #EricGarner, #FreddieGray, #SandraBland, #ChristianTaylor, and #TamirRice are putting a name to injustice. The same thing happened when Troy Davis was executed in Georgia and thousands took to the streets with signs and shirts that said, "I am Troy Davis."

Putting a name to injustice, in a very public way, happened again with Kelly Gissendaner. Her story, her humanity, awakened thousands of people to the madness of execution. Prior to Kelly, only fifteen women had been executed since 1976.[10] But the twisted nuances of her case made her death especially poignant. Kelly was

Kelly Gissendaner | Alfredo Prieto | Juan Garcia | Licho Escamilla | Jerry Correll | Raphael Holiday convicted in a 1997 Atlanta murder plot that targeted her husband. Though she was sentenced to death, it is clear that with a little better legal coaching, she could have plea-bargained for her life. That's exactly what her husband's *actual* killer, Gregory Owens, did. She got death, and he's up for parole in eight years.[11]

It just doesn't feel as if your life should depend on how well you play the legal cards, but it sure seems to. One of the things that made the news around the time of Kelly's scheduled execution was her final meal, which was strikingly human—a Burger King burger, cornbread and buttermilk, popcorn, a salad with Newman's Own dressing, and lemonade. Beyond her final cravings, what quickly made international news was the impact she had on others, as women in prison with her talked about her faith and character, some saying she saved their lives as they considered ending them. Those who loved her spoke of her faith, her character, and her repentant heart. Her children lamented the trauma of losing yet another parent. But the all-male pardons board chose death.

Then, in a freak, unprecedented event, her execution was canceled because of snow—in Georgia. Not surprisingly, that continued the media buzz. And it gave her friends, suddenly hopeful, another few days to build momentum. They spoke again of their love for her. Folks she was in prison with told of how she'd saved their lives, speaking encouragement and dignity to them through the bars as they contemplated suicide. And her faith became public: the fact that she'd gotten a theological degree while in prison and had become a spiritual force to be reckoned with. They described how her smile lit up the darkness. Oh—and there's the wonderful friendship she sparked with renowned theologian Jürgen Moltmann (whose book *The Crucified God* is a classic). There's a great picture of them together as he visited with her.

Within three days, there were nearly one hundred thousand signatures calling for her life to be spared. Kelly's friends, along with several hundred Georgia faith leaders, delivered fifty boxes of petitions to City Hall. And the best part is, many of those leading the charge, prior to this, were not "activists" or "protesters"—they were people of faith, pastors, grandmothers, kids who just knew killing Kelly wasn't right.

That is what moved the hearts and minds of so many.

As the clock ticked and the final hours passed, Kelly's execution grew imminent. Tears rolled down scores of faces, including mine. And then—another interruption! One of the physicians announced that the lethal injection chemicals had become "cloudy." Even though they had been tested and Georgia was accustomed to executing regularly, the execution, once again, was canceled.

Even as I write this, tears still flow.

Thousands of folks around the world—many of them following #KellyOnMyMind—rejoiced as her life was spared. It was clear that the world is a better place with her in it. One of my friends in the media world said that an unprecedented four thousand–plus news stories circulated.

A journalist asked me, "Was it a miracle or was it good organizing that stopped the death of Kelly Gissendaner?"

My answer: "Why can't it be both?"

There were many things we learned that week. And one of them was that prayer needs to be at the heart of this movement, as well as good organizing. We are up against some very dark forces. We are battling some principalities and powers. We are exorcising the demons of death and revenge. We need God.

There are hundreds of other people on death row who deserve the same attention and momentum and prayer that Kelly got. In

Christopher Brooks | James Freeman | Brandon Jones | Gustavo Garcia | Travis Hittson order for that to happen, we need to know their names, their stories. We have to make the death penalty personal.

And we need to *keep* fighting. Just after I finished writing the first draft of this book, we discovered that we'd lost the next round in this fight. Kelly Gissendaner was executed on September 30, 2015. She died singing "Amazing Grace."

Let's Start a Grace Revolution

We need courage as we stand on the side of life. We need to take some risks and have some hard conversations with people in power—and maybe even with people we live with. It takes courage to get involved, to go into the streets and talk change. There is so much at stake.

I'm reminded of the courage of my friends down in North Carolina, who have been going to jail (as prisoners, mind you) as they nonviolently pray and put their bodies in the way of executions.

Their movement started with the feeling that they just couldn't watch any more of these spectacles of death. From that feeling grew action.

My pal Jonathan Wilson-Hartgrove and his community, called Rutba House, are located down in Durham, North Carolina, not far from the maximum-security prison that houses North Carolina's death row. In fact, Jonathan teaches some classes for Duke to men on death row. Their community also shows hospitality to family members as they visit their soon-to-be-executed loved ones the week of an execution. He says, "Watching a family go through that week with their loved one feels strangely like living through Holy

Week. By mandate of North Carolina statute, the prisoner is served a last supper on Thursday night, strapped to a gurney on Friday morning, and executed before a small gathering of witnesses."[12]

He and his fellow community members were struck by the way the execution rite mimics Christ's passion, almost as if the salvation of the people depended on this human sacrifice. They began to see the death penalty as a contemporary form of idolatry. As Jonathan says, "We wanted people to know that Jesus died once and for all so that no one else would have to. We didn't want to participate in the idolatry any longer."

And they didn't. At first they began praying against the demonic forces of death at work, forces that competed with the message of grace and redemption at the heart of the gospel.

But then, as often seems to be the case, prayers turned into action. On the night in 2005 when the state was scheduled to execute Kenneth Lee Boyd, the thousandth person to be executed since the 1976 reinstatement of the death penalty, fifteen Christian leaders dressed in sackcloth and ashes knelt before the prison and blocked the entrance to where the execution was to take place. They were arrested and taken to jail.

When the next execution was scheduled, they did it again. This time they sang the old hymn "Were You There When They Crucified My Lord?" and held a worship service, honoring the One who gave his life as a ransom for many. Again they went to jail. Over and over they were prepared to go to jail, and soon, with bail set at five thousand dollars, they were prepared to stay there. The momentum continued to build. After more than six months and a total of sixty-five arrests at four different executions, they were finally brought to trial to argue their case. Jonathan and his fellow abolitionists

Charlie Brooks | John Evans | Jimmy Gray | Robert Sullivan | Robert Williams | John Smith did not dispute the facts of the case (trespassing, blocking the entrance, etc.), but they tried a line of argument that is notorious for *not* working in these types of cases. They argued that their actions were justified and necessary. In 2006, the judge stunned everyone by agreeing to hear the case.

Jonathan explained on behalf of the group that they were Christians, and as such could not support state-sanctioned executions that expressly mimicked Christ's passion. He went on to say that Christian convictions compel Jesus's followers to take direct action to prevent any murder. They had openly trespassed at the prison, they explained, to try to prevent a murder that they believed was unjust and idolatrous.

At one point the judge interjected: "Before we proceed, could you tell me how you read Romans 13?" As we saw earlier, this is a common, not-surprising question, except for the fact that it came from a judge on the stand. Jonathan had a surge of energy, knowing that there was hope if the judge wanted to talk about the Bible. And there *was* hope.

Jonathan quoted from Paul's injunction in Romans 13 to "be subject to the governing authorities" (Rom. 13:1) and pointed out that Martin Luther King Jr. had taught that it is the Christian's duty to break an unjust law and thereby put the law on trial so that a court can evaluate its justice. And then Jonathan said, "We are here today, Your Honor, to submit to your authority and ask for a decision about the justice of the death penalty." The judge nodded and asked them to present their case.

On the stand, defendants spoke of their relationships with people on death row and their families. They spoke of the murder victims' family members they knew who also agreed that execution is not the best form of justice or healing. They explained that they had exhausted all legal means to stop the executions of the four men whose killings they ultimately tried to prevent by putting their bodies nonviolently in the way of the wheels of death. But more than anything, they spoke of Jesus in that courtroom. They talked—in part in response to questions from the prosecutor about Paul's writing and theology—about the good news that all human sacrifice had been brought to an end at the cross.

Eventually the defendants asked the judge if they could bring a theologian to testify as an expert witness. And the judge allowed it! None other than Stanley Hauerwas made his way to the stand. While that name may mean little to folks who could care less about theology, Hauerwas is a legend in some circles, having written some fifty books and serving as the distinguished Gilbert T. Rowe Professor Emeritus of Theological Ethics at Duke Divinity School.[13]

Dr. Hauerwas explained the overwhelming opposition to the death penalty held by the early Christians, together with most major teachers of the church throughout history, including Pope John Paul II. He laid it all out there, saying, "The Church has always had a problem with capital punishment. After all, the State executed our Lord."[14]

With his characteristic southern charm, as if sipping sweet tea in a rocking chair on the porch, Hauerwas kept the court fascinated. He recounted for the judge an exhaustive history of Christian civil resistance, from the Underground Railroad and sit-ins to conscientious objection to war and disarmament of nuclear weapons.

The testimony was really something special. He concluded with these words: "This is what Christians do when their convictions run up against the systems of this world. They get in the way." Bam.

With that the defendants rested their case and waited for the judge's verdict.

Elmo Sonnier | James Adams | Carl Shriner | Ivon Stanley | David Washington | Ernest Dobbert

The judge, on returning to the courtroom after his deliberations, began by saying that he generally didn't like to say much from the bench, being careful not to turn that bench into a pulpit. But, he explained, in this case he wanted to diverge from the norm. He told the defendants that he admired their courage and conviction and was honored to hear their case. He explained that it was not in his power to make a ruling on the justice of the death penalty, but merely to judge on the trespassing charges. He found them all guilty but he suspended sentences. It was almost as if he were winking as he dropped the gavel.

Little victories like this one began to slowly change the tide. Following this case, one North Carolina lawyer who had spent years working to stop executions congratulated the defendants and said he believed that the death penalty was on its way out. In fact, he said he didn't think it would last another year in North Carolina. Less than six months later, in August 2006, North Carolina had its last execution to date.

What's interesting about North Carolina is that it wasn't just activists in the streets who abolished the death penalty. It was theologians, lawyers, victims, and Sunday school teachers. And it was doctors too. One of the final blows to the death penalty in North Carolina was dealt by the medical community. As has been the case in many states, various doctors and nurses came to believe that it is immoral to participate in execution—and they spoke out in protest. Many of them said that not only is it immoral, but it is a violation of the medical oath to "do no harm."

The North Carolina Medical Board issued a statement backing the protesters' conviction that it would be a breach of medical ethics for any physician to participate in an execution.[15] The state's protocol mandates that a physician be present for an execution to take place. So . . . for now, that's what's stopping death. No doctors means no executions, and thus we have a moratorium in North Carolina.

So we need radical theologians. We need activists. We need courageous doctors. And abolitionist lawyers.

We *all* have a voice in the freedom choir.

It's going to take all of us—and the Spirit of the living God working with us—to stop the wheels of death. Let's make death penalty history together.

In the name of the executed and risen Savior. Amen.

Oh, and remember the two stories we started with?

George Junius Stinney, the fourteen-year-old executed by electric chair in 1944. Remember him?

One of Stinney's only remaining relatives reopened his case in 2013, in an attempt to clear his name—something she felt compelled to do since she had been with him on the day he was convicted of killing two girls. Reviewing the evidence (or lack of evidence, as it turned out), a South Carolina judge passionately vacated the boy's sentence. Judge Carmen Mullen wrote: "I can think of no greater injustice than the violation of one's Constitutional rights which has been proven to me in this case."[16] Seventy years after he was executed, George Junius Stinney's sentence was vacated.

And as for Terri Roberts, whose son Charlie was responsible for the Amish school shooting, she continues to meet every other Thursday with Rosanna, who is now fifteen years old. Every year in the fall, around the anniversary of the shooting, Terri has tea with the Amish moms in her home.[17] Terri just wrote a book called *Forgiven*.

And now Terri's other son, Charlie's brother Zach, is doing a film on his mom, called *Hope*.

Velma Barfield | Timothy Palmes | Alpha Stephens | Robert Willie | David Martin

Acknowledgments

L et me begin by saying I've been a learner when it comes to the issues raised in this book. And I've tried to be a really good one. I've read dozens of books, digested hundreds of articles, and watched countless films, docs, and TV specials.

Most importantly, I've talked to *people*. I have interviewed people on all sides of the issue. I've talked with victims of horrific crimes and with folks who have done horrific crimes—and with folks who have been convicted of horrible crimes they had nothing to do with.

I've listened to tapes . . . and I've listened to tears.

I have sat up many late nights haunted by the stories I've heard. And just as I've been haunted, I have also been inspired by the stunning stories of grace shared in these pages.

When it comes to those I need to thank, why save the best for last? My wife, Katie Jo, has been a constant support—she's a shining star. Her smile lights up the world. She inspired me to get involved in issues of mass incarceration and the death penalty. Katie is one of the most grace-full people I know. And she's one of the funniest. Nothing helped me more than the comic relief she imposed upon me, sending me photoshopped pictures of what she might look like as a zombie, or interrupting my deep, important writing time with juggling and plate spinning. She has reminded me that laughter has power over the darkness. And she has held me when the darkness has felt heavy, as we've cried over yet another execution.

I have many people to thank, but these are the only ones I'll mention by name: Bryan Stevenson, Stacy Anderson, Heather Beaudoin, Bill Pelke, Billy Neal Moore, Sister Helen Prejean, Kathleen Lucas, Jonathan Wilson-Hartgrove, Desmond Tutu, Dale Recinella, Michael McRay, Terry Rumsey, Terri Roberts, Kathy Spillman, Ron McAndrew, Elaine Enns, Art Laffin, Scott Bass, Diann Rust-Tierney, and Steve Dear. These are some of my heroes. I will be donating a large portion of the royalties from this book to all the great groups these folks represent. (Those groups are listed separately.)

My assistants, Christine Holbert and Rebekah Devine, helped me in all sorts of ways, and my editor, Mickey Maudlin, is a legend. My buddy Chris Haw, one of the preeminent theologians in the country, helped me with some of the theological meanderings—so if there's anything wrong there, it's his fault. Scott Langley offered all his photos for free—which I'm using in presentations, websites, and visuals related to the content of this book. His photos bring the death penalty to life and show how tragic it truly is. And of course I'm grateful to all the men and women behind bars whom I have grown to love, especially Duane Buck on Texas's death row, who first caught my attention.

There are folks who have been working on the death penalty for decades who have written their own books, and others who could write volumes but are too busy trying to save lives. In these pages I've done my best to put the spotlight on these folks—lawyers and legislators, prophets and prisoners, chaplains and ex-executioners.

I have been a student of murder victims' families who have taught me about grace.

I have been a student of folks exonerated from death row who have taught me about injustice.

I have been a student of the men and women on America's death row who have taught me about hope.

I have been a student of the dead—those who have been murdered both legally and illegally—whose lives and deaths have taught me that there is another way.

Works Cited

(and Other Books Worth Reading)

Alexander, Michelle. *The New Jim Crow: Mass Incarceration in the Age of Colorblindness.* New York: New Press, 2010.

Blackmon, Douglas A. *Slavery by Another Name: The Re-enslavement of Black Americans from the Civil War to World War II.* New York: Doubleday, 2008.

Cabana, Donald A. *Death at Midnight: The Confession of an Executioner.* Boston: Northeastern Univ. Press, 1996.

Cahill, Thomas. *A Saint on Death Row: The Story of Dominique Green.* New York: Doubleday, 2009.

Campbell, Will D., and Richard C. Goode. *And the Criminals with Him: Essays in Honor of Will D. Campbell and All the Reconciled.* Eugene, OR: Cascade, 2012.

Cone, James H. *The Cross and the Lynching Tree.* Maryknoll, NY: Orbis, 2011.

Gilligan, James. *Violence: Reflections on a National Epidemic.* New York: Vintage, 1997.

Gushee, David P. *The Sacredness of Human Life: Why an Ancient Biblical Vision Is Key to the World's Future.* Grand Rapids, MI: Eerdmans, 2013.

Jones, Tony. *Did God Kill Jesus?* San Francisco: HarperOne, 2015.

Jones, W. Paul. *A Different Kind of Cell: The Story of a Murderer Who Became a Monk.* Grand Rapids, MI: Eerdmans, 2011.

Katongole, Emmanuel. *Mirror to the Church.* Grand Rapids, MI: Zondervan, 2009.

MacNiven-Johnston, Glynn. *Maria Goretti: Teenage Martyr.* London: Catholic Truth Society / Ignatius Press, 1997.

Marlowe, Jen, Martina Davis-Correia, and Troy Davis. *I Am Troy Davis.* Chicago: Haymarket Books, 2013.

Marshall, Christopher D. *Beyond Retribution: A New Testament Vision for Justice, Crime, and Punishment.* Grand Rapids, MI: Eerdmans, 2001.

Moore, Billy Neal. *I Shall Not Die: Seventy-Two Hours on Death Row.* Bloomington, IN: AuthorHouse, 2005.

Osler, Mark William. *Jesus on Death Row: The Trial of Jesus and American Capital Punishment.* Nashville: Abingdon, 2009.

Pelke, Bill. *Journey of Hope: From Violence to Healing.* Bloomington, IN: Xlibris, 2003.

Pickett, Carroll, and Carlton Stowers. *Within These Walls: Memoirs of a Death House Chaplain.* New York: St. Martin's Press, 2002.

Prejean, Helen. *Dead Man Walking: An Eyewitness Account of the Death Penalty in the United States.* New York: Vintage, 1994.

———. *The Death of Innocents: An Eyewitness Account of Wrongful Executions.* New York: Random House, 2005.

Recinella, Dale S. *The Biblical Truth About America's Death Penalty*. Boston: Northeastern Univ. Press, 2004.

———. *Now I Walk on Death Row: A Wall Street Finance Lawyer Stumbles into the Arms of a Loving God*. Grand Rapids, MI: Chosen, 2011.

Roberts, Terri. *Forgiven: The Amish School Shooting, a Mother's Love, and a Story of Remarkable Grace*. Bloomington, MN: Bethany House, 2015.

Sarat, Austin. *Gruesome Spectacles: Botched Executions and America's Death Penalty*. Redwood City, CA: Stanford Law Books, 2014.

Sider, Ronald J. *Completely Pro-Life: Building a Consistent Stance on Abortion, the Family, Nuclear Weapons, the Poor*. Eugene, OR: Wipf & Stock, 2010.

———. *The Early Church on Killing: A Comprehensive Sourcebook on War, Abortion, and Capital Punishment*. Grand Rapids, MI: Baker Academic, 2012.

Stevenson, Bryan. *Just Mercy*. New York: Random House, 2014.

Taylor, Mark Lewis. *The Executed God: The Way of the Cross in Lockdown America*. Minneapolis, MN: Fortress, 2001.

Tutu, Desmond. *No Future Without Forgiveness*. New York: Random House, 1999.

Tutu, Desmond, and Mpho Tutu. *The Book of Forgiving: The Fourfold Path for Healing Ourselves and Our World*. Edited by Douglas C. Abrams. San Francisco: HarperOne, 2014.

Volf, Miroslav. *Exclusion and Embrace: A Theological Exploration of Identity, Otherness, and Reconciliation*. Nashville: Abingdon, 1996.

Wiesenthal, Simon. *The Sunflower*. New York: Schocken, 1976.

Wright, N. T. *What Saint Paul Really Said*. Grand Rapids, MI: Eerdmans, 1997.

Zehr, Howard. *Changing Lenses: A New Focus for Crime and Justice*. Scottdale, PA: Herald Press, 1990.

———. *The Little Book of Restorative Justice*. Intercourse, PA: Good Books, 2002.

There are countless heroic organizations around the country working for alternatives to the death penalty, and for grace, forgiveness, and restorative justice. Royalties from this book will be shared with some of the organizations that have inspired and shaped it. Among them are the groups listed below (with mission statements taken directly from the organizations' websites):

Center for Death Penalty Litigation

http://cdpl.org/
The Center for Death Penalty Litigation is a nonprofit law firm that provides direct representation to inmates on North Carolina's death row, as well as consulting with and training attorneys who practice capital litigation across the state.

Death Penalty Focus

http://deathpenalty.org/
Hubbed in California and founded in 1988, Death Penalty Focus is committed to the abolition of the death penalty through public education, grassroots organizing and political advocacy, media outreach, and domestic and international coalition building.

Death Penalty Information Center

www.deathpenaltyinfo.org
The Death Penalty Information Center is a national nonprofit organization serving the media and the public with analysis and information on issues concerning capital punishment.

The 8th Amendment Project

www.proteusfund.org
A coordinated national campaign to end the death penalty, including litigation, legislation, and policy reform, outreach, and partnerships.

Equal Justice Initiative

www.eji.org
The Equal Justice Initiative is a private, nonprofit 501(c)(3) organization that provides legal representation to indigent defendants and prisoners who have been denied fair and just treatment in the legal system.

Equal Justice USA

http://ejusa.org
Equal Justice USA cuts through polarization to build a criminal justice system that works. For *everyone*.

Forgiveness Project

http://theforgivenessproject.com
The Forgiveness Project is a United Kingdom–based charity that uses storytelling to explore how ideas around forgiveness, reconciliation, and conflict resolution can be used to impact positively on people's lives, through the personal testimonies of both victims and perpetrators of crime and violence.

Innocence Project

www.innocenceproject.org
The Innocence Project is a national litigation and public policy organization dedicated to exonerating wrongfully convicted individuals through DNA testing and reforming the criminal justice system to prevent future injustice.

Journey of Hope . . . from Violence to Healing

www.journeyofhope.org
Journey of Hope . . . from Violence to Healing is an organization that is led by murder victim family members that conducts public education speaking tours and addresses alternatives to the death penalty.

Murder Victims' Families for Human Rights (MVFHR)

www.mvfhr.org
MVFHR is an international, nongovernmental organization of family members of murder victims and family members of the executed, all of whom oppose the death penalty in all cases.

Murder Victims' Families for Reconciliation (MVFR)

www.mvfr.org
MVFR is a community led by family members of murder victims and the executed that advocates for the repeal of the death penalty.

National Coalition to Abolish the Death Penalty

www.ncadp.org
The National Coalition to Abolish the Death Penalty's mission is to abolish the death penalty in the United States and support efforts to abolish the death penalty worldwide.

Nebraskans for Alternatives to the Death Penalty (NADP)

http://nadp.net
NADP provides speakers for educational talks and events, organizes testimony for legislative committee hearings, coordinates member education and involvement, and lobbies the Nebraska Legislature.

Pennsylvanians for Alternatives to the Death Penalty

www.padp.org
Pennsylvanians for Alternatives to the Death Penalty is a grassroots nonprofit organization dedicated to ending executions in Pennsylvania. PADP believes that there are safe and fair alternatives to execution.

People of Faith Against the Death Penalty

www.pfadp.org
The mission of People of Faith Against the Death Penalty is to educate and mobilize faith communities to act to abolish the death penalty in the United States.

Southern Center for Human Rights

www.schr.org/
The Southern Center for Human Rights is a nonprofit, public interest law firm dedicated to providing legal representation to people facing the death penalty, challenging human rights violations in prisons and jails, seeking through litigation and advocacy to improve legal representation for poor people accused of crimes, and advocating for criminal justice reform on behalf of those affected by the system in the Southern United States.

Tennesseans for Alternatives to the Death Penalty

http://tennesseedeathpenalty.org
Tennesseans for Alternatives to the Death Penalty seeks to "honor life by abolishing the death penalty."

Texas Defenders Service

http://texasdefender.org/
Texas Defenders Service seeks reform of criminal justice policy at all levels, fights to prevent unjust executions, and works to stop the execution of the mentally ill. And they win in the US Supreme Court.

Witness to Innocence

www.witnesstoinnocence.org
Witness to Innocence is the nation's only organization dedicated to empowering exonerated death row survivors to be the most powerful and effective voice in the struggle to end the death penalty in the United States.

Notes

Chapter 1: Something Just Doesn't Feel Right

1. Details about the George Junius Stinney Jr. case are from Terrell Jermaine Starr, "Executed at 14," posted Oct. 19, 2012, http://newsone.com/2061550/george -junius-stinney-jr-birthday.

2. Details about the shooting and its grace-filled aftermath are from my interview with Terri Roberts on Feb. 3, 2015. You can read more in her book *Forgiven: The Amish School Shooting, a Mother's Love, and a Story of Remarkable Grace* (Bloomington, MN: Bethany House, 2015).

3. This statement, released through the Associated Press, circulated broadly and is reprinted in "Shooter's Wife Thanks Amish Community," posted Oct. 14, 2006, www.washingtonpost.com/wp-dyn/content/article/2006/10/14/AR2006101400510 .html.

4. I interviewed David Weaver-Zercher at Messiah College on Feb. 18, 2015.

5. Donald Kraybill, Steven Nolt, and David Weaver-Zercher, *Amish Grace: How Forgiveness Transcended Tragedy* (San Francisco: Jossey-Bass, 2007).

6. Michael Rubinkam, "Amish School Shooter's Kin: Horror, Then Healing," posted Dec. 9, 2013, http://bigstory.ap.org/article/amish-school-shooters-kin-horror-then -healing; Daniel Burke, "Mother Cares for Her Son's Amish Victims," updated Sept. 29, 2011, http://usatoday30.usatoday.com/news/religion/story/2011–09–29/amish -schoolhouse-shooting/50609184/1.

7. A few years ago, my pal Chris Haw and I wrote a book about political imagination called *Jesus for President* (Grand Rapids, MI: Zondervan, 2008), and we included a section on the Amish called "Amish for Homeland Security," winking at how the world might be different had we conjured up the Amish imagination after September 11. For our sake here, we might also suggest, "Amish for Supreme Court"! Pretty sure that would mean the end of the death penalty.

Chapter 2: Let's Begin with the Victims

1. This quote, along with quotes later in the chapter from Miriam Thimm Kelle, Bruce Grieshaber, Martin Luther King III, and the letter to the New Jersey legislature, as well as dozens of others we weren't able to include here, can be found at the Equal Justice USA website, www.ejusa.org.

2. Taking my cue from the organization Murder Victims' Families for Reconciliation (MVFR), I use the word "victim" to include "close relative of homicide victim" or "co-victim of homicide." This is consistent with the definition used by most state laws and in the victim assistance community.

3. One of the most helpful resources I have found from victims themselves is this article published by Murder Victim's Families for Reconciliation: Robert Renny Cushing and Susannah Sheffer, "Dignity Denied: The Experience of Murder Victims' Family Members Who Oppose the Death Penalty" (Cambridge, MA: MVFR, 2002). It is also available for free online: www.ncadp.org/resources/entry/dignity-denied. Sojourner Truth asked the second question in 1851 when addressing a convention of women in Ohio, challenging them to consider the rights of *all* women, not just white women.

4. In the powerful article entitled "Dignity Denied," referenced in the previous note, the authors collect the stories of some courageous murder victims' family members who oppose the death penalty.

5. In fact, the section of the Victims of Crime Act that deals with eligibility for compensation says that a crime victim program is eligible for federal funding if, among other things, the organization "promotes victim cooperation" with law enforcement, which certainly would require a victim's cooperation with prosecutors seeking the death penalty. A victim's failure to support that agenda could be seen as a refusal to cooperate. Cushing and Sheffer, "Dignity Denied," 8.

6. You can watch and read Amy Goodman's stunning interview with Bob—" 'The Death Penalty Is a Hate Crime': Bob Autobee Speaks Out to Spare Life of Son's Killer," (Mar. 5, 2014)—on the *Democracy Now* website: www.democracynow.org/2014/3/5 /the_death_penalty_is_a_hate. And here's a great video of Bob's meeting with the man who killed his son, and the protest of his execution: http://www.deathpenalty .org/article.php?id=712.

7. Cushing and Sheffer, "Dignity Denied," 9.

8. https://www.victimsofcrime.org/our-programs/public-policy/amendments.

9. This was a significant case, as it was the first time that murder victims' family members mounted a court challenge over the fact that their opposition to the death penalty had placed them outside the definition of "victim" and excluded them from legal proceedings.

10. Cushing and Sheffer, "Dignity Denied," 11.

11. Cushing and Sheffer, "Dignity Denied," 13.

12. www.cnn.com/2015/09/29/us/georgia-execution-kelly-gissendaner/.

13. As noted earlier, the three groups I am most familiar with and work most closely with are Journey of Hope, Murder Victims' Families for Reconciliation, and Murder Victims' Families for Human Rights. I also admire the international work of the Forgiveness Project.

14. I've heard Sister Helen say this in person, but also she mentions it in this PBS interview available online: www.pbs.org/wgbh/pages/frontline/angel/interviews /hprejean.html.

15. http://mvfhr.blogspot.com/2007/09/power-of-choice.html.

16. http://mvfhr.blogspot.com/2009/10/its-unlikeliest-legacy.html.

17. http://mvfhr.blogspot.com/2008/01/building-bridges-for-peace.html.

18. http://mvfhr.blogspot.com/2010/04/message-was-plain.html.

19. https://www.journeyofhope.org/who-we-are/murder-victim-family /ron-carolyn-callen/.

20. http://ldbpeaceinstitute.org/content/our-staff.

21. http://mvfhr.blogspot.com/2010/10/there-are-human-beings-involved.html.

22. http://peacefultomorrows.org/members/loretta-filipov/.

23. https://www.journeyofhope.org/who-we-are/murder-victim-family /aba-gayle/.

24. http://mvfhr.blogspot.com/search?q=susan+hirsch.

25. http://mvfhr.blogspot.com/2008/03/dead-man-walking-play.html.

26. More info on Bess is here: https://www.journeyofhope.org/who-we-are /murder-victim-family/bess-klassen-landis/. There's a great article about how Bess and her sisters have become a powerful voice for healing and forgiveness: Emily Dougherty, "After Murders, Families Find a Healing Path," posted on Mennonite Weekly Review, Mar. 23, 2009, www.mennoworld.org/archived/2009/3/23/after -murders-families-find-healing-path/?print=1.

27. Interview with Art Laffin on Mar. 28, 2014.

28. Yolanda is an active member of Murder Victims Families for Reconciliation. More info can be found in this video interview on their website—https://www.face book.com/mvfrus/posts/576174655762011—and in this article from The Root, posted Sept. 22, 2014: http://www.theroot.com/articles/culture/2014/09/jacquetta_thomas _case_family_still_waiting_for_justice_23_years_later.html. Here's a video of Yolanda and Greg speaking together: http://www.wral.com/news/local/ video/12323975/.

29. http://mvfhr.blogspot.com/search?q=marietta.

30. http://peacefultomorrows.org/stories/robin-theurkauf-are-we-at-war/. This quote and more about her life and memorial service are here: www.yale.edu/divinity /news/090716_news_theurkauf.shtml.

31. www.willsworld.com/~mvfhr/gallery-Warner.pdf.

32. http://deathpenaltyusa.blogspot.com/2007/01/creating-more-victims -part-ten.html.

33. https://www.journeyofhope.org/who-we-are/murder-victim-family /suezann-bosler/.

34. https://www.journeyofhope.org/who-we-are/murder-victim-family /maria-hines/.

35. http://theforgivenessproject.com/stories/cathy-harrington-usa/.

36. http://theforgivenessproject.com/stories/judith-toy-usa/.

37. http://theforgivenessproject.com/stories/terry-caffey-usa/.

38. http://theforgivenessproject.com/stories/rebecca-demauro-usa/.

39. See my article "Death Penalty for Dzhokhar Tsarnaev: A Call for Radical Mercy," posted May 19, 2015, http://www.huffingtonpost.com/shane-claiborne/death -penalty-for-dzhokhar-tsarnaev-a-call-for-radical-mercy_b_7336662.html.

40. Details here are from my interview with Bill Pelke, who is not only a hero but has now become a friend. Interview with Bill Pelke, Aug. 5, 2013. You can see our Skype conversation at http://www.redletterchristians.org/bill-pelke-wants-the -best-for-his-grandmothers-killer-paula-cooper.

41. Interview with Bill Pelke, Aug. 5, 2013.

42. Pope John Paul II spoke out against Paula's execution.

43. Here's the heartbreaking story of Paula Cooper's life after prison, and her death: Liliana Segura, "From Death Row at 16 to Suicide," posted June 12, 2015, https://theintercept.com/2015/06/12/paula-cooper-dead-at-45/.

44. Bill founded Journey of Hope, which brings together victims' families, families of the executed, and exonerated folks. See www.journeyofhope.com. After Paula's death he said that Journey of Hope is the legacy both of his Nana and of Paula

Cooper. He noted, "There would be no Journey of Hope without Paula Cooper. . . . It's just amazing how many lives she touched."

Chapter 3: Death and Grace in the Bible

1. Dale Recinella, *The Biblical Truth About America's Death Penalty* (Boston: Northeastern Univ. Press, 2004).

2. The "Bible Belt" is defined by Merriam-Webster as "an area chiefly in the southern United States whose inhabitants are believed to hold uncritical allegiance to the literal accuracy of the Bible." Recinella defines it as the area of the United States consisting of the eleven states and Oklahoma territory of the Confederacy, and the slave-holding border states. His point is clear, where the population of Christians is highest is precisely where death sentences and executions are highest. The percentage statistic is from Richard C. Dieter, "The 2% Death Penalty: How a Minority of Counties Produce Most Death Cases at Enormous Costs to All" (Washington, DC: Death Penalty Information Center, 2013).

3. Dale Recinella has been a great resource and an inspiration. His book *The Biblical Truth About America's Death Penalty* is one of the best resources out there on what the Bible really says about capital punishment, and how our contemporary practice of execution is in stark contrast.

4. Interview with Bryan Stevenson, Mar. 14, 2014.

5. Paul Young, "Love Is Conditional. Relationships Aren't," posted Sept. 22, 2015, http://storylineblog.com/2015/09/22/love-unconditional/.

6. Nearly every society has a "founding murder" story. In addition to Cain and Abel, consider Romulus and Remus, Oedipus and Laius, Marduk and Tiamat, among others.

7. A genealogy appears in the first chapter of Matthew, a passage that at first might be a little bit boring, but when it gets to David it says, "David was the father of Solomon, whose mother had been Uriah's wife" (Matt. 1:6). There's a little gospel humor here, as Uriah was the man David had killed. Clearly that was a sin. God did not forget. But God's grace is bigger than our sins.

8. There are dozens and dozens of appeals of court decisions in capital cases (nearly one hundred in fifteen years) that have involved legal challenges based on the grounds that the prosecutor used religious remarks to support leveling a death sentence. These include multiple references to specific scriptures: eight cases of "eye for eye," nine cases of Exodus 21, eight cases of Genesis 9, six cases of Numbers 35, and other cases of Romans 13. In one Alabama case, the prosecutor said simply that "God believed in capital punishment." See *The Biblical Truth About America's Death Penalty*, 5–6.

9. Recinella, *The Biblical Truth About America's Death Penalty,* 67.

10. Recinella, *The Biblical Truth About America's Death Penalty,* 69.

11. *Ancient Hebrews,* note 100. 52–53 (as quoted in Recinella, *The Biblical Truth About America's Death Penalty*, 72).

12. *Ethics and Halakhah,* 156 (as quoted in Recinella, *The Biblical Truth About America's Death Penalty*, 72).

13. *Ethics and Halakhah,* 156 (as quoted in Recinella, *The Biblical Truth About America's Death Penalty*, 72). One of the most prominent voices against the death penalty in Florida has been Jack Gordon, who speaks from his Jewish faith: "From a Jewish theological perspective, capital punishment is not something you should be for. . . .

Even though there's an eye for an eye and a tooth for a tooth in the Bible, the history of Jewish jurisprudence, Talmudically, is that if the court sentences someone to death more frequently than every sixty or seventy years, then they're supposed to get a new court." Gordon is quoted in Recinella, *The Biblical Truth About America's Death Penalty*, 33.

14.   In *The Biblical Truth About America's Death Penalty*, Recinella looks closely at the biblical text itself; at the Talmud, which is the written collection of the oral law (he uses the Talmud Bavli Schottenstein edition); and at the Mishnah, which is the compilation of multi-century commentary from the teachers concerning the law.

15.   Here are a few of Brother Dale's fascinating discoveries:

The Great Sanhedrin, sort of the Supreme Court of the Jews, consisted of seventy-one members, and it was housed in the temple.

Procedure for the death penalty contained specific restrictions:

- At least two eyewitnesses whose testimony agreed on virtually every detail were needed.
- Confessions of the accused were of no validity or effect.
- Circumstantial evidence was not allowed.
- Premeditation had to be proved by showing that the accused was warned before committing the crime that the penalty would be execution.
- Conviction required a majority of two votes by the judges, but release required a majority of only one (again, that bias toward the defendant).
- Certain categories of people were exempt: minors, the mentally unstable, people with special mental needs, and certain people acting under duress.

Felony murder was excluded. This category of murder encompasses the intentional killing of an unintended person, the intentional killing by indirect means, reckless homicide, and liability of any accomplice. These were punishable, but not by death as is the case in many U.S. states. An example of this is a robbery with three criminals, in which a store clerk is killed. Even if the death is accidental, *all* can be found guilty of felony murder today, including those who did no harm. If one of the robbers is accidentally killed, it is even possible for the fellow robbers to be charged with felony murder. None of these would be possible under the biblical practice of the death penalty.

Four methods of execution were allowed for in the biblical practice of the death penalty: stoning, burning, decapitation, and strangulation. None of these methods is used in the contemporary practice of the death penalty in North America, another major hurdle for fundamentalists who want to do death by the letter of the law. Rabbis thought stoning was the harshest and strangulation the mildest. Even the rabbinical practice evolved in decency, to virtual nonexistence. If you dig deeper you can find punishments as harsh as cutting a person's tongue out, burning a person alive, and beating evil out of someone; furthermore, there is an evolution in the way that we do it—that is, no longer publicly. It's as if there's something in us that hesitates to kill. (Maybe that's because there *is* something in us that doesn't want to kill.)

If all this is interesting to you and you want more, check out *The Biblical Truth About America's Death Penalty*. (Have I mentioned that I really like Dale's book?)

16.   Recinella, *The Biblical Truth About America's Death Penalty*, 91.

17.   Maimonides, "Sanhedrin," chap. 14, par. 13, 41.

18.   Recinella, *The Biblical Truth About America's Death Penalty*, xvi. Interesting note: the man convicted of this horrific crime and sentenced to death was recently exonerated. After being proved innocent by DNA evidence, Henry McCollum and his mentally disabled half-brother are both free men, but they lost twenty-one years of their lives (Henry spent more years in jail than outside since he was nineteen when the crime happened). www.miamiherald.com/opinion/opn-columns-blogs/leonard-pitts-jr/article23877205.html.

19.   Leonard Pitts Jr., "What Do You Think of the Death Penalty Now, Justice Scalia?" *Miami Herald,* June 13, 2015.

20.   See, for example, Galatians 5:14: "For the entire law is fulfilled in keeping this one command: 'Love your neighbor as yourself.'"

21.   Saeed Kamali Dehghan, "Iranian Killer's Execution Halted at Last Minute by Victim's Parents," posted Apr. 16, 2014, www.theguardian.com/world/2014/apr/16/iran-parents-halt-killer-execution.

Chapter 4: The Limits of an Eye for an Eye

1.   See Brigid Delaney, "Bryan Stevenson: If It's Not Right to Rape a Rapist How Can It Be OK to Kill a Killer?," posted Feb. 16, 2015, www.theguardian.com/world/2015/feb/17/bryan-stevenson-if-its-not-right-to-a-rapist-how-can-it-be-ok-to-kill-a-killer.

2.   Howard Zehr, *Changing Lenses: A New Focus for Crime and Justice* (Scottdale, PA: Herald Press, 1990), 126.

3.   See especially Exod. 21:23–25; Lev. 24:17, 19–21; Deut. 19:21.

4.   Interview with Bryan Stevenson, Mar. 14, 2014.

5.   See R. Albert Mohler Jr., "Why Christians Should Support the Death Penalty," posted May 1, 2014, http://religion.blogs.cnn.com/2014/05/01/why-christians-should-support-the-death-penalty. I do want to affirm something that Al Mohler said, which I did not do in the original response I wrote. He called out the dysfunction of the current practice of the death penalty when it comes to race and inequity—something to be applauded. And worth quoting: "Christians should be outraged at the economic and racial injustice in how the death penalty is applied. While the law itself is not prejudiced, the application of the death penalty often is. There is very little chance that a wealthy white murderer will ever be executed. There is a far greater likelihood that a poor African-American murderer will face execution. . . . This is an outrage, and no Christian can support such a disparity." Those are the words of Southern Baptist leader Al Mohler! Sadly, his response is a radical reconstruction of the system rather than abolition. But perhaps that will change. One can hope.

6.   My piece can be read here: Shane Claiborne, "If It Weren't for Jesus, I Might Be Pro-Death Too," posted May 12, 2014, www.redletterchristians.org/werent-jesus-might-pro-death/.

7.   This idea is thoroughly explored in the book I wrote with Chris Haw, *Jesus for President: Politics for Ordinary Radicals* (Grand Rapids: Zondervan, 2008).

8.   Dale Recinella, *The Biblical Truth About America's Death Penalty* (Boston: Northeastern Univ. Press, 2004), 101.

9.   Building here on the good scholarship of Dale Recinella, among others.

10.   Michael Frost, *Jesus the Fool* (Sutherland, Australia: Albatross, 1994), 138–44.

Chapter 5: The Most Famous Execution in History

1. For more info on crucifixion you can read the historian Josephus, or scholars like Richard Horsley and John Dominic Crossan, or for those looking for a shortcut, you can just check out Wikipedia: https://en.wikipedia.org/wiki/Crucifixion.

2. Josephus, Jewish War V.11: "the soldiers out of rage and hatred, *nailed* those they caught, one after one way, and another after another, to the crosses, by way of jest."

3. https://en.wikipedia.org/wiki/Crucifixion.

4. Daniel Berrigan said this in a legendary way during his "Meditation on a Martyr" speech here in Philadelphia, which was a tribute to Franz Jagerstatter, executed by the Nazis. http://nightslantern.ca/meditation.htm.

5. See the website of the Ku Klux Klan if you really must (or just take my word for it): www.kkk.com.

6. Tony Jones, *Did God Kill Jesus?* (San Francisco: HarperOne, 2015). I've borrowed some of Tony's categories and built on some of his thoughts here. He calls himself a "proctologist" for the church. If this stuff is interesting to you, Tony's book is worth a read.

7. There's an entire section about botched executions, including the details on this one, here: www.deathpenaltyinfo.org/some-examples-post-furman-botched -executions.

8. Mary Jo Melone, "A Switch Is Thrown, and God Speaks," *St. Petersburg Times,* July 13, 1999, 1B.

9. "Nonviolent Atonement" is one of the hottest theological conversations happening, thanks to folks like James Alison and René Girard. I also appreciate my friend Scot McKnight's book *Your Atonement Is Too Small.*

10. 1 Cor. 13:12, NASB.

11. Mark Lewis Taylor, *The Executed God* (Minneapolis: Fortress, 2001), 101.

12. James Cone, *The Cross and the Lynching Tree* (Maryknoll, NY: Orbis, 2011), 2.

13. John Neafsey has written a whole book on Ellacuria's ideas, entitled *Crucified People.*

14. Cone, *The Cross and the Lynching Tree,* 31.

15. Cone, *The Cross and the Lynching Tree,* xviii.

16. Cone, *The Cross and the Lynching Tree,* 96.

17. Jones, *Did God Kill Jesus?,* 197.

18. www.americanrhetoric.com/speeches/mlkihaveadream.htm.

19. Clarence Jordan, *Cotton Patch Gospel: The Complete Collection* (Macon, GA: Smyth and Helwys, 2014).

20. Rene Girard was prolific in his writing. He died as I was finishing this book, Nov. 4, 2015. A good place to start is his book *I See Satan Fall Like Lightning.*

21. N. T. Wright, *What Saint Paul Really Said* (Grand Rapids, MI: Eerdmans, 1997), 110–11.

22. Christopher D. Marshall, *Beyond Retribution: A New Testament Vision for Justice, Crime, and Punishment* (Grand Rapids, MI: Eerdmans, 2001), 67.

23. A great book on the power of the Eucharist in connecting us to victims of violence is William Cavanaugh, *Torture and the Eucharist* (Oxford, UK: Blackwell, 1998).

24. Details about Maria Goretti's life and death, and about her killer, are from Glynn MacNiven-Johnston, *Maria Goretti: Teenage Martyr* (London: Catholic Truth Society / Ignatius Press, 1997).

25. MacNiven-Johnston, *Maria Goretti,* 28.

Chapter 6: The Early Christians and Execution

1. David Neff, "Rethinking Capital Punishment," posted Mar. 14, 2014, www.christianitytoday.com/ct/2014/march/rethinking-capital-punishment.html.

2. Ronald J. Sider, *The Early Church on Killing: A Comprehensive Sourcebook on War, Abortion, and Capital Punishment* (Grand Rapids, MI: Baker Academic, 2012). I ride the wave of Sider's thorough research in the discussion that follows. Unless otherwise noted, all subsequent quotations in this chapter are from *The Early Church on Killing*, and the page numbers after each quote refer to that book.

3. This quote is from a wonderful compilation of early Christian writings and sto- ries compiled by Eberhard Arnold, founder of the Bruderhof Community. Eberhard Arnold, ed. *The Early Christians in Their Own Words* (Rifton: Plough, 2011). The book is available for free online: www.plough.com. And I bet if you visit them they'll give you a hard copy.

4. The Maximilian story gets even better. He was being executed for refusing to fight in the military, and he asked his father to give the executioner all the new, un- used military clothing, since he wouldn't be needing it (Sider, 155).

5. Clemens Alexandrinus and Eusebius (Ecclesiastical History II.2) both tell how the executioner witnessed the courage and unrecanting spirit of James and was then convinced of Christ's resurrection and was executed along with James. www.credohouse.org.

6. Neff, "Rethinking Capital Punishment," Mar. 14, 2014, http://www.christianity today.com/ct/2014/march/rethinking-capital-punishment.html.

7. Joel Harrington, *The Faithful Executioner* (New York: Macmillan, 2013).

8. This story is from an interview with Nyasha, who has become a dear friend and hero of mine. Interview with Nyasha Manyau, March 18–19, 2014.

9. Nyasha told me that when he asked her to pray with him, she felt crushed be- cause her attitude had been "so wrong" when she went to meet him on that Father's Day. I left this little detail out in my original manuscript. When Nyasha read a draft of her story, she made me put it back in. It's almost inconceivable that she would sug- gest she could have had a "better attitude" when going to meet this man who had caused such agonizing pain. Heroic humility.

10. Several years later, he asked Nyasha to baptize him. She did so gladly. And two days later he died.

11. As did nuclear weapons. South Africa concluded that such weapons have no place in the society they hope to build . . . and thus its leaders destroyed their nuclear arsenal.

Chapter 7: Death on the Run

1. On the web, *TIME* magazine has an interactive chart of all the executions since 1700. They even break it down by method. http://time.com/82375/every-execution -in-u-s-history-in-a-single-chart/.

2. The best site I've found for info and stats on the death penalty is appropriately named: Death Penalty Information Center. You'll find everything from historic data to breaking news. And it's free. Facts for this chapter are from this site, unless another source is given: www.deathpenaltyinfo.org.

3. If you're wondering where your state stands or how many folks are on death row, check out the state-by-state directory here: www.deathpenaltyinfo.org/.

4. For a full list of exonerees: www.deathpenaltyinfo.org/innocence-list
-those-freed-death-row.

5. And the number of wrongful convictions soars if you include folks not on
death row, many of whom pleaded guilty to a lesser crime they did not commit in
order to avoid any chance of execution.

6. http://www.amnestyusa.org/research/reports/death-sentences-and
-executions-2014.

7. Using information from Death Penalty Information Center (1,319 of the 1,422
executions are in fifteen states, and 1,379 of 1,422 are in twenty states).

8. From *State of Connecticut v. Eduardo Santiago,* argued Apr. 23, 2013, officially
released Aug. 25, 2015, http://www.jud.ct.gov/external/supapp/Cases/AROcr/CR318
/318CR306.pdf.

9. Richard C. Dieter, "The 2% Death Penalty: How a Minority of Counties Produce
Most Death Cases at Enormous Costs to All" (Washington, DC: Death Penalty Information Center, 2013), v.

10. Harris County, Texas, has had over 115 executions since 1976, making it by far
the deadliest county in the country.

11. All statistics, unless otherwise noted, are from www.deathpenaltyinfo.org.

12. Not that you would like to see more horrific ways we kill people, but here are
two sources I used: http://list25.com/25-of-humanitys-most-brutal-methods-of
-execution/ and https://en.wikipedia.org/wiki/Methods_of_Execution. Other brutal
but less common legal means of execution include disembowelment (pulling out
of organs and intestines), falling (being thrown off a high place or into a pit), flaying
(removing the skin from the body), poisoning, smothering by ash (suffocating from
ashes from a fire), and back-breaking (a Mongolian method of execution that avoided
spilling blood).

13. *TIME* magazine has a chart mapping the over 15,000 executions in U.S. history
at http://time.com/82375/every-execution-in-u-s-history-in-a-single-chart/.

14. Dale Recinella, *The Biblical Truth About America's Death Penalty* (Boston: Northeastern Univ. Press, 2004), 66.

15. Chief Justice Warren used this phrase in *Trop v. Dulles* in 1958: "the Amendment must draw its meaning from the evolving standards of decency that mark the
progress of a maturing society" (356 U.S. 86, 101). And it was used in *Atkins v. Virginia*
to ban executions of mentally challenged individuals. Among other places, more info
here: www.americanbar.org/content/dam/aba/publishing/criminal_justice_section
_newsletter/crimjust_juvjus_EvolvingStandards.authcheckdam.pdf.

16. I'm thankful for the great work of the Death Penalty Information Center
(www.deathpenaltyinfo.org) in compiling information, history, and current news on
the death penalty. I built this timeline with much help from these fine folks.

17. www.deathpenaltyinfo.org.

18. www.deathpenaltyinfo.org.

19. Pew Research Center, "Shrinking Majority of Americans Support the Death
Penalty," posted Mar. 28, 2014, www.pewforum.org/2014/03/28/shrinking-majority
-of-americans-support-death-penalty/.

20. Damla Ergun, "New Low in Preference for the Death Penalty," posted June
2014, http://abcnews.go.com/blogs/politics/2014/06/new-low-in-preference-for
-the-death-penalty/.

21. www.deathpenaltyinfo.org.

22. www.deathpenaltyinfo.org/colorado-governor-indefinitely-stays
-execution-over-concerns-about-flawed-system.

23. Pew Research Center, "Continued Majority Support for Death Penalty," posted Jan. 6, 2012, www.people-press.org/2012/01/06/continued-majority-support-for -death-penalty.

24. www.deathpenaltyworldwide.org/country-search-post.cfm?country =Japan.

25. Mari Yamaguchi, "Iwao Hakamada Freed from Death Row in Japan After Record 48 years," posted Mar. 27, 2014, www.huffingtonpost.com/2014/03/27/iwao -hakamada-freed_n_5039719.html.

26. These three statements and many others like them are available at www.deathpenaltyinfo.org. This originally appeared in the *New York Times:* W. Brennan, "What the Constitution Requires," *New York Times,* April 28, 1996.

27. http://www.deathpenaltyinfo.org/statements-death-penalty-supreme -court-justices#scalia.

28. The source for Bill's story is the presentation he gave at the event in DC on June 30–July 3, 2014, and multiple conversations since then. He is a champion for grace and inspires me every time I get to talk to him. There is an award-winning short film about Bill and his brother Manny entitled *Last Day of Freedom.* You can find it at www.lastdayoffreedom.net.

29. Manny's attorney was later disbarred and sued for racism, but none of that in time to save Manny's life.

30. Manny was buried with full military honors. His body rests in Wareham, Massachusetts.

31. Bill later told me more of the story, dating back to before he met David. As he lay locked in his room one day, paralyzed in a deep depression, he prayed that God would send someone to help him. He was thinking maybe a pastor, a friend. Laughing at the top of his lungs, he relayed to me the irony: "God sent this Christian brother a Buddhist friend from Texas to save me!" In Bill's words: "He saved my life by making me promise that I would not kill myself. I knew he needed me as I needed him." They have been the best of friends ever since. To hear Bill's story as told by David, see www.youtube.com/watch?v=m4Y4KAmeEfk.

Chapter 8: Race, the Death Penalty, and Lynching

1. As noted in chapter 5, I am indebted to the work of James Cone in helping me understand the connection between lynching and the death penalty, and how both of these help us see Jesus with new eyes. See James Cone, *The Cross and the Lynching Tree* (Maryknoll, NY: Orbis, 2011).

2. From Dale Recinella, *The Biblical Truth About America's Death Penalty* (Boston: Northeastern Univ. Press, 2004), 257, we learn that in Kentucky from 1865 to 1940 there were 229 executions and 353 lynchings. Lynchings outnumbered executions 82 to 6 in the 1870s and 92 to 40 in the 1890s. Of 771 people of identified race known to be executed for rape from 1870 through 1950, 701 were black. For robbery, 31 of 35 were black. For burglary, 18 of 21 were black.

3. In 2015, Bryan Stevenson and the fine folks at the Equal Justice Initiative re- leased the most thorough report on lynching to date. I used much of their research and work here. The full report is "Lynching in America: Confronting the Legacy of Racial Terror." You'll find it and so much other great info at http://www.eji.org.

4. One of the initiatives of the Equal Justice Initiative is to dedicate historic markers around the country where lynchings took place. They are also gathering

soil from these sites with the names of the victims. When I visited EJI in 2015, we collected soil from six lynchings and heard the vision for memorializing this part of our national history. Before we can heal, we must first remember.

5. Equal Justice Initiative, "Lynching in America," 2.

6. "Lynchings: By State and Race, 1882–1968," University of Missouri-Kansas City School of Law, retrieved July 26, 2010. Statistics provided by the Archives at Tuskegee Institute.

7. Equal Justice Initiative, "Lynching in America," 5.

8. Three reports are from Equal Justice Initiative, "Lynching in America," 33.

9. There are documented cases of over ten to twenty thousand spectators at some lynchings, according to Cone, *The Cross and the Lynching Tree*, xiv.

10. Equal Justice Initiative, "Lynching in America," 34.

11. Cone, *The Cross and the Lynching Tree*, 9.

12. From *The Crisis* 10, no. 2, June 1915; quoted in Cone, *The Cross and the Lynching Tree*, 1.

13. Quoted in Cone, *The Cross and the Lynching Tree*, 7.

14. Cone, *The Cross and the Lynching Tree*, 120.

15. Equal Justice Initiative, "Lynching in America," 35.

16. Equal Justice Initiative, "Lynching in America," 46.

17. Equal Justice Initiative, "Lynching in America," 59.

18. Equal Justice Initiative, "Lynching in America," 59–60.

19. Equal Justice Initiative, "Lynching in America," 60.

20. Cone, *The Cross and the Lynching Tree*, 8.

21. Recinella, *The Biblical Truth About America's Death Penalty*, 254.

22. Recinella, *The Biblical Truth About America's Death Penalty*, 258. A side note on this one: Alabama Governor James Folsom commuted the sentence after announcing that he was "snowed under" by more than three thousand letters urging him to spare Mr. Wilson's life.

23. Recinella, *The Biblical Truth About America's Death Penalty*, 252.

24. Interview with Bryan Stevenson, Mar. 14, 2014.

25. Recinella, *The Biblical Truth About America's Death Penalty*, 271.

26. https://www.aclu.org/blog/fighting-too-much-justice.

27. Released by Equal Justice Initiative in August 2010, the report is available on their website: www.eji.org. The information here in regard to jury selection is all from this report.

28. The U.S. Supreme Court's 1986 decision in *Batson v. Kentucky* ruled that prosecutors cannot exclude any potential juror because of his or her race.

29. Equal Justice Initiative, "Illegal Racial Discrimination in Jury Selection," 42.

30. Equal Justice Initiative, "Illegal Racial Discrimination in Jury Selection," 42.

31. Recinella, *The Biblical Truth About America's Death Penalty*, 273. Recinella cites a study in Alabama that found that black people constitute 2 percent of prosecutors, 4 percent of judges, 26 percent of the population, 63 percent of those in prison, and 70 percent of those executed.

32. This story about Hector Black is from several great conversations with my pal David Bowden, a friend of Hector and Suzie. You can hear Hector tell his own story here to Bianca Giaever at Radiolab: www.radiolab.org/story/317629-dear-hector/.

Chapter 9: The Death Penalty's Hall of Shame

1. For this quote and many other great quotes by Dr. King and others on capital punishment, check out www.ncadp.org/blog/entry/outraged-by-executions-on-dr.-martin-luther-kings-birthday.

2. Emily Friedman, "Brandon Rhode Executed After Suicide Attempt Left Him Brain Damaged," posted Sept. 27, 2010, http://abcnews.go.com/US/brandon-joseph-rhode-executed-denied-stay-arguing-brain/story?id=11736714.

3. This list of botched executions, and many others not included here, came from Professor Michael L. Radelet. More info can be found on www.deathpenaltyinfo.org/some-examples-post-furman-botched-executions.

4. Romell Broom has written a book with Clare Nonhebel entitled *Survivor on Death Row,* in which he tells his story of living for thirty years on death row and surviving his own execution.

5. Tracy Connor, "Oklahoma Governor Halts Richard Glossip Execution at Last Minute," posted Sept. 30, 2015, www.nbcnews.com/storyline/lethal-injection/pope-francis-tries-stop-richard-glossips-oklahoma-execution-n436166.

6. Sister Helen Prejean has written a great book called *The Death of Innocents* (New York: Random House, 2005). *The Death of Innocents* is about what it was like to accompany three men to their death who were most likely innocent of the crimes they were executed for.

7. These cases of executing people who were likely innocent or were even posthumously pardoned because they were proven innocent can be found, with many other cases, at www.deathpenaltyinfo.org/executed-possibly-innocent.

8. Herrera's case and nine others can be found here: http://listverse.com/2010/01/12/10-convicts-presumed-innocent-after-execution/.

9. On the Death Penalty Information Center site (http://www.deathpenaltyinfo.org/node/2047) there is also the Final Words project by Marc Asnin, who collected the last words of 527 people killed in Texas from 1982 to 2015.

10. Justice Harry Blackmun's statement is here: www.law.cornell.edu/supct/html/91-7328.ZD.html.

11. www.deathpenaltyinfo.org/executed-possibly-innocent#Davis.

12. Dale Recinella, *The Biblical Truth About America's Death Penalty* (Boston: Northeastern Univ. Press, 2004), 200–201.

13. Nancy Leong and Justin Marceau, "Will Texas Execute a Mentally Ill Man?," posted Dec. 1, 2014, www.theatlantic.com/national/archive/2014/12/will-texas-execute-scott-panetti/383285/.

14. Recinella, *The Biblical Truth About America's Death Penalty,* 221.

15. Recinella, *The Biblical Truth About America's Death Penalty,* 222.

16. Override is legal in Alabama, Delaware, and Florida but is uniquely used in Alabama to regularly overturn jury verdicts to impose a death sentence.

17. www.eji.org/overridereport.

18. Rebecca Buckwalter-Poza, "With Judges Overriding Death Penalty, Alabama Is an Outlier," posted July 27, 2014, www.npr.org/2014/07/25/335418230/with-judges-overriding-death-penalty-cases-alabama-is-an-outlier.

19. Recinella, *The Biblical Truth About America's Death Penalty,* 240.

20. Prejean, *The Death of Innocents,* 17.

21. Recinella, *The Biblical Truth About America's Death Penalty,* 230.

22. Interview with Bryan Stevenson, Mar. 14, 2014.

23. Recinella, *The Biblical Truth About America's Death Penalty,* 234–35.

24. Nomaan Merchant, "Ethan Couch, 'Affluenza' Teen Who Killed 4 in Crash, Given No Jail Time," posted Feb. 5, 2014, www.huffingtonpost.com/2014/02/05/ethan -couch-affluenza-teen_n_4729821.html.

25. Recinella, *The Biblical Truth About America's Death Penalty,* 173.

26. We'd like to believe that innocent people are freed because the system works. But in the case of Joe Amrine and many like him, it is volunteer lawyers, students, journalists, and documentarians who worked to expose their innocence and stop their executions. More can be seen on Mr. Amrine's case in the acclaimed documentary "Unreasonable Doubt: The Joe Amrine Case," which may be said to have played a key role in stopping his wrongful execution.

27. Recinella, *The Biblical Truth About America's Death Penalty,* 175.

28. For further reading on innocence and other tragic miscarriages of justice, check out Barry Scheck, Peter Neufeld, and Jim Dwyer, *Actual Innocence: Five Days to Execution, and Other Dispatches from the Wrongly Convicted* (New York: Doubleday, 2000).

29. Timothy McVeigh, "Essay on Hypocrisy," written while in federal prison in Florence, CO, Mar. 1998. Also, Timothy J. McVeigh, "An Essay on Hypocrisy," *Media Bypass,* June 1998.

30. The information and quotations from Bud Welch are taken from the wonderful Forgiveness Project: http://theforgivenessproject.com/stories/bud-welch-usa/.

31. Six months after the bombing, a poll taken in Oklahoma City of victims' families and survivors showed that 85 percent wanted the death penalty for Timothy McVeigh. Six years later that figure had dropped to nearly half, and now—with the execution in the past—most of those who supported his execution have come to believe it was a mistake. In other words, they didn't feel any better after McVeigh was taken from his cell and killed. http://theforgivenessproject.com/stories/bud -welch-usa/.

Chapter 10: Putting a Face on the Issue

1. Kim Bellware, "Marty Stroud, Prosecutor Who Put Innocent Man on Death Row: 'Whole System Is Fatally Flawed,' " posted Apr. 1, 2015, www.huffington post.com/2015/04/01/marty-stroud-prosecutor_n_6988752.html.

2. For this quote and many other great quotes by Dr. King and others on capital punishment, check out www.ncadp.org/blog/entry/outraged-by-executions-on -dr.-martin-luther-kings-birthday.

3. The info for this story is from our time together and an interview with Billy on September 26, 2014. Reverend Moore has a book (and CD) titled *I Shall Not Die* (Bloomington, IN: AuthorHouse, 2005). He continues to inspire me.

4. Amy Goodman interview on Democracy Now, "Prosecutor Seeks Stay of Execution for Texas Prisoner Duane Buck, Sentenced to Death for Being Black," posted Apr. 1, 2013, www.democracynow.org/2013/4/1/prosecutor_seeks _stay_of_execution_for.

5. Here's a good piece on the evolution of the Catholic catechism: www.the freelibrary.com/Catechism+takes+harder+line+on+death+penalty.-a019811897.

6. Charles J. Ogletree Jr., "Condemned to Die Because He's Black," posted July 31, 2013, www.nytimes.com/2013/08/01/opinion/condemned-to-die-because-hes -black.html.

Chapter 11: Putting a Face on the Innocent

1.   Dale Recinella, *The Biblical Truth About America's Death Penalty* (Boston: North-eastern Univ. Press, 2004), 183–84.

2.   Recinella, *The Biblical Truth About America's Death Penalty*, 183–84.

3.   Information here for Curtis McCarty is from our time together in Nebraska on April 19–20, 2013, and from the website of the wonderful people at Innocence Project: www.innocenceproject.org/cases-false-imprisonment/curtis-mccarty.

4.   David Kohn, "Under the Microscope: Forensic Scientist Accused of Mishandling Cases," *60 Minutes*, May 8, 2001, www.cbsnews.com/news/under-the-microscope-08-05-2001/.

5.   In addition to the Innocence Project and Journey of Hope where you can find information on other exonerees, I am also thrilled to support the work of Witness to Innocence (www.witnesstoinnocence.org), which was established to support other survivors of death row.

6.   www.newsweek.com/one-25-executed-us-innocent-study-claims-248889.

7.   Kim Bellware, "Marty Stroud, Prosecutor Who Put Innocent Man on Death Row: 'Whole System Is Fatally Flawed,' " posted Apr. 1, 2015, www.huffingtonpost.com/2015/04/01/marty-stroud-prosecutor_n_6988752.html.

8.   Matt Schudel, "Glenn Ford, Wrongfully Convicted in Louisiana Murder Case, Dies at 65," posted July 4, 2015, https://www.washingtonpost.com/national/glenn-ford-wrongfully-convicted-in-louisiana-murder-case-dies-at-65/2015/07/04/0dfa3cec-2266-11e5-84d5-eb37ee8eaa61_story.html.

9.   www.deathpenaltyinfo.org.

10.   Here's one of the video links of Ricky walking out of jail after thirty-nine years on death row: https://www.youtube.com/watch?v=2yV_HLDjMlw.

11.   Press release from Nov. 20, 2014, posted here: www.deathpenaltyinfo.org/documents/OHInnocPR.pdf.

12.   Recinella, *The Biblical Truth About America's Death Penalty*, 198–99.

13.   Recinella, *The Biblical Truth About America's Death Penalty*, 166.

14.   Recinella, *The Biblical Truth About America's Death Penalty*, 181.

Chapter 12: The Haunted Executioners

1.   Ron McAndrew, testimony in support of Senate Bill 236, Montana House of Representatives Judiciary Committee, Mar. 25, 2009, http://ejusa.org/state-leader/testimony/ron-mcandrew. For more info on Ron McAndrew, visit www.ronmcandrew.com.

2.   All the information here is from my interview with Ron McAndrew on May 1, 2014, and other sources as noted.

3.   This McAndrew quote and the several that follow are from Jason Silverstein, "Ron McAndrew Is Done Killing People," posted Jan. 14, 2014, www.esquire.com/blogs/news/ron-mcandrew-is-done-killing-people.

4.   Donald A. Cabana, *Death at Midnight: The Confession of an Executioner* (Boston: Northeastern Univ. Press, 1996), 156.

5.   Kathryn Westcott, "How and Why Gardner Was Shot," posted June 18, 2010, www.bbc.com/news/10254279.

6.   Don Cabana describes how impossible it is to really become desensitized to death. On one occasion, when he was warden, he and his staff decided to place two

rabbits, in a cage, in the gas chamber as a way to prepare the death team to take a real human life. But it backfired as they all watched the rabbits flopping violently about. One of the staff said after the test, "Jesus Christ, can you imagine what the hell that does to a man?" Cabana replied, "No, and I don't want to imagine. . . . I just want it to be over." Donald A. Cabana, *Death at Midnight: The Confession of an Executioner* (Boston: Northeastern Univ. Press, 1996), 162.

7.   Sometimes it's the defendants who are blindfolded. In 2015, in Indonesia, two men made news around the world as they and six others were killed by firing squad for alleged drug charges: Andrew Chan (who was ordained as a priest during his decade in jail) and Myuran Sukumaran. They asked that their heads not be covered so they could see the executioner face to face. They sang "Amazing Grace" and "Bless the Lord, O My Soul" as they died. Kate Lamb, "Indonesia Executions," posted Apr. 29, 2015, www.theguardian.com/world/2015/apr/29/indonesia-executions-prisoners -bali-nine-sang-amazing-grace-last-moments.

8.   Cabana, *Death at Midnight*, xi, italics added.

9.   Cabana, *Death at Midnight*, 17.

10.   Cabana, *Death at Midnight*, 16.

11.   Cabana, *Death at Midnight*, 187.

12.   Pamela Colloff, "The Witness," posted Sept. 2014, www.texasmonthly.com /articles/the-witness. The two quotes in this section are from that article.

13.   Bryan's statement, and much more about Mr. Hinton, is on the Equal Justice Initiative site: www.eji.org/deathpenalty/innocence/hinton. And here's a powerful video of Mr. Hinton's release: http://abcnews.go.com/Nightline/video/30-year -death-row-inmate-celebrates-days-freedom-30548291.

Chapter 13: A New Vision of Justice

1.   Bryan said this when I was with him and a group of faith leaders on Dec. 15, 2015.

2.   In his great book with a wonderful title, Emmanuel Katongole shows what Rwanda has to teach the world about trauma, faith, and restorative justice. See *Mirror to the Church* (Grand Rapids, MI: Zondervan, 2009).

3.   David P. Gushee, *The Sacredness of Human Life* (Grand Rapids, MI: Eerdmans, 2013), 367–68.

4.   Gushee, *The Sacredness of Human Life,* 368. Gushee notes one exception: Adolf Eichmann, who was executed in 1962 for his pivotal role in the killing of Jews.

5.   Howard Zehr, *The Little Book of Restorative Justice* (Intercourse, PA: Good Books, 2002), 37. The quote here, along with the great wisdom that follows are thanks to Howard Zehr and succinctly compiled in this little book (and unpacked more thoroughly in his many other books and articles, which I highly recommend).

6.   Zehr, *Little Book of Restorative Justice,* 36.

7.   www.azquotes.com/quote/930527.

8.   Zehr, *Little Book of Restorative Justice,* 4.

9.   I wrote about this in my book with Chris Haw, *Jesus for President* (Grand Rapids, MI: Zondervan, 2008), 252.

10.   The story of Joe Avila was told to me in an Interview with Elaine Enns, Mar. 28, 2014. She's written much more about restorative justice in her book *Ambassadors of Reconciliation* (co-authored with her partner, Ched Myers).

11.   Elaine Enns, interview with author, Mar. 28, 2014.

12. Zehr, *Little Book of Restorative Justice*, 40–41.

13. John F. Kennedy quote is from a letter to a Navy friend, quoted in Arthur M. Schlesinger Jr., *A Thousand Days: John F. Kennedy in the White House* (Boston: Houghton Mifflin Company, 1965), 88, and available here: www.jfklibrary.org/Research /Research-Aids/Ready-Reference/JFK-Quotations.aspx.

14. This quote is from none other than his Facebook page: www.facebook.com /drcornelwest/posts/119696361424073.

15. I recommend anything by Desmond Tutu, but for my purposes here I found two books especially helpful: *No Future Without Forgiveness* (New York: Random House, 1999) and, coauthored with Mpho Tutu, *The Book of Forgiving*, ed. Douglas C. Abrams (San Francisco: HarperOne, 2014).

16. Tutu and Tutu, *The Book of Forgiving*, 140.

17. This story is from my time with Mary in Minneapolis on Jan. 5, 2016, and an interview with her on Jan. 27, 2016. You can hear her and Oshea tell their story here: https://storycorps.org/listen/mary-johnson-and-oshea-israel/.

18. More info on Mary's organization, From Death to Life, is here: www.from deathtolife.us/enter.htnl.

Chapter 14: Making Death Penalty History

1. These words from Pope Francis, along with many other quotes, statements, and speeches by religious and civic leaders, can be found here: www.deathpenalty info.org/node/6086.

2. There is a great cover story from *The Atlantic* titled "Cruel and Unusual," June 2015. It goes into fascinating (and troubling) detail about lethal injection secrecy, even documenting states that have now been raided for illegally purchasing execution drugs. Here's a crazy story I learned when I was in Nebraska visiting with the men on death row: Nebraska purchased its lethal injection medication illegally. The supplier was an unlicensed medicine man in India, who didn't have the necessary facilities (like refrigeration) to produce the chemicals safely. Nonetheless, a European company brokered the deal, legitimizing the product. However, the European Union intervened; they called it an illegal drug deal, since they do not allow medication to be exchanged for the purpose of execution. Nebraska executions were stalled as a result, and eleven men's lives hinged on a legal battle over whether the state could use drugs that it had purchased illegally. Can you believe that?! Thankfully, Nebraska has since abolished the death penalty.

3. Katie Fretland, "Scene at Botched Oklahoma Execution of Clayton Lockett Was 'a Bloody Mess,'" posted Dec. 13, 2014, www.theguardian.com/world/2014/dec/13 /botched-oklahoma-execution-clayton-lockett-bloody-mess.

4. Kelly Phillips Erb, "Considering the Death Penalty: Your Tax Dollars At Work," posted May 1, 2014, www.forbes.com/sites/kellyphillipserb/2014/05/01/considering -the-death-penalty-your-tax-dollars-at-work/.

5. Francis X. Rocca, "Pope Francis Calls for Abolishing Death Penalty and Life Imprisonment," posted Oct. 23, 2014, http://ncronline.org/blogs/francis-chronicles /pope-francis-calls-abolishing-death-penalty-and-life-imprisonment.

6. Jonathan Merritt, "Poll: Younger Christians Less Supportive of Death Penalty," posted Jan. 18, 2014, www.religionnews.com/2014/01/17/among-us-christians -declining-support-death-penalty. Other related polls found here: www.death

penaltyinfo.org/public-opinion-support-death-penalty-low-among-christians
-particularly-younger-members.

7. Jonathan Merritt, "Younger Christians Less Supportive of Death Penalty, Poll," posted Jan. 18, 2014, www.huffingtonpost.com/2014/01/18/christians-death
-penalty-_n_4622902.html.

8. Jonathan Alter, "Six Catholics, Three Jews and Not Much Memory at the Supreme Court," posted May 10, 2014, www.thedailybeast.com/articles/2014/05/10
/six-catholics-three-jews-and-not-much-memory-at-the-supreme-court.html.

9. Jonathan Merritt, "Younger Christians," www.huffingtonpost.com/2014/01/18
/christians-death-penalty-_n_4622902.html.

10. The last woman executed in Georgia, and the only other one in Georgia's history, was Lena Baker. An African American maid, Baker was sentenced to death by an all-white, all-male jury in 1944, despite her claims of self-defense and obvious abuse. Sixty years later, in a rare move, Georgia's parole board posthumously pardoned her, finding "grievous error" in the process. Hindsight is twenty-twenty; unfortunately, death is irreversible.

11. Patrick Frye, "Kelly Gissendaner Death Unfair? Boyfriend Gregory Owen Did the Murder, Gets Parole in Eight Years," posted Mar. 4, 2015, www.inquisitr.com
/1894125/kelly-gissendan-death-unfair-boyfriend-gregory-owen-did-the-murder
-gets-parole-in-eight-years/.

12. Interview with Jonathan Wilson-Hartgrove, Aug. 24, 2015.

13. In 2001 *Time* magazine named him "America's Best Theologian," to which he is reputed to have responded, "How the hell would they know?"

14. This Hauerwas quote and the next are from an interview with Jonathan Wilson-Hartgrove, Aug. 24, 2015.

15. Max Blau, "North Carolina Bill Pushes to Execute Inmates Without Doctors," posted May 8, 2015, www.theguardian.com/world/2015/may/08/north-carolina
-bill-execution-no-doctors.

16. Campbell Robertson, "South Carolina Judge Vacates Conviction of George Stinney in 1944 Execution," *New York Times,* posted Dec. 17, 2014, www.nytimes.com
/2014/12/18/us/judge-vacates-conviction-in-1944-execution.html.

17. Terri and I got to meet in 2015 for a magnificent event. Together with my blacksmith friends at RAW Tools (www.rawtools.org), we took a forge and heated up the barrel of a gun together, then beat it into oblivion. We turned the gun into a plow! See Carol Kuruvilla, "Guns Beaten into Garden Tools by Peacemakers in Pennsylvania," updated Mar. 21, 2015, www.huffingtonpost.com/2015/03/21/raw-tools
-gun-garden-tools_n_6914636.html. Maybe next year we'll melt down an electric chair.